INCOME MAINTENANCE

INCOME MAINTENANCE

Interdisciplinary Approaches to Research

Edited by

LARRY L. ORR
ROBINSON G. HOLLISTER
MYRON J. LEFCOWITZ

with the assistance of
KAREN HESTER

Institute for Research on Poverty Monograph Series

MARKHAM PUBLISHING COMPANY/Chicago

INSTITUTE FOR RESEARCH ON POVERTY MONOGRAPH SERIES

Allen, ed., *Psychological Factors in Poverty*
Edelman, *Politics as Symbolic Action: Mass Arousal and Quiescence*
Lampman, *Ends and Means of Reducing Income Poverty*
Handler and Hollingsworth, *The Deserving Poor: A Study of Welfare Administration*
Orr, Hollister, and Lefcowitz, eds., with the assistance of Karen Hester, *Income Maintenance: Interdisciplinary Approaches to Research*
Williams, ed., *Language and Poverty: Perspectives on a Theme*

This book is one of a Series sponsored by the Institute for Research on Poverty of the University of Wisconsin pursuant to the provisions of the Economic Opportunity Act of 1964. Additional funds for the research reported in this volume were made available by the Department of Health, Education, and Welfare.

cC

CONTRIBUTORS

D. Lee Bawden
Associate Professor of Economics
University of Wisconsin

Ernest Bonner
Planner
*City Planning Department,
City of Cleveland*

Glen G. Cain
Associate Professor of Economics
*On leave from University of
Wisconsin at Princeton University*

David Elesh
Assistant Professor of Sociology
University of Wisconsin

Leonard J. Hausman
Assistant Professor of Economics
and Social Policy
*Heller School of Social Work,
Brandeis University*

Robinson G. Hollister
Professor of Economics
*Woodrow Wilson School
of International Affairs,
Princeton University*

Hirschel Kasper
Professor of Economics
Oberlin College

David Kershaw
Project Director,
Negative Income Tax
MATHEMATICA

Jack Ladinsky
Associate Professor of Sociology
University of Wisconsin

Myron J. Lefcowitz
Associate Professor of Social Work
University of Wisconsin

Raymond Munts
Professor of Social Work
University of Wisconsin

Donald A. Nichols
Associate Professor of Economics
*On leave from University of
Wisconsin at Yale University*

Hugh O. Nourse
Professor of Economics
University of Missouri

Larry L. Orr
Economist
Research Division, OEO

Irving Piliavin
Professor of Social Work
University of Wisconsin

Thomas I. Ribich
Associate Professor of Economics
*University of North Carolina,
Chapel Hill*

Seymour Spilerman
Associate Professor of Sociology
University of Wisconsin

James A. Sweet
Assistant Professor of Sociology
University of Wisconsin

ACKNOWLEDGMENTS

Although the papers included here are clearly the work of each author, they were also products of considerable group effort. From the start, regular seminars were scheduled. The immediate focus at first was to lay out a range of issues. As this emerged, project members assumed responsibility for issues falling within their area of expertise and in which they were interested.

Eventually, the more general sessions were supplemented by three seminars which concentrated more specifically on work effort and savings, fertility and family structure, and community effects. These seminars became the major operating arenas of the project. As participants developed their ideas, their approaches to the specific issues became topics for critical examination at the appropriate seminar.

A comment on the tone which pervaded the seminars is in order. Within the bounds of good taste, the operating norm was an unmerciful critique of the ideas presented. The give and take, however, was so clearly aimed at the development and improvement of the ideas presented that the loss was only momentarily felt. The importance of this process for the final output is to the credit of all who were involved. Without minimizing the individual contributions, there is no doubt in our minds that the intellectual interaction which emerged within the seminar framework pushed all of us to the limit of our capacities.

In addition to the contributors to this volume, others who provided stimulation and guidance in the discussion of the issues were: Charles Cnudde, Joel Handler, A. James Heins, Donald Hester, David Horner, William Klein, Robert Lampman, Theodore Marmor, Charles Metcalf, Richard Perlman, Herman Turk, Harold Watts, and Burton Weisbrod.

Supplementing the work and discussions of the professionals was the project staff. First and foremost was Joan Grant, who was assistant to the project director. Gretchen Rudolph filled the essential role of project secretary. Completing the cadre were our research assistants: Ernst Berndt, Frank Cooper, Anna Craig, Norman Madrid, Juliet Mak, and Bill Peyton.

This group was ably supported by the Institute's administrative and clerical staff. Special thanks are due to Felicity Skidmore and Dwight Ziegler. Margeret Witte supervised the typing of the original report plus the present manuscript. At different times we have had the editorial assistance of Jeanne DeRose, Nancy Kreinberg, and Ann Jacobs.

A special acknowledgment is due to Harold Watts. Our debt to him is only partially due to his participation in the seminars and to the availability of the Institute staff which he put together and directed. Dr. Watts was responsible for the initial negotiations with HEW and from beginning to end was a constant source of sound advice and encouragement.

Finally, this project could not have been done without the substantial input—personal as well as contractual—of James F. Garrett, Helen Nicol, and Jodie Allen from HEW. These papers are based on work which was supported by funds granted to the Institute for Research on Poverty by the Social and Rehabilitation Service of the Department of Health, Education, and Welfare. In addition, work on the manuscript was supported in part by funds granted to the Institute by the Office of Economic Opportunity pursuant to the provisions of the Economic Opportunity Act of 1964. The conclusions, however, are the sole responsibility of the authors.

L. L. O.
R. G. H.
M. J. L.
K. H.

FOREWORD

In summer of 1968 the Institute for Research on Poverty, under a grant from OEO, began its Graduated Work Incentive Experiment, aimed at determining the labor-supply response to a range of alternative simple income transfers. Thus by winter 1969, when it became clear that the Department of Health, Education, and Welfare was likely to undertake a large-scale program of experimentation in the area of income maintenance, the Institute's work was well underway. In light of the existing experiments and the anticipated major expansion in the capability to carry out further experiments, it seemed quite reasonable to attempt to develop a carefully defined agenda for further experimentation. To develop such an agenda rationally and within a reasonable amount of time clearly required a major effort involving several types of social science talent. It also seemed clear that government agencies, under considerable day-to-day pressures, could not hope to mount and sustain such an effort on their own, because of the diversity of talents and the length of continuous effort required. A group at the University of Wisconsin proposed to undertake the task, guided by the Institute for Research on Poverty, in which many of them had already been working. HEW agreed to support this undertaking and a nine-month effort resulted, during which social scientists from other departments of the University of Wisconsin and from other universities across the country were drawn in to supplement the efforts of the original Poverty Institute group.

With important data from the Graduated Work Incentive Experiment becoming available, it will soon be necessary to develop analytical models which will enable us to use all obtainable information in the experimental sample. While this volume is in no sense a report from the Experiment, it critically treats many of the same questions, both financial and nonfinancial. I am encouraged to report that these seminars succeeded in bringing a variety of academic scholars from diverse disciplines into concerted, fruitful contact. Interdisciplinary activity has a rather bad name, and may richly deserve it, but there are conditions under which it can be successful.

This collection of papers provides a welcome assurance of the contribution such a group can make toward solving urgent social problems from our so-called ivory tower.

Madison, Wisconsin   Robert H. Haveman, Director
                                                Institute for Research on Poverty
                                                August, 1971

CONTENTS

PART ONE

INTRODUCTION: THE INCOME MAINTENANCE PROJECT

Robinson Hollister

The purpose of this introduction is twofold. First, it is to serve the usual function of introducing the reader to the rationale for the organization of the contents of the volume. Second, I want to try to provide, in a relatively short space, some idea of the character of the project from which the papers which make up this volume emerged. It is the conviction of those of us who participated in the project that conveying to the readers a sense of the process by which this interdisciplinary work was accomplished is as important as making available to them the actual substance of the papers produced.

I. BACKGROUND AND ORGANIZATION OF THE PROJECT

In the winter of 1969 it became clear that the Department of Health, Education and Welfare was likely to obtain within the next fiscal year the authority to undertake a large scale program of experimentation in the area of income maintenance. At that time, the New Jersey Graduated Work Incentives experiment was well underway and the rural counterpart to the New Jersey experiment was about to begin. In light of the existing experiments and the anticipated major expansion in the capability to carry out further experiments, it seemed quite reasonable to attempt to develop a carefully defined agenda for further experimentation. To develop such an agenda rationally and within a reasonable

3

amount of time clearly required a major effort involving several different types of social science talent. It also seemed clear that government agencies, under considerable day-to-day pressures, could not hope to mount and sustain such an effort on their own, both because of the diversity of talents and the length of continuous effort required. A group at the University of Wisconsin proposed to undertake the task under the aegis of the Institute for Research on Poverty, in which many of them had already been working. The Department of Health, Education and Welfare agreed to support this undertaking and a nine-month effort resulted, during which social scientists from other departments of the University of Wisconsin and from other universities across the country were drawn in to supplement the efforts of the original Poverty Institute group.

A. A Comprehensive Listing of Behavioral Responses

In the plainest terms, the question posed for this project was: "What do we need to know to improve the system of income maintenance in the United States and how should we go about finding it out?" This is a staggeringly broad question, and a major problem from the outset was just how to get a reasonable grasp on an issue of this magnitude. We sought to fulfill our mandate to be "comprehensive" in our analysis without becoming so hopelessly general and abstract as to fail to produce a useful product.

After some frustrating forays which focused first on program objectives and then on target populations, it became evident to us that what we really sought to isolate was the full range of possible *behavioral responses* to various configurations of social policy in the area of income maintenance.

Comprehensiveness was best to be achieved, then, by developing as complete a listing as possible of such potential behavioral responses. Once that comprehensive list was compiled, we could proceed to explore the state of knowledge about such responses and progressively bring the focus of our inquiries down to the operational level. The process of exploring and narrowing the focus will be outlined below, but first the development of the comprehensive list of behavioral responses will be described briefly.

In order to talk about the effects of income maintenance programs, it is necessary to categorize the major types of program characteristics (or policy parameters). Any income maintenance program would probably be characterized by a specific set of legislative or administrative rules which covered the following broad categories:

1. The definition of income
2. The period over which income is accounted

3. The definition of the family unit
4. The level of income transfer guarantee for a family and the implicit tax rate on additional income
5. The administrative features of the program
6. The interaction and means of coordination with other social programs
7. The methods of financing of the program

Admittedly, some of these categories may seem arbitrarily narrow (e.g., accounting period) and others excessively broad (e.g., administrative features). We do not wish to argue the merits of this particular categorization but simply to illustrate the procedure.

With these broad categories of program characteristics in mind, we attempted to list the various behavioral responses which might be elicited by particular choices of characteristics within each of these categories. To facilitate this process, it proved useful to define several broad categories of behavioral response and to construct the accompanying matrix framework (Fig. 1).

The important thing about this matrix of program characteristics and behavioral responses is that it proved a helpful device for insuring that we developed a comprehensive list of potential behavioral responses to potential decisions concerning program characteristics; for each category of program characteristics we considered the potential impact of various sorts of decisions on each category of behavioral response. Some of the cells of the matrix turned out to contain virtually no significant issues for research, while others proved to contain a very substantial list of possible implications for behavior. In some ways, of course, the matrix is an oversimplified device. In reality, "Interaction and Coordination with Other Social Programs" should be considered another dimension rather than a column of the matrix—since the character of the behavioral responses will depend on the particular income maintenance plan characteristics as well as the character of the other social programs. Furthermore, drawing this as a matrix fosters the impression that each of the cells is to be considered completely independent, whereas, in fact, there is likely to be a great deal of interdependency; e.g., the work effort response to the guarantee and tax rates is likely to be affected by the way in which income is defined. Finally, while this was a useful device for organizing the research initially, we did not allow it to become a rigid framework to which all further development of the research had to conform. Therefore, the reader will not find that the papers which follow can be fit neatly into different cells of this matrix. Rather, given papers will touch upon behavioral responses which are drawn from several different cells of the matrix and some of the behavioral responses on the

Figure 1. Matrix of behavioral responses to the structure of income maintenance plans

Behavioral responses / Program characteristics	(1) Definition of income	(2) Accounting period for income	(3) Definition of family unit	(4) Guarantee and tax rates	(5) Administrative features	(6) Interaction and coordination with other social programs	(7) Methods of financing
A. Work effort and migration							
B. Effects on family unit							
C. Expenditure and savings pattern							
D. Community effects							
E. Miscellany							

list derived from the matrix are not explicitly discussed in any of the selection of papers provided in this volume.

At this point no further attempt to specify the description of the comprehensive response list will be made. Many of the details are reflected in the papers which make up the rest of this report. Before passing to a discussion of the stages of analysis which followed the development of the comprehensive list of behavioral responses, there are several points related to this analytical stage which should be mentioned.

1. The development of an adequate listing of responses required the insights provided by a wide spectrum of behavioral sciences. Therefore, proceeding in this fashion called, right from the outset, for the participation of sociologists, psychologists, economists, social workers, lawyers, regional and urban planners, and political scientists. This approach gave immediate focus to the interdisciplinary character of the project.

2. The responses listed were those which could possibly be evoked by particular configurations of program characteristics. In addition to those, there are responses which would be related solely to the higher income provided by any income maintenance program. Thus it was necessary to add a set of responses related to pure income effects to the list of responses to program characteristics.

3. Even at this stage, one of the fundamental lessons learned from this project began to emerge. Any attempt to design social legislation faces a very difficult task in trying to reconcile potential conflicts between concern with equity and concern with incentive effects. In attempting to create social legislation which is equitable, one tries to insure that "persons in like circumstances" are treated equally. The problem, of course, is to define what "like circumstances" are. The concern to clearly define "like circumstances" in the body of the social legislation itself has recently received particular attention (and especially with respect to income maintenance) because of the desire to reduce the degree of discretionary behavior on the part of state and local administrators to a minimum.[1] The difficulty is, however, that when one specifies in legislation how certain situations will be treated with respect to income transfer or taxes (or other social costs or benefits), potential incentives are created for individuals to change their behavior so as to put themselves into defined situations which will maximize their transfer (or social benefit) or minimize their tax (or social cost).

As the comprehensive list of possible behavioral responses was spelled out, the potential for conflict between the desire for equity and the concern with behavioral response to incentive became increasingly clear.

---

[1] Joel Handler and Aaron E. Goodstein, "The Legislative Development of Public Assistance," *Wisconsin Law Review,* Vol. 1968, No. 2, pp. 414–60.

This problem, of course, is not confined to income maintenance but extends to all social policies; rules and regulations of social policies in general have unintended, as well as intended, incentive effects on behavior and serve to meet reasonable concepts of equity in differing degrees. It seems that these problems—which have become evident in the investigation of income maintenance reform—have received relatively little attention in other areas of social policy.

B. Exploring Knowledge of Behavioral Responses and Deriving Priorities for Experimentation

In compiling the comprehensive list of behavioral responses we had cast our net as broadly as possible in an attempt to insure that no potential intended or unintended effects of income maintenance reform were overlooked. At the next stage, however, the problem was to explore the state of knowledge about the various types of behavioral responses. Obviously, within the time and structure of the project, it was not possible to explore in detail all the potential responses which had been listed. In some areas of behavioral response to income maintenance, e.g., work effort, considerable exploration had already been carried out, both in the social science literature in general and with respect to the New Jersey and Rural Income Maintenance experiments in particular. In other areas, project participants sought to summarize broadly the relevant studies, and in some areas, judgments were made to focus more narrowly on particular behavioral responses which seemed likely to be of a major policy importance.

At the same time that we were exploring the state of knowledge about various types of behavioral responses (i.e., providing some basis for the answer to the question "what do we need to know?"), we began the process of narrowing the focus down to the operational issues of research and experimentation (i.e., beginning to try to answer the question: "How should we go about finding it out?"). The process of narrowing from the comprehensive list of possible responses to an explicit set of priorities for experimentation required the application of a mixture of explicit criteria and judgment. The explicit criteria utilized are more fully discussed in the paper in this volume by Larry Orr, "Strategy for a Broad Program of Experimentation in Income Maintenance"; therefore, I will only roughly characterize the process by which priorities were derived.

First of all, it was necessary to make some judgmental calibration of the likely *size* of a potential behavioral response and to balance that against a judgment about the social significance of such a response, if it were sizable. The combination of these judgments would roughly determine the policy relevance of the response issue. I should note that these were not necessarily purely subjective judgments. Here the background explorations of the state of knowledge concerning the issue often provided guidance for calibration of the likely size of the response.

For issues that passed the application of the criteria of policy relevance, it was necessary to consider how best to carry out research on this issue. We felt that this particular step was of critical importance for this project. One of our major objectives was to highlight the fact that in many cases experimentation is simply *not* the appropriate research approach. In some cases, this may be because the issue can be resolved with more traditional research methods, utilizing data generated by normal social and economic processes. In other cases, the theory or methods of measurement are so poorly developed that adequate experimental models cannot be specified. In still other cases, the phenomenon at issue may simply be one which cannot be adequately simulated in any experimental context. This attempt to clarify those situations in which experimentation was *not* appropriate appeared particularly important in light of the fact that, following the first round of publicity concerning the New Jersey experiment, it seemed that nearly every federal agency thought any issue that came to mind called for the mounting of "an experiment."

Once the general research approach for a particular issue was specified, it was possible, in a few of the cases for which an experiment was required, to begin the first steps toward actual experimental design. This is best illustrated in the paper by Glen Cain, "Experimental Income Maintenance Programs to Assess the Effect on Fertility."

The end result of the process of narrowing from the comprehensive list to the operational level of experimentation was a list of priorities for further experimentation in income maintenance, a set of priorities which had been determined jointly by policy relevance and research feasibility. The priorities are reported and discussed in Orr's "Strategy" paper in Part Two.

II. ORGANIZATION OF THIS VOLUME

The papers included in the volume are a selection from among those produced during the course of the project[2] and some have been subsequently somewhat refined.

---

[2] Three papers—Bawden, "The Rural Negative Income Tax Experiment," Nourse, "Impact of a Negative Income Tax on the Number of Substandard Housing Units," and Elesh et al., "The New Jersey–Pennsylvania Experiment"—had been prepared under Institute for Research on Poverty sponsorship prior to this project but were included because they cover areas that fall within the mandate of the project.

Part One papers are intended to describe the context and character of the project. Following this introduction, two papers describe the New Jersey Graduated Work Incentives project and its rural counterpart. These are included to allow the reader to familiarize himself with the general character of these experiments, as when the project reported on in this volume began these experiments had been started and most of the papers included here assume some knowledge of the experiments.

Part Two is devoted to the priorities for experimentation. Orr's paper gives the general overview of, and rationale for, the development of the priorities. The other papers in this section are a selection of the sorts of materials which were developed in the process described above which yielded the priorities Orr summarizes; they are not comprehensive, but rather serve to illustrate the various sorts of elements which were needed for this process. Thus the papers should be read not only for the substantive material on the area they cover, but also for the variation in emphasis on methods of approach. In addition, the papers included here dealt with topics which eventually became matters of priority because they met both the criterion of policy relevance and the criterion of experimental feasibility.

The papers included in Part Three, entitled "Community Effects," dealt with topics which turned out not to be of experimental priority. In some cases, this was on the grounds of policy relevance judgments, but generally it was because analysis indicated that experimentation was not the appropriate research approach at this time. In his paper on community effects, Lefcowitz indicates a number of the difficulties which beset our attempts to get a clear grasp on approaches to issues in this rather amorphous category. The papers included may be somewhat arbitrarily divided into a group of three which deal with aggregate economic effects of increases (or decreases) in individual incomes associated with income maintenance reforms and a second group which deal with non-economic "community effects" from such reforms.

Whereas the papers in the previous parts are largely based on an initial concern with certain types of behavioral and institutional responses, the papers in Part Four focus on the specific characteristics of potential income maintenance programs and, in some cases, their coordination with other social programs. One of the major objectives of the project, from the outset, was to detect as many as possible of the unintended incentive effects and unperceived inequities which might emerge from seemingly harmless decisions concerning specific program characteristics. The obverse of this concern was, of course, to uncover any potential (but perhaps unrecognized) mechanisms inherent in program characteristics which might be harnessed to serve in the promotion of desired social goals. The papers in Part Four provide ample evidence of both these dimensions, positive and negative.

Both as a warning to the reader and as an apology on the part of the contributors, it should be noted that these papers necessarily differ in several respects from most academic output. First, it is usual academic practice to focus attention in writing on those topics for which the procedures of analysis and substance which can be brought to bear are strongest and to avoid those areas in which knowledge is weakest. For the purposes of this project, it was just as important to state clearly what is *not* known as it was to point up those areas for which existing knowledge could provide reasonable guidance to policy decisions. Second, since both the participants in the project and the potential users of the project output were drawn from diverse subject backgrounds, it was felt useful in many cases to present in the papers relatively simple statements of facts and theories which might be well known to members of one academic discipline but unknown to, or poorly understood by, those unfamiliar with the literature in that area. Thus papers which appeared superficial to some participants proved to be quite enlightening to others. Finally, in certain areas, the state of knowledge was found to be extremely rudimentary and those attempting to provide some guidance in the area were forced to commit views to paper that were far more speculative and preliminary than those they would normally produce for scholarly output. While each of these features might be regarded as weaknesses of these papers from an academic viewpoint, they were, in the context of the project, features of strength—for in no other way could the gaps in knowledge relevant to important policy decisions be brought to light; they were, then, the first steps taken toward filling the gaps.

III. SECONDARY FEATURES OF THE PROJECT

There were a number of secondary features of the project which seemed important to the participants and may be of interest to the reader.

1. Some specific issues which emerged in the process of analysis were, in our judgment, adequately resolved, i.e., they did *not* require further research; we were ready to make immediate policy recommendations. The fact that the method by which the income accounting period is calculated is likely to have important effects on behavior (as discussed in the essay "Problems in Income Reporting and Accounting," by Lee Bawden and David Kershaw) was first realized in the process of planning the New Jersey and Rural experiments. However, during the course of this project a method of accounting was developed which seemed

highly likely to strike a reasonable balance of equity and incentive and most participants felt ready to recommend this method for any income maintenance reform. (The New Jersey experiment, which had been running for a year already, was immediately shifted over to this accounting procedure.) Likewise, as a result of analysis in this project, the desirability of emphasizing deductibility as a mechanism for handling such things as medical care and day care became evident. It was possible to pass these views on to governmental agencies currently developing specific reform proposals, and in this sense the project provided some immediate as well as long-term policy payoffs.

2. To our knowledge, the particular process which we went through in analyzing the area of income maintenance is unique; it has not been carried out before with respect to other social policies. We see two features which are unique: first, the process of starting with the development of a comprehensive listing of behavioral responses and narrowing to priorities for research by exploration of the state of knowledge about responses and application of criteria of policy relevance and methodological feasibility; second, the fact that this was, in a sense, a *pre-research* analytical effort—we attempted to isolate both issues and methods of research approach to those issues in order to provide guidance in the allocation of resources to, and the undertaking of, the actual research effort.

3. We believe that we found some useful ways to structure an analytical effort in a university setting. The organization of the effort was mainly in terms of several loosely structured meeting groups. These initially began with rather broad discussions of the issues (eventually leading to the comprehensive response list approach) and then, as work progressed, individual participants made more or less formal presentations on particular issues, and the papers provided in the report emerged from the subsequent discussion and further refinement of the work. The looseness of the organization made it possible to attract a greater number and variety of university talents to the process—they could adjust their degree of participation in light of their other time constraints and their degree of stimulation. The fact that the analysis was to be "comprehensive" stimulated them to think broadly and freely (an exercise of considerable appeal to academics who are often narrowly confined in pursuing a research topic in depth), but the fact that a set of experimental priorities was required provided the degree of concreteness and rigor necessary to force their work toward operational usefulness. This structure and mixture of elements seem particularly conducive to the slow and steady development of truly effective interdisciplinary work.

4. Combining points 2 and 3, we can see that this type of project

may provide government agencies with a new type of input. What is suggested is a means of obtaining a product whose character is between the short-term studies provided by consultants and the longer term output of substantial research projects. Using the type of structure outlined, it seems possible to obtain within six to nine months a reasonably comprehensive review of an area of social policy and a clear indication of steps to be taken to increase knowledge which is needed to improve policy in that area. This sort of product is difficult to obtain under the daily pressure of government operations, and the structure utilized seems to allow the harnessing of scholars from a multiplicity of disciplines to such a task. One of our hopes in making this volume available to a wider public is that it will serve as an example, however crude, which will stimulate the undertaking of similar analytical efforts in other areas of social policy. As participants in this project, we know that such efforts would increase the knowledge about, and sensitivity to, issues of public policy on the part of academics. We hope and expect that it will be concluded that government agencies and society as a whole will find that such efforts will provide substantial benefits in terms of increased rationalization of the process of development of public policies.

THE NEW JERSEY–PENNSYLVANIA EXPERIMENT: A FIELD STUDY IN NEGATIVE TAXATION

David Elesh, Jack Ladinsky, Myron J. Lefcowitz, and Seymour Spilerman

The fight against poverty has become the single most important item on the agenda of this country. In reaction to widespread dissatisfaction with traditional welfare programs, the antipoverty innovations of the 1960's emphasized direct action and involvement of the poor. These orientations gave rise to the community action programs. More recently, reflecting the realization that such programs at best can meet the needs of only a small proportion of the poor, attention has turned to income maintenance both for humanitarian reasons and to break the cycle of poverty. This paper reports some preliminary findings from the first field experiment with an income maintenance program, the New Jersey and Pennsylvania negative income tax experiment.[1] Before moving to a discussion of the

Version of a paper presented at the Association for the Study of the Grants Economy Symposium at the annual meeting of the American Association for the Advancement of Science, December 27, 1969. The research reported here was supported by funds granted to the Institute for Research on Poverty at the University of Wisconsin by the Office of Economic Opportunity pursuant to the provisions of the Economic Opportunity Act of 1964.

[1] The experiment is a joint effort of the Institute for Research on Poverty at the University of Wisconsin, MATHEMATICA, and the Office of Economic Opportunity under the general direction of Harold Watts. Responsibility for the experiment is thus shared with others; responsibility for the accuracy of this report is ours alone.

14

experiment, however, it is appropriate to place it in the context of alternative income maintenance programs.

I. ALTERNATIVE INCOME MAINTENANCE PROGRAMS

The United States already has a substantial system of income maintenance and public assistance which derives essentially from the social security legislation of the 1930's. It is necessary to review these programs and evaluate their effectiveness in combating poverty in order to understand the many problems which a new and comprehensive income maintenance program must solve.

A. Structural versus Distributive Programs

As James Tobin has pointed out, the United States has dealt with low income in two ways (Tobin, 1968). First, *structural* remedies have been sought, such as altering monetary and fiscal policies, encouraging education, and providing training and rehabilitation. These programs attempt to alter the earning capacity of the poor by increasing the demand for labor and by raising their skill levels. Second, *distributive* remedies have been used to make up income deficiencies through cash or in-kind payments or by subsidies to productivity or employment.

Structural programs can be further divided into those which are *market* solutions and those which are *individual* solutions to poverty. Market solutions to low income are attempts to end market imperfections. Among these are the manipulation of monetary and fiscal policy to maintain a high level of aggregate demand; anti-discrimination legislation to end discrimination in employment or restrictions on entry into the organized craft occupations; minimum wage legislation; attempts to increase the size and efficiency of the employment service system in matching employers with job vacancies and potential applicants. Individual solutions take the form of building up human capital through programs in health, education, and skill training.

1. Structural programs. There are many who feel that structural solutions are the most adequate for solving the problem of poverty because they deal directly with the failures of the economy or the causes of low earning power. Unfortunately, experience reveals that there are two major weaknesses to such solutions. First, there are certain obstacles that limit the effectiveness of structural solutions, at least for the current generation in poverty. The poor have large families, broken homes, physical and mental handicaps, and other problems which are generally untouched by higher minimum wages, better employment services, anti-discriminatory legislation, economic progress, or by a larger Gross National Product. Distributive mechanisms are necessary to meet the needs of the poor who are not reached by these endeavors. Second, structural solutions are long term and not always successful, given our current economic and educational knowledge. They involve restructuring labor markets and creating new training systems. Meanwhile the poor must survive. Only distributive programs can guarantee decent standards of survival in the short run.

We have substantial experience today with economic development and manpower development programs, and it is clear that they fall far short of serving the needs of the poor. Although persons in poverty decrease during periods of high aggregate demand, the hard core poor remain substantially untouched. In the 1960's almost all of the decrease in the poverty population was among male-headed households. About the same number of persons in female-headed households were poor in 1966 as in 1959 (Orshansky, 1968). Reduction of unemployment is also accompanied by inflationary trends that further reduce the value of the earnings of poor households. More significant perhaps is the possible policy reaction to inflation which can increase unemployment and thus would hit the poor disproportionately.

Minimum wage legislation, an important feature of American economic policy, rarely helps the poor who either work less than full time or have large families. At present minimum wage levels their incomes would not be sufficient to keep them above the poverty line. Moreover, minimum wage increases can work to the detriment of the poor. Possessing low skills, they are the first to be released if employers, faced with paying higher wages, tighten up their work forces to increase efficiency. Thus, greater industrial coverage under the minimum wage law could well mean greater unemployment and underemployment for the working poor.

With regard to manpower development programs, the results have been disappointing. The Department of Labor estimates that there are 11 million poor for whom work is a feasible way out of poverty. Only some 4.5 million have been enrolled in federal manpower programs since 1962, of whom about 3 million have been in work experience programs like Neighborhood Youth Corps. These programs emphasize payments for services performed rather than intensive training for work outside the programs. Of the 4.5 million enrolled in manpower programs, only 1.4 million, less than one-third, were in intensive training under the Manpower Development and Training Act (MDTA), Job Corps or similar programs, and not all finished the training, nor were all who finished placed in jobs. Of the 1.4 million in these structured work training programs, only 50 percent, or 700,000, completed the programs and were placed in jobs (President's Commission, 1969:246).

Manpower and economic development programs undoubtedly play an important role in aiding the poor to earn more and hold respectable jobs. But alone they are not a solution to poverty in America.

2. Distributive programs. There are three general forms which distributive programs take in America today:

Social insurance programs, such as Old Age, Survivors and Disability Insurance (OASDI, or Social Security), and Unemployment Insurance. These programs cover risks that are predictable and outside of individual control; they replace lost earnings from retirement, unemployment, death, or disability. All are in some way tied to work and earnings in that they are financed by employee and employer taxes or contributions specified by law.

Income subsidy programs, such as Public Assistance, and Veterans Pensions. With few exceptions these programs provide cash income transfers only to particular categories of needy persons who are deemed worthy of public assistance—the blind, disabled, and dependent children. The overwhelming majority of income subsidy programs are financed jointly by federal, state and local governments; all are administered at the state and local level. None are mandatory programs. The federal government grants matching funds to states meeting a small number of requirements, but does not require that states pay benefits up to federally determined levels.

According to the Heineman Commission there are "over 300 separate programs of cash Public Assistance receiving federal funds, covering different categories of the population under widely varying standards" (President's Commission, 1969:286). The most important of these is Aid to Families with Dependent Children (AFDC). The program is designed to keep children in their own homes by providing financial assistance to needy families with dependent children under eighteen. Initially intended for widows with children, it at first excluded any but fatherless families, unless the fathers were incapacitated. Since 1961, however, families with able-bodied fathers who are unemployed and unable to find work have been included. This is the AFDC-UP program (Unemployed Parent). A 1967 amendment to the Social Security Act further defined the "Unemployed Parent" as one who has been fairly recently connected with the labor force, so that if the father has not previously had a job, he cannot receive benefits under this program, even if he is "ready, willing and able to work."

In addition, the 1967 amendments established the Work Incentive Program (WIN). Local welfare agencies were authorized to refer unemployed parents deemed capable of work to state employment offices for placement in jobs or training. All WIN enrollees receive training incentive payments in addition to their welfare benefits. AFDC parents, however, have to accept placement via WIN in order to retain their welfare status.

Income-in-kind programs, such as food stamps, Medicaid, and public housing. Some in-kind programs provide full subsidy (surplus commodity distribution and Medicaid), while others provide only partial subsidy (public housing, rent supplement, food stamps, and Medicare). In-kind programs for the poor exist for two reasons. First, it is argued that certain services, such as housing, will not be provided to the poor by the private market in the quantity and price that they can afford. Second, it is argued that the poor will not allocate their money properly, so it is necessary to control choice and quality in such areas as housing, food purchase, and medical care.

3. Evaluation of Distributive Programs. All three distributive programs are either irrelevant, grossly inadequate, or detrimental to the poor. First, let us consider social insurance programs. The failures here are twofold. Because the poor have irregular work histories and low earnings, they gain little from Social Security or unemployment insurance. In addition, few insurance programs provide adequate payments even for workers who have had a solid work history and adequate earnings. Unemployment insurance is particularly weak for the poor, because it is not universally available and often not available for long enough periods of time. In 1968 nearly two-thirds of the unemployed were not covered by unemployment insurance due primarily to benefit expirations (President's Commission, 1969). We do recognize, however, that social insurance does keep many people out of poverty; but it is not relevant to our current problem.

There are two major problems with income subsidy programs: inadequate benefits and inadequate coverage. In 1965, 56 percent of all households below the poverty line before receiving cash transfers were *still* below after receiving them. Thirty-two percent of the pre-transfer poor received *no* government payments at all (Orshansky, 1968:28). Average payments per recipient for AFDC equaled $43 monthly in January 1969, ranging from $10 in Mississippi to $65 in Massachusetts (President's Commission, 1969). The poor with intact families cannot qualify for coverage in most states. AFDC-UP does provide for unemployed able-bodied male heads, but eligibility is very restricted, and only 25 states have programs. Less than 100,000 families are covered by this component of public welfare (President's Commission, 1969:22). The lack of any program for the working poor with intact families appears to have three dysfunctional side-effects. First, it creates work disincentives; second, it encourages family disruptions; third, it has a deleterious social effect, because some broken families can qualify for categoric relief and have incomes that exceed those of intact, working families with the same needs.

There are other unfortunate aspects of the public assistance system. Administrative costs are high, in part because it is a decentralized program, and in part because so much effort is put into screening and surveillance for eligibility. It is often undignified and imposes severe behavioral restraints on recipients. The means test and rules about how benefits can be spent are restrictive of freedoms other citizens enjoy; often regulations are unrealistic in that they impose constraints most citizens could not live up to. Finally, the program lacks uniformity and clarity and grants a great deal of discretionary power to local administrators which is often misused. On this point, Harold Watts has stated (Watts, 1969b):

> Much of the dissatisfaction with our current welfare system stems directly from discretion at the lower levels of authority. The inequities resulting from uneven and sometimes capricious use of this discretion are bad enough, but it can also be argued with some merit that the experience of face-to-face dealing with one who has the authority to withdraw or grant a principal means of support itself encourages and even promotes the very habits and attitudes of dependency our society is at some pains to eliminate.

In-kind programs are the least satisfactory of all distributive schemes. The Heineman Commission has recommended that special programs providing food to poor families be phased out in favor of cash assistance. The Commission also has expressed a preference for gradual elimination of housing programs when income supplements approach adequate levels and the private market can meet the demand for low-cost housing (President's Commission, 1969: 22). Many in-kind programs are not only demeaning and falsely assume that the poor lack proper values, but they are also wasteful and ineffective. The Heineman Commission found that surplus food is often thrown away because people do not like it; eligible families do not buy food stamps because they have to give up too many nonfood purchases to do so; and sick people often fail to use health facilities because they are unpleasant or too far away (President's Commission, 1969: 367).

B. Alternative Income Supplement Strategies

In light of the deficiencies of present income maintenance programs, attention recently has turned to consideration of various comprehensive income supplement strategies that would provide nationwide annual minimum incomes to all Americans based on family need or an alternative criterion. The three most widely discussed schemes are:

1) *Guaranteed employment,* a program that would make the federal government the employer of last resort for those who could not find jobs
2) *Children's allowances,* which would provide to families a specified grant of money for each child
3) *Negative income tax,* the program of concern in this paper, which provides specified supplements to annual income based on family size, and includes a financial incentive to work feature which reduces payments by some fraction of a dollar for each dollar earned, to insure that those who work always have more income than those who do not

1. Criteria for evaluating programs. In order to evaluate the relative advantages and disadvantages of each scheme properly, we need a set of criteria applicable to all. Scholars in the field of income maintenance have emphasized a variety of criteria (Marmor, 1969; Weisbrod, 1969; President's Commission, 1969). In the absence of a generally accepted set, we offer the following tentative list of factors for evaluating any new income maintenance program:

1) *Adequacy of benefits*—where will the poor be in relation to the poverty line after payments, or what percent of lost earnings will be replaced by the program
2) *Scope of coverage*—what percent of the poor or the risk population will be covered by the program
3) *Leakage*—how efficient is the program in terms of the percent of total costs spent on administration and in payments to nonpoor as opposed to direct benefits to the poor
4) *Cost*—how much will the program cost the taxpaying public
5) *Dignity and restraints on behavior*—does the program dispense funds without disagreeable surveillance or screening procedures; does the program restrict freedom of movement or choice in the labor or consumer market
6) *Adverse side effects*—does the program have inadvertent consequences such as disruption of family organization, discouragement of labor force participation, or encouragement of labor force withdrawal in order to qualify for funds; does the program interfere with other programs or create undesirable patterns of migration
7) *Clarity of application and minimization of discretionary*

power—does the program minimize, if not eliminate, the power of administrators to determine final treatment of recipients, are there clear and precise rules that specify the allocation of benefits in the program

8) *Equity*—are there precise rules for horizontal equity, i.e., the equal treatment of all who are equally placed; are there rules for vertical equity, i.e., clear-cut and reasonable criteria by which groups are differentiated in terms of needs

9) *Automatic flexibility*—is there built into the program anticipations of changing statuses of recipients and economic conditions which provide for automatic shifts in benefits

10) *Economic stability*—does funding or operation of the program have adverse effects on the economy or labor markets

No attempt has been made to be exhaustive in this list. We have intentionally avoided listing specific program attributes having to do with definition of income and family unit, benefit structure, length of the accounting and payment period, how the program shall be paid for, and other features that are quite obviously critical in the final operation of a program. At present it is not possible to know with any certainty the outcomes for each program on each criterion listed, much less for those details not listed. We lack precisely the kind of evidence for program evaluation that is being collected in the New Jersey–Pennsylvania experiment. However, it is possible to make some estimates of how each program might fare the above criteria so long as we keep in mind the possible influences of variations in program details.

Space does not allow a detailed application of these criteria to the three comprehensive income maintenance schemes. We present instead a brief summary of the most important weaknesses and strengths of each program.

2. Guaranteed employment. The major advantages of a guaranteed employment program are its utilization of manpower and the fact that income would be dignified by work rather than stigmatized as "given away." The major weaknesses of a guaranteed employment program have to do with adequacy, scope, and adverse side effects. Unless a guaranteed employment program were tied to a generous wage supplement scheme it could not provide the occupationally unskilled poor with incomes above the poverty line. Nor would making the federal government an employer of last resort assist the one-third of poor families who simply do not have employable members. Finally, if, as employer of last resort, the federal government paid unskilled workers wages or supplements sufficient enough to bring incomes above the poverty line, these jobs might very well attract many low paid semiskilled and unskilled workers from the private sector, an undesirable side effect that would require the imposition of restrictive eligibility rules and tests of need for qualification. These weaknesses appear to outweigh any social gains from linking income to work.

3. Children's allowances. The major advantage of a children's allowance program is that it sets up a simple, easily administered, and dignified right to income based on size of family, a criterion that is not considered by employers in setting wages of workers. There are, however, a number of weaknesses, with respect to adequacy, leakage, and adverse side effects. A good deal depends upon the size of the allowance. If payment per check is as low as in Canada and most other nations (excluding France) it would be inadequate to lift most poor families out of poverty. The major weakness, however, is that children's allowances are very inefficient for getting at poverty. To make the program universal means paying most of the money to nonpoor families and retrieving it through positive taxation. In addition, certain unfortunate side-effects are possible. Some concern has been expressed that it might depress wages or decrease work incentives. Effect on wages would depend upon how the program is financed. Wages are more likely to be affected if the taxes are tied to payrolls (Green, 1967). Affects on work incentives depend upon whether allowances are so high as to make total allowance income equal to or higher than work income. The dilemma is precisely that in order to be of real assistance to the poor, allowances would have to be high enough to "compete" with wage income, which suggests that despite its good qualities a children's allowance program does not deal efficiently with the poverty problem.

4. Negative income tax. This scheme has many obvious advantages. It would be universal in coverage, provide a dignified way to transfer funds to the poor without screening or surveillance, avoid possible disruption of family organization, and, with the work incentive factor built in, encourage voluntary labor force participation. It also minimizes the discretionary power of administrators and provides clear and precise rules of horizontal and vertical equity. As in the federal income tax system, shifts in the organization of the program or recipient status vis-à-vis the program could be easily and automatically accommodated.

As a move in this direction, the Nixon Administration introduced legislation last year to reform the existing welfare transfer programs by instituting what amounts to a negative income tax for families with children under eighteen. This Family Assistance Plan (FAP) provides a minimum income guarantee of $1,600 for a family of four. In addition, the bill includes a 50 percent tax rate on earnings plus a set-aside of up to $60 a month from earnings. Thus the break-even point for a four-person family is $3,920. Although the legislation is currently stalled in the Senate, there seems to be little doubt that change in the income maintenance is pointed along the negative income tax route.

The major problems with a negative income tax program have to do with adequacy and cost. Adequacy would depend entirely upon where the break-even points are set. Most programs now being discussed would not do away with poverty. They are typically minimal supplements to earned income. To wipe out poverty via the negative income tax would be expensive, possibly costing in the neighborhood of $25 billion.

II. EXPERIMENTAL OBJECTIVES OF THE NEW JERSEY–PENNSYLVANIA STUDY

Whatever the presumed benefits of a negative tax scheme, there are a variety of questions that must be answered before its adoption. With some oversimplification, they can be summarized into one: what is the cost of a negative tax program? To answer this question, we must specify a particular program—a particular tax rate, guarantee level, and a set of eligibility criteria—and examine empirically the work effort under the program.

If tax rates, guarantee level, and eligibility criteria were all that were needed to calculate cost, empirical research would be unnecessary, aside from the determination of the number of eligibles. Nor would research be required if it were possible to determine the work response of participants from theory, but neither economic nor sociological theory is sufficiently developed to provide us with quantitative forecasts in these areas. Both economic and sociological theory will give us qualitative predictions: we expect some people to choose less work as the cost of not working decreases, but we cannot say by how much. We need to know how the response will vary with the tax rate-guarantee level combination and, within combinations, by labor market status, age, race, ethnicity, education, residential location, family size and composition, occupational history, values, etc.

The usual types of economic and sociological data—governmental and private censuses and surveys—are not adequate to these questions, for it is extremely unlikely that we could find natural analogs of sufficient size and permanence to be comparable to the exogenously induced changes in a family's unearned income which would be provided in a negative tax program. What evidence we have on the unearned part of a family's income indicate that it is of little consequence for families of low annual income (Weisbrod and Hansen, 1967). Consequently, we are led to an experimental design for research into the response to a negative income tax.

The particular experiment reported here is chiefly concerned with the broad question of work effort response. The dimensions of this question are extremely complex and we shall just list some of the major issues with which the experiment is concerned. This list by no means exhausts all of the important questions associated with work effort response. There are a large number that the experiment, by design, cannot address. We shall return to this problem later.

First, if cash transfers carry with them work disincentives, how do these vary by tax-rate-guarantee combinations? Second, will primary and secondary wage earners respond differently? Theory would lead us to expect that wives working as secondary earners will leave the labor force more readily than their husbands since half their income typically goes to cover the costs of working (Addiss, 1963). Does this happen and does it happen differentially by transfer treatment? Third, if job opportunities are scarce, do benefits induce migration to areas of tighter labor supply? Fourth, do the guarantees stimulate job changes which produce a fuller utilization of available skills and/or enhancement of skills in order to command a higher price? Fifth, do the guarantees stimulate enrollments to training courses for the purposes of upgrading skills?

Cross-cutting these five issues are questions of response by race, ethnicity, education, age, occupational history, and values. As the poor are neither uniform in their characteristics nor a random sample of the United States population, estimates of costs must take their composition into consideration. We must learn whether different groups respond in the same way to a particular transfer scheme. We are likely to find that no one program minimizes the disincentives for all groups. If this is the case, examining the intergroup variation in response should provide a basis for constructing ancillary programs to fill in the deficiencies of whatever scheme seems most feasible in terms of the largest number of the poor. Even given the same net aggregate response for two different transfer schemes, we may want to choose, for exogenous policy reasons, the scheme which would minimize the disincentive in one group and maximize it in another. For example, we might want to minimize the disincentive among the young and maximize it among the potentially retired.

Still other questions refer as much to the social as to the fiscal costs associated with a negative tax. For example, we want to know the effect of the transfers on family structure, particularly among blacks. If job-conditioned income instability contributes to marital disruptions as currently thought, we will want to know if a transfer scheme will reduce them. On the other hand, it is possible for the transfers to increase marital conflict. Since the transfer income does not stem from the activities of an individual, questions may arise regarding rights to it. How this potential conflict will be resolved, and how the resolution will differ by ethnic and racial group, are of interest to us.

In addition, we are examining consumption and savings patterns, use of time, fertility and child spacing, political consciousness and participation. Again, questions mentioned here do not exhaust the complexity of questions relating to program costs or other concerns; they merely represent some of the major areas of investigation. Also, because of their importance, some questions will be researched even though the experiment is not designed to address them efficiently. For example, while we will look into the issues of fertility and child spacing, these questions really call for an experiment of greater duration. And while we will examine the impact of income transfers on the economic and political structures of the sampled neighborhoods, the problem truly requires an experiment which supports all of the eligibles in an area—which the present one does not.

III. THE DESIGN OF THE EXPERIMENT[2]

Since the major purpose of the experiment is to assess work effort response and since most of the poor are in intact families in urban areas, the experiment is restricted to male-headed families with a nonstudent male head, 18–58 years of age, able to work, and with a normal[3] family income no more than 150 percent of the poverty line for each family size. This line is based on a formula established in basic outline by Mollie Orshansky of the Social Security Administration.[4] It is calculated by tripling the cost of a food plan deemed nutritionally adequate for individuals in different sex-age categories, summed for each family, with a 15

---

[2] See Watts (1969) for a more detailed description of the experiment at its conception.

[3] "Normal" income refers to an empirical approximation to a long-run income concept such as Friedman's Permanent Income. A regression is being developed to describe the average relation between family income and a fairly eclectic set of household characteristics; they are fitted to give a good approximation at the low end of the income distribution. "Normal" income is an interpolation between (1) a household's income as predicted by this and (2) its actual income over the most recent year as reported in a special screening interview.

[4] Mollie Orshansky, "Counting the Poor: Another Look at the Poverty Profile," *Social Security Bulletin,* January 1965; id., "Who's Who Among the Poor: A Demographic View of Poverty," ibid., July 1965.

Table 1. Nonfarm Poverty Lines in 1968,
by Family Size

Family size	Experiment	Federal[a]
2	$2,000	$2,272
3	2,750	2,774
4	3,300	3,553
5	3,700	4,188
6	4,050	4,706
7	4,350	5,789
8 or more	4,600	5,789

[a] U.S. Bureau of the Census, "Poverty in the United States: 1959–1968," *Current Population Reports*, Series P-60, No. 68 (U.S. Government Printing Office, 1959), p. 11.

percent discount for families living on farms. Moreover, the poverty threshold is adjusted each year to reflect price changes.

The poverty line used in the experiment is slightly different than that used by the Federal government. The variation resulted from a desire to round off the odd numbers plus some feeling that a realistic cash transfer program would not increase benefits proportionate to increases in family size. Both the experimental "poverty line" and the average Federal threshold in terms of 1968 prices are presented in Table 1.

The sample has been drawn from poverty tracts in Trenton, Paterson, Passaic, and Jersey City, New Jersey; and Scranton, Pennsylvania. The first part of the sample was drawn in Trenton in August 1968; the final segment was selected in Scranton in September 1969. Our experience is that roughly 80 percent of the eligibles will fall between 100–150 percent of the poverty line.

The basic design contains one experimental and two control groups. Once eligibility is determined from a special screening interview, families are randomly assigned to one of eight negative tax plans which together define the experimental group or to one of the two control groups. The experimental group contains 659 families; the first control group consists of 650 families, the second of 100.

The eight tax plans are combinations of tax rates and guarantee levels which, in our judgment, encompass the area of greatest policy interest. Tax rates range from 30 to 70 percent, and guarantee levels vary from 50 to 125 percent of the poverty line (thus for a family of four, the range of guarantees would be from $1,741 to $4,352). Table 2 shows the combinations selected for experimentation. Table 3 gives the guarantee levels by family size.

After families have been assigned to groups, all (experimental and

Table 2. Negative Income Tax Plans in the
New Jersey Experiment
("X" marks plans in use)

Guarantee levels	Tax rates		
	30%	50%	70%
.50 poverty line ($1,741)[a]	X	X	
.75 poverty line ($2,611)	X	X	X
1.00 poverty line ($3,482)		X	X
1.25 poverty line ($4,352)		X	

[a] Figures in parentheses are guarantee levels for a family of four.

control) receive a pre-enrollment interview. The purpose of this interview is to obtain baseline data in a variety of areas uncontaminated by knowledge of the experiment or the inception of transfers. Subsequently, the experimental families are visited by enrollers who explain the program to them and solicit their cooperation. If obtained (less than 7 percent refuse), they receive payments for three years. Their only obligation is to report their income and family composition each month and to submit to quarterly interviews.

The first control group is also interviewed quarterly. The size of this group (650 families) reflects a concern for attrition which grew as sampling and interviewing progressed.

One of the most difficult methodological problems in studies of this kind arises from the possibility that what transfer effects are observed may be due to the experiment rather than to payments themselves. Since we are asking people about their work quarterly (and if they are not working, whether they have looked for work), it is not beyond the realm of possibility that our interviews might stimulate responses. We cannot eliminate such effects, but we can measure them by means of the second control group, which will be interviewed annually. Initially it will be selected from the same list of eligibles as the other groups; however, no

Table 3. Guarantee Levels by Household Size

Guarantee levels	Household size						
	2	3	4	5	6	7	8+
.50 poverty line	$1,055	$1,450	$1,741	$1,952	$2,136	$2,294	$2,426
.75 poverty line	$1,582	$2,175	$2,611	$2,928	$3,204	$3,441	$3,639
1.00 poverty line	$2,110	$2,901	$3,482	$3,904	$4,273	$4,589	$4,853
1.25 poverty line	$2,637	$3,626	$4,352	$4,880	$5,341	$5,736	$6,066

effort will be made to maintain the same group over the three years. It would be extremely difficult, given the once-a-year contact, and not really necessary. A comparable sample is all that is required, and it can be drawn freshly each year.

Because of a concern for ethnic and racial difference in responses, an effort was made to balance the sample in this regard. Properly speaking, we employed a form of stratified random sampling in order to ensure adequate numbers of black, Puerto Rican, and white families. Had this not been done so, there would have been an excess of Puerto Ricans and too few whites. Currently, the sample composition is 36 percent black, 32 percent Puerto Rican, and 32 percent white.

Finally, our design recognizes that the experiment exists in competition with current welfare programs, and during its existence, these programs may provide higher support levels. The likely result of such a situation would be that some families will elect to receive welfare in preference to the experiment's benefits. Rather than simply drop these families from our program and lose all of the effort invested in and information obtained from them, we chose to continue these families as part of the experimental group, but pay them only the minimum benefit. It would, of course, be of little use to pay them more, since welfare would only cut their payment by an equivalent amount. We do not believe this is by any means an optimal solution to the problem, but as yet we do not know of a better one.

IV. FINDINGS AND METHODOLOGICAL ISSUES

While detailed statistical analysis of the data collected thus far is yet to be undertaken, our experience does permit us to report some preliminary findings relevant to a national negative tax program and to current and future experiments. We shall divide these findings into two groups: (1) those which relate to both possible national programs and to other experiments and (2) those which refer more directly to other experiments. In the latter section, we shall also address some methodological problems with experiments in general and our experiment in particular. The preliminary nature of the findings cannot be overemphasized. It would be inappropriate to draw strong inferences from them.

A. National Programs and Experiments

The critical experimental question is, of course, the work effort response to the negative tax payments. Two measures of this response are currently available: (1) changes in the size of our average payment and (2) relative change in the average earned family incomes for the experimental and control groups. If wage earners drop out of the labor force and substitute negative tax payments for earned income, the size of our average payment should rise over time. Moreover, average earned family income in the experimental group should decline relative to average earned family income in the control groups.

Based on fifteen months' experience in Trenton and in Paterson and Passaic, we can say that there is little evidence that wage earners are leaving the labor force. On the contrary, our average payments have been quite stable over time, and average earned family incomes have risen and at approximately the same rate for both the experimental and control groups. It appears that the increases in family incomes are due to increases in the prevailing wage rates. Thus both measures of work effort indicate so far that it is undiminished by negative tax transfers.

In addition, there is no evidence that families have treated the payments as a windfall, even during the very first payment periods. Fears of spending sprees or "unusual" expenditures have not been justified. It appears that families budget the payments as they do any other item of income.

From the standpoint of national program cost, another important experimental issue is the probable participation rate of the eligible population. Projections of program costs vary markedly depending upon the particular tax rate, guarantee level, and population groups the estimator chose to incorporate. But all estimators assume complete participation of the eligible population. This is a perfectly reasonable assumption if a national program is structured to make payments automatically. For example, benefits might be computed and paid as a result of filing the annual tax return. However, if application for benefits is discretionary, then the assumption is not viable and current cost estimates may be excessively high.

Because participation in the experiment is voluntary, we did not assume full participation of the eligible population. Given the percentage of the eligibles utilizing current welfare programs, unemployment compensation, and tax rebate procedures, this just did not seem reasonable. Rather we expected that those families whose normal income was close to their break-even point, or whose income fluctuations brought them close to their break-even point, might not find the size of the payment worth the bother to apply for it. And as income rose, we expected an increasing number of families with self-definitions as nonpoor would reject our payments.

Thus far these expectations have been confirmed and the results are observable in terms of the families who have dropped out of the experiment or refused to participate. As of October 1970, 91 of the roughly 725 experimental families have withdrawn from the experiment. Of these, 67 were at or above their break-even point just prior to quitting the program. Of the 24 families who were below their break-even point— that is, who received more than the minimum payment—15 dropped out either because they moved and could not be located[5] or because they moved out of the continental United States.[6] For only 15 of the 16 families at or above their break-even point was a move the basis for attrition. (Of these 16, 8 moved and could not be located; this figure should be compared with the four withdrawals among the 24 receiving more than the minimum payment which involved a family that moved and could not be located.) While evidence based upon such small numbers is suggestive at best, it does not seem unreasonable to propose that families receiving the minimum payment may not believe as strongly as families receiving higher payments that keeping the experimenters informed of their whereabouts is worth the bother. Analysis of the refusals provides further substantiation for the general point. Over all cities, 71 percent of the families who refused to participate (54 families) would have received only the minimum payment in any case. Of the remainder, virtually all were families on welfare who did not feel it to their advantage to change to our programs.

Altogether, the number of families who have dropped out is roughly 13 percent of the experimental group. It would be extremely difficult to project these figures into estimates for a national program. Families whose incomes exceeded the experimental criterion when eligibility was determined but whose incomes subsequently dropped below it are excluded. Thus net attrition may be less than 7 percent. On the other hand, the exigencies of the research design have required that we make every effort to persuade families to remain in the experiment. Matters are further complicated by the fact that those who withdrew are spread across eight experimental tax plans, so no plan contains enough cases for reliable estimates. Nonetheless, it is clear that if participation in a national program is voluntary, there may well be significant underutilization—as is the case with other voluntary transfer programs.

---

[5] Families are considered to have dropped from the experiment if they move without leaving a forwarding address and if an elaborate search procedure we have developed fails to reveal their whereabouts.

[6] We make no effort to follow those families that leave the continental United States.

B. Experiments

However valuable it may be for an estimate of national program participation, attrition is a disaster for an experiment. Not only may samples become too small to permit reliable estimates of effects, but if attrition is at all selective (and we have seen that it is), the estimates that can be calculated on those remaining in the experiment may be seriously biased. The problem is particularly acute in the control groups, since there are fewer benefits to induce cooperation. Thus far, we have lost 69 control group families out of 632.

The experiment began with payments to all families, experimental and control, of $5 per interview, in the rather naive (it now appears) hope that this amount would be sufficient to hold the cooperation of the main control group. It was not. Moreover, the minimum payment of $5 a month did not seem to be enough to sustain the cooperation of many experimental families. Therefore a decision was made to substantially increase the incentives. Now the main control group is paid a $10 per month "filing fee" for keeping our office informed of their addresses, and the minimum experimental payment is $20 per month. While we are hopeful that these solutions will alleviate the problem, it is as yet too early to judge their effects. Admittedly, the remedy slightly distorts the experimental approximation to reality, since it can be said that now all families are receiving payments. However, the problem does not appear to be significant. The amount involved probably is not large enough to affect estimates, and in any event, responses are likely to be more readily observed in terms of the variation in payments than in terms of their absolute levels.

For the experimental group, information is another means to cut attrition. The program was explained to sample families at some length prior to their enrollment, but a substantial amount of ignorance, confusion, and suspicion remained and further explanations were made in a number of cases. While most of the suspicion appears to have been allayed, a recent sampling of families revealed that a great deal of ignorance still exists. Such ignorance does little to motivate cooperation, and, consequently, we are considering making new explanations to everyone. Clearly, if such knowledge, or the lack of it, affects participation in the experiment, it is likely to affect participation in a national program.

Also related to the question of attrition is the length of the period between income reports and payments. Originally, families were asked to report their incomes monthly; payments were made biweekly. But we quickly discovered that many families, particularly those receiving the minimum payment, found the schedule onerous. Fearing—and finding—

attrition we attempted to ease the situation by only requiring those receiving minimum payments to report their incomes every three months. Interestingly, we found more opposition to the new plan than to the old. Investigation revealed that with the reduced contact under the new plan families perceived the requests for data as even greater disruptions of their normal scheme of things than they had under the old plan. In addition, since we require each family to submit their pay stubs along with their income reports, we found that they had difficulty keeping track of them over the three-month period. As a result, we returned to the monthly schedule.

Despite their deficiencies, these procedures do represent an improvement over those developed during the planning stage of the experiment. It was intended that both reports and payments would be made on a monthly basis. But pilot interviews suggested that the families would find the schedule bothersome. So we asked ourselves how we could emphasize the benefits of the program. We concluded that we had to make the program more visible and salient to the families. One way to accomplish this is simply to increase rather than decrease contact. But to increase contact by increasing the frequency of the required income reports is to emphasize a negative aspect. Accordingly, we decided to shorten the payment interval; rather than monthly, payments are made every two weeks. Reaction to the change has been remarkably good. Most of our families are paid their earnings weekly or every two weeks, and many have told us that the schedule helps them to integrate our payments into their budgets. Judging from reactions like these, the payment schedule may well have avoided a source of attrition.

More generally, our experience suggests that the length of the interval between payments may significantly affect participation in national programs or future experiments. Keying the transfer interval to the prevailing job payment period could be beneficial.

There are a number of additional questions of interest to both economists and sociologists which derive from the conditions of a negative income tax experiment rather than from negative taxation per se.

Negative tax experiments must exist in the context of alternative welfare programs which they cannot control and which may offer competing benefits. Changes in these competing programs therefore may seriously affect the behavior of experimental families. For example, during this past summer, New Jersey raised the support level of its AFDC-UP program. As a result, the AFDC-UP payments now exceed the benefits in a number of tax plans in the experiment. This situation has led a number of families to drop our payments in favor of New Jersey's. Although almost all of these families continue to be interviewed, the loss of these families from our tax plans clearly endangers the validity of the estimates we hope to make as to the effects of these plans. Moreover, the loss of families is likely to be systematic, since differences in the educational attainment and sophistication of families imply that the distribution of knowledge about alternative welfare programs is not random. Thus estimates made on the basis of families remaining in the tax plans may well be biased. It is entirely possible that our experiment and others like it could be seriously impaired by current, competing welfare programs.

Another set of problems derives from the possibility of communication among persons on the experiment. As described earlier, some of the tax plans are considerably more generous than others. Obviously, individuals are disturbed when they learn that their families are being supported at a lower level than their neighbors. One family quit the experiment for this reason. Related to this phenomenon is the case of the employer who, discovering that one of his employees was receiving benefits from us, decided the man did not need his job and fired him.

Many of these problems are less likely to occur or if they did would have little significance in a national program of negative taxation. However, they are endemic to experimentation in this area, and they do make the problem of obtaining experimental guidance for a national program more difficult.

Some of the difficulties associated with supporting only a proportion of the eligible population in a neighborhood relate to our ability to predict community effects which may emerge under an income maintenance program. A range of neighborhood responses to the infusion of financial resources into poor areas is possible. Services which are currently lacking in these areas may improve, the quality of housing may be raised, or, alternatively, the exploitation of the poor may simply become more rewarding. Similarly, it is possible that with an increase of resources in poor neighborhoods, the ability to maintain self-interest organizations will improve, possibly resulting in a multiplier effect whereby poor neighborhoods translate some of their new income into political power.

However, many of these effects cannot be adequately studied since only a proportion of the eligible population in any neighborhood is supported by the experiment. Some of the possible neighborhood responses may require a minimum critical value of disposable income before they can occur. The aggregate amount of money provided to a neighborhood may be too low to allow us the opportunity to study community organization effects.

Another kind of problem deriving from support of only a proportion of the eligible population stems from pressures that have been exerted to place specific individuals under the support program. Organized political groups in a few instances have viewed the experiment as a potential source of favors for important constituents. Pressure has been exerted to admit particular individuals into the experiment or onto the program staff. Fortunately, we have been able to resolve these problems without affecting the integrity of the experiment. However, the potential for such interference will have to be considered in planning future experimental research on income maintenance.

V. THE ETHICAL ISSUE

In closing, we would like to mention a critical issue that heretofore has received little attention: the ethical questions in social experimentation. One set of problems arises from the fact that we are intervening in major ways into the lives of human beings—even if it is ostensibly for their betterment. For example, do we have any responsibility for what happens to persons in the experiment after the payments have ended when they know or at least were repeatedly told that the benefits will only be paid for a given time period? More specifically, if, for those eligible for welfare, there is a time gap between the end of our payments and the start of welfare, do we have a responsibility to assist them financially? What are our obligations if families develop patterns of life that cannot be sustained without the experimental payments?

We raise these issues as warnings to future experimenters rather than as problems capable of universal solutions. We note only that we hope to report at a later time on our particular solutions.

VI. REFERENCES

Addiss, Luise K. Job-related expenses of the working mother. *Children*
    1963   (November–December): 219–223.
Green, Christopher. *Negative Taxes and the Poverty Problem.* Washington,
    1967   D.C.: The Brookings Institution.
Marmor, Theodore R. Income Maintenance Alternatives: Concepts, cri-
    1969   teria, and program comparisons. University of Wisconsin,
              Institute for Research on Poverty, Discussion Paper No. 55.
Orshansky, Mollie. The shape of poverty in 1966. *Social Security Bulletin*
    1968   (March): 3–31.
President's Commission on Income Maintenance Programs. *Poverty amid*
    1969   *Plenty: The American Paradox* (November).

Tobin, James. Raising the incomes of the poor. Pp. 77–116 in Kermit
    1968   Gordon (ed.), *Agenda for the Nation*. Garden City, N.Y.:
              Doubleday.
Watts, Harold W. Graduated Work Incentives: An experiment in negative
    1969a   taxation. *Am. Econ. Rev. Proc.* (May): 463–72.
Watts, Harold W. Testimony Before the Committee on Ways and Means,
    1969b   House of Representatives, U.S. Congress, on H.R. 14173,
              "Family Assistance Plan."
Weisbrod, Burton A. Collective action and the distribution of income: a
    1969   conceptual approach. University of Wisconsin, Department of
              Economics, unpublished ms.
Weisbrod, Burton A., and W. Lee Hansen. An Income-Net-Worth Ap-
    1968   proach to Measuring Economic Welfare. *Am. Econ. Rev.* (De-
              cember): 1315–29.

THE RURAL NEGATIVE INCOME TAX EXPERIMENT

D. Lee Bawden

Increasing concern about the exclusivity, inequity, and inadequacy of the welfare structure has stimulated a search for alternative income maintenance schemes to augment or replace current public assistance programs. One of these alternatives is the negative income tax. An historic social experiment financed by the Office of Economic Opportunity was begun in New Jersey in 1968 to test the workability and consequences of this program for families residing in urban areas. This paper reports on a second experiment, the purpose of which is to measure the effects of alternative negative income tax (NIT) programs upon rural people.

I. THE NEGATIVE INCOME TAX

The negative income tax may be thought of as a downward extension of the positive income tax. There would be both positive and negative rates and there would be some income level unique for each family size, above which taxes would be paid and below which money subsidies would be received. There are several variations of the negative income tax described in the literature but all have the same basic components: (1) a guaranteed minimum level of income (G) that varies with family size, (2) a negative tax rate (T) applied against earned income,[1] and (3) a

---

This paper appears as "Income Maintenance and the Rural Poor: An Experimental Approach," in *American Journal of Agricultural Economics,* 52: 438–41, August 1970. Reprinted by permission.
[1] In some proposals the tax rate varies as earned income rises.

break-even level of earned income (B), above which no transfer payment is received. The relationship between these three variables may be stated in algebraic terms as follows:

$$G/T = B$$

As can be seen, setting of the level of any two of these variables determines the outcome of the third. The amount of transfer payments (P) in relation to earned income (E) under such a scheme is

$$P = G - (T \times E) \geq 0$$

and $P = 0$ when $E = B$.

It might be useful to illustrate the negative income tax with an example. The presently established poverty line for a family of four is about $3,600. Let us suppose that there is a negative income tax program that guarantees a family of four three-fourths of this level, or $2,700. Assume further that the established negative tax rate is 60 percent. If the family earned no income it would be paid $2,700 per year. For every dollar the family earns, payments would be reduced by $0.60. If the family earned $1,000 in income, payments would be $2,700 minus ($0.60 × $1,000), or $2,100. Family income would be $1,000 plus $2,100, or $3,100. If the family earned $2,700, the minimum guarantee, it would still receive a payment of $1,080 [$2,700 − ($0.60 × $2,700) = $1,080]; hence family income would be $3,780. If the family earned the established poverty amount of $3,600, it would still receive a subsidy of $540 [$2,700 − ($0.60 × $3,600) = $540] and total family income would be $4,140. In fact, payments would not cease for that family until its income reached $4,500. This can be derived directly from the above formula by setting $G = \$2,700$, $T = .6$, and solving for B.

This simple illustration points out both the major strength and the major weakness of the negative income tax. The strength is that the negative income tax contains an incentive for individuals to work because they are allowed to keep some of their earned income. The weakness is that, if this is done, one must lower the guarantee below the poverty line, or pay money to families above the poverty line, or (as in the above example) both. Twenty-seven hundred dollars is below the minimum poverty line for a family of four; yet with a 60 percent tax rate, payments would be made to families earning up to $4,500. Obviously, the marginal benefit of a dollar paid to a family earning $4,400 is less from a welfare standpoint than a dollar paid to a family earning no income. Yet there seems no way to resolve this paradox and provide an incentive to work.

Finally, a basic concept of the negative income tax is that it is paid to the poor regardless of *why* they are poor. Presumably eligibility would be based on individual declarations of income much the same as the positive tax system now operates.

II. REASONS FOR A RURAL NIT EXPERIMENT

The New Jersey experiment is expected to yield a great deal of information about the effects of various negative tax plans on attitudinal and behavioral characteristics of *urban* wage earners. There is reason to believe, however, that these results may not be directly applicable to the rural sector, in which one-third of the nation's poor resides. One expected difference between rural and urban residents is in their work response to such a program, because of differences in alternative employment opportunities and in the proportion of self-employed people. An accurate estimate of the magnitude of disincentive, both rural and urban, is crucial to estimating the cost of a nationwide program.

A negative income tax is also expected to have a substantial effect on the rate and composition of migration, both intra- and inter-community. Net migration out of rural areas during the 1960's probably has exceeded 10 million people and gross migration may be double that amount. Since there is considerable interest by policymakers in ways to reduce and/or direct this flow, it seems important to learn the effects of NIT payments upon rural-urban migration.

Also, it is not readily apparent that the specific program most effective for addressing urban poverty problems is best suited for rural poverty. For example, a large number of rural residents with low incomes are operators of farms or businesses in small towns. Administration of a program for the self-employed (especially those farmers who receive their entire annual income at harvest time) is likely to be different from that for wage earners.

Finally, the urban experiment restricts eligibility to families of two or more members, with a male head between the ages of 18 and 58. Since a large number of poor households are headed by a female of working age and by those over 58 years of age, a study of their work behavior is also necessary for an accurate estimate of the cost of a nationwide NIT program. There seems to be no obvious way to infer from male work behavior the effect of this program upon female and older heads.

The need for experimentation in addition to that being conducted in New Jersey and Pennsylvania was recognized by the Ford Foundation, which made a grant to the Institute for Research on Poverty at the University of Wisconsin to plan for a rural experiment. Under this grant, ten staff members representing economics, agricultural economics, sociology, political science, law, and social work combined in an interdisciplinary effort to design this experiment.

III. THE RURAL NIT EXPERIMENT

A dispersed sample of 825 families was selected for the rural experiment; 600 of these are headed by a male between 18 and 58 years of age, 110 by a female in the same age range; 115 by a male or female over 58 years of age. The sample was drawn during the summer and early fall of 1969; the first payments were made in November and December. The experiment will continue for three years, at an estimated total cost of $3.3 million. Funding is by the Office of Economic Opportunity.

The experiment is patterned after the one in New Jersey. It has the same basic objectives, a comparable experimental design, a similar procedure for determining income and making payments, and is to be of identical duration. It differs from the urban experiment in that eligibility is extended to single-person households as well as those headed by females and the aged. Minor variations also exist in the definition of earned income and in the accounting period.

Each of the major facets of this experiment is briefly discussed below.

A. Objectives of the Experiment

The primary objective is to measure the effect of alternative tax rates and minimum guarantees upon the work incentive of rural residents and to compare and contrast these findings with those of the urban experiment. This issue is of paramount importance because of the commonly held belief that payments, even with the negative tax, will significantly reduce the work effort of able-bodied males. Another objective is to measure the effect on school performance of children of poor rural families.

Of secondary importance are a number of other objectives, one of which is to learn the effect of payments on the rate and composition of migration, with particular attention to differences in response among age groups. Changes in expenditure patterns are also of interest—the distribution among savings, investment, and consumption; relative expenditures on necessities and luxuries; marginal expenditures on medical and dental care; and the effect upon credit versus cash buying. Other objectives include the effect of NIT payments upon adult education (including job training), family structure (separation and divorce rates), involvement in social, business, and political organizations, family health, and attitudes towards oneself and others.

B. Location

The sample was drawn from two separate locations, one in the South (North Carolina), the other in the Midwest (Iowa). The alternative of taking a nationwide rural sample was rejected in deference to administrative ease and a smaller operating budget. The choice of two areas rather than one was made because policymakers may distinguish between northern and southern rural residents. Furthermore, regional and ethnic differences in work incentive, migration, and other behavioral characteristics can be tested. The South was chosen because it contains a higher incidence of rural poverty than any other area in the United States; the Midwest, because it is (as classified by the USDA) "a relatively affluent area with a poor white minority."

Criteria for selection of the specific counties in each region included the size and number of rural towns, their proximity to large cities, density of the farm population, diversity of agriculture, and representativeness of the entire region with respect to incidence of poverty, unemployment, racial mix, age distribution, and educational level.

C. Experimental Design

Families were selected randomly from predesignated areas and, if deemed eligible for the program, were randomly assigned to a control group or to one of the program alternatives. Individuals will remain on that assignment for the duration of the experiment, and will be eligible for payments for the 36-month period regardless of their subsequent geographic location, as long as it is within the United States.

Family income at the time of screening could not exceed one and one-half times the established poverty line. Poverty levels for various family sizes are shown in Table 1. These poverty levels will be adjusted annually to account for increases in the national cost of living.

Family members (other than the head or spouse) age 21 or older who leave the original tax unit will be entitled individually to a separate head-of-household payment; those 18–20 will be granted "other adult" status. A family head or spouse who leaves the original unit will be eligible for a payment of one-half the amount that a head and spouse were entitled to when both were in the unit (e.g., for a group at 100 per-

Table 1. Poverty Levels

| Size of household | Poverty levels dollars per year | |
	Marginal	Total
Household head	$1,319	$1,319
Spouse	844	2,163
First dependent	738	2,901
Second dependent	581	3,482
Third dependent	422	3,904
Fourth dependent	369	4,273
Fifth dependent	316	4,589
Sixth dependent	264	4,853
Seventh dependent	211	5,064
Eighth dependent	158	5,222
Additional dependents	0	5,222
Other adults	844	—

cent of the poverty line the guarantee would be one-half of $2,163, or $1,082, if the head or spouse left).

To ensure a wider variation in environment, the sample density is fairly sparse, but not so much so as to make selected individuals oddities in their communities. The sample is stratified by income level.

D. Program Alternatives

Five program alternatives, involving three tax rates and three guaranteed minimums, are being tested. These are shown in Table 2 for a family of four. About 50 percent of the families were assigned to a control group and 50 percent to various plans, with less proportionate sampling in the more expensive plans. It is anticipated that about 750 of the original 825 families will remain in the program for the entire experimental period.

Table 2. Program Alternatives

| Poverty levels | Tax rates | | |
| | 30% | 50% | 70% |
	Guarantee level/cut-off		
One-half		$1,741/$3,482	
Three-fourths	$2,611/$8,703	$2,611/$5,222	$2,611/$3,730
Full		$3,482/$6,964	

E. Definition of Income

Income is defined as the total net income in cash or kind received by the household from all sources (including social security payments, unemployment compensation, and veterans' benefits). For some groups, imputed income is added to reported income for purposes of figuring program payments. Homeowners have an imputed rental value added to their income. For those with assets, 10 percent of net capital wealth is added annually to income to reflect potential capital consumption, the latter reflecting the thesis that the poor should, in part, "live off their assets rather than the Government."[2]

The first $20,000 of business assets, the first $10,000 equity in owner-occupied homes, $1,000 in cash or savings, and all personal effects are excluded from net capital wealth for purposes of this imputation.

F. Payment Interval and Income Accounting

Payments are based on income and the number of dependents, as reported on returns filed by the participants. These returns are filed every four weeks, showing gross receipts (wages for salaried employees, cash sales for businessmen and farmers) and (for the latter) *cash* expenses. The self-employed report depreciation and other noncash costs once a year, after filing their positive tax returns. All households are paid bi-weekly, but the accounting period for computing income, upon which those payments are based, is treated as an experimental variable.

The basic accounting plan for both the rural and urban experiments is a three-period moving average, each period representing four weeks. In addition, seventy-five families in the rural experiment receive payments based solely on income earned in the preceding four weeks.[3]

G. Measurement and Analysis

The experimental households are interviewed quarterly to gather information on the previously mentioned attitudinal and behavioral characteristics. Information will also be gathered from sources other than

---

[2] For a discussion of the various forms that this may take, see Weisbrod and Hansen [2].

[3] The income accounting procedure embodies a "carryover" provision. Earned income in excess of the break-even, or cut-off, level is carried forward for a maximum of one year and is added to income in any period in which such income falls below the break-even level. NIT payments are based on earned income plus any amount assigned to that period from the carryover.

the families, such as schools, hospitals, public organizations offering services to the poor, and other relevant institutions and organizations.

IV. CONCLUDING COMMENTS

Social experimentation of the nature and magnitude of these negative income tax studies is unique; previous experiments involving human beings have been limited to business games and consumer panels. Such experiments encounter some special problems—bias due to the Hawthorne effect, contamination by publicity, exogenous changes in the community (e.g., in employment opportunities or in the level of welfare support), bias because of sample attrition, and limitations on the time period over which the experiment can be conducted.[4]

It is hoped that the rural and urban negative income tax experiments will generate information, not only on the probable cost and effects of a nationwide negative income tax program, but also on the broader issue of the feasibility of social experimentation.

---

[4] For an in-depth consideration of the problems of social experimentation, especially regarding income maintenance, see Orcutt and Orcutt [1].

V. REFERENCES

[1] Orcutt, Guy H., and Alice G. Orcutt, "Incentive Experimentation for Income Maintenance Policy Purposes," *Am. Econ. Rev.,* 58:754–72, September 1968.
[2] Weisbrod, B. A., and W. L. Hansen, "An Income-Net Worth Approach to Measuring Economic Welfare," *Am. Econ. Rev.,* 58:1315–29, December 1968.

PART TWO

INTRODUCTION: STRATEGY FOR A BROAD PROGRAM OF EXPERIMENTATION IN INCOME MAINTENANCE

Larry L. Orr

I. INTRODUCTION

The initiation of the graduated work incentives experiment being conducted by the Institute for Research on Poverty and MATHEMATICA in New Jersey and Pennsylvania[1] has raised the prospect (some might say the specter) of an ambitious program of experimentation in social programs in general, and income maintenance programs in particular. Indeed, the enthusiasm for this relatively novel technique in some quarters threatens, at times, to outrun the capabilities of the embryonic reservoir of experience and expertise in this largely untried methodology.

It is important to understand from the outset exactly what "experimentation" means and to distinguish experimentation from the related, but distinctly different, concept of "demonstration." An experiment attempts, through the exogenous manipulation of the environment facing various economic, social, or political decision-making units, to measure their behavioral responses to variations in a particular program or program feature. Viewed in terms of a multiple regression model, the experiment seeks to generate data for the estimation of the response (de-

[1] For a detailed description of this project, see Harold W. Watts, "Graduated Work Incentives: An Experiment in Negative Taxation," *American Economic Review Proceedings* (May 1969), pp. 463–72.

pendent) variable as a function of a number of independent variables, some of which are policy parameters which can be manipulated experimentally. To achieve this goal, the experiment must obviously include several different "treatments" (at a minimum, one "experimental" treatment and a "control" or "status quo" treatment), in order to obtain estimates of differential responses. Where it is possible to define a quantifiable continuum in both the policy parameters and the behavioral response variable, it is desirable to select a number of treatments corresponding to different values or combinations of the policy parameters in order to estimate a continuous (generally nonlinear) "response surface." For example, the New Jersey experiment includes nine distinct treatments (including the control group), defined by different combinations of the income guarantee and the "special tax rate" under a negative income tax, with the objective of estimating the earned income response surface over the guarantee-tax rate plane. The importance of such experimental variation is that it yields information about behavioral responses to a variety of possible program variations, both those included in the experiment and, by interpolation or extrapolation (in the continuous case), others not included.

By contrast, what I shall call "demonstrations" typically involve little or no controlled variation of policy parameters. A uniform treatment is applied to a specified group or geographic area, often without even an attempt to define a comparable control group. Thus, it is difficult to test hypotheses rigorously in a demonstration; at best, one gets a qualitative feel for the consequences of the single program variant applied, and some idea of the administrative feasibility of the program.

While demonstrations of this type may be useful for certain purposes, in this paper I shall confine my attention to experiments in which hypotheses relating to behavioral responses to specified policy parameters can be rigorously posed and tested.

II. CRITERIA FOR THE SELECTION AND DESIGN OF EXPERIMENTS

Experimentation in income maintenance is an extremely expensive research undertaking, not only in financial terms, but in terms of research talent, which at the moment is a very scarce resource in this area. It follows that experiments should be used sparingly and be carefully designed to maximize their informational output. A prime criterion for the selection of a particular hypothesis for experimental testing, then, is whether that hypothesis can be adequately tested by nonexperimental (and, therefore, generally less expensive) methods. If relevant nonexperimental data exist, the presumption is against using experimentation to generate new data. That is, in many cases "natural experiments" can be found which provide the means of analyzing important questions, and such data should be fully utilized before experimentation is considered. The other side of this coin is, of course, that even if nonexperimental data are not available, experimentation is feasible only if it can be reasonably expected to provide a definitive test of the hypothesis in question.

For hypotheses where both of these conditions are satisfied, one is faced with the problem of assigning research priorities which rank them according to some set of criteria. I would suggest that the following criteria be applied, roughly in the order presented.

A. Policy Relevance

The overriding objective of research in the field of income maintenance is to provide guidance to policymakers in the revision and modification of income maintenance programs. Therefore, an obvious and appropriate criterion in developing experimental research is the usefulness of the information to be obtained from such research as an input into the policy decision-making process. This does not mean catering to political whims or pressures. It simply means that certain behavioral responses will bear more heavily on the desirability of any particular income maintenance plan than will other responses; ceteris paribus, these responses should receive higher experimental priority. The focus of the New Jersey experiment upon work effort response is a case in point; clearly, the response of recipients' earned income will have a major impact upon the cost of a negative income tax, as well as its political acceptability in terms of the dominant Puritan ethic. Moreover, because this response might be expected to be greatest among families with male heads in their working years, the New Jersey experiment was limited to that population.

B. Replicability

As a second criterion, I suggest what Hollister and Cain have called the "replicability criterion."[2] This criterion would restrict experimentation to those program features which can feasibly be replicated on a national scale. Any number of programs can be devised and instituted on

---

[2] Robinson Hollister and Glen Cain, "The Methodology of Evaluating Social Action Programs," University of Wisconsin, Institute for Research on Poverty (April 1969).

an experimental basis which, because of their cost or administrative complexity, could not reasonably be considered to be feasible alternatives for national policy. For example, one might hypothesize that a very intensive job training and counseling program would be an effective offset to the work disincentives of cash transfers. It may well be that, even if such a program could be carried out experimentally, it would simply not be feasible to provide such services to all recipients of a national transfer program.

A corollary of the replicability criterion is that, to obtain valid estimates of the effects of a national program, it must be possible to replicate the hypothesized feature of the national program in the experimental setting. For example, most income maintenance programs currently under consideration provide an income guarantee which is adjusted for family size. One might hypothesize that this program feature will tend to raise fertility by lowering the cost of childbearing. Clearly, however, an experiment which provides payments for only, say, three to five years would not be a valid simulation of the corresponding national program. To the extent that family planning is influenced by economic decisions at all, it presumably takes into account expected family income over the entire period of the child's dependency; transfer payments in a short-term experiment would seriously understate the financial incentive to bear children which would be present in a permanent program. On the other hand, an opposite bias is also introduced by the transitory nature of the experiment: since only those additional children born within the experimental period would be eligible for payments, there would be an incentive to speed up the timing of childbearing, resulting in a spurious increase in birth rates during the experiment. Again, this incentive would not exist in a permanent program. The possibility of devising an experiment designed to avoid these pitfalls will be discussed later in this paper.

C. Adequacy of Existing Theory and Measurement Techniques

In certain areas, the current state of the art severely circumscribes the possibilities for experimentation. In many cases, we have a vague notion that a particular policy parameter may have important behavioral effects, but we have only a general idea of the connection between the two, and the possibly only very crude quantitative measures of the effect itself. For example, one such area is the whole question of the effects of income maintenance on the institutional structure of the community. It seems plausible that large-scale income transfers will have important effects upon the interactions of recipients and non-recipients within a whole range of economic, social, and political institutions. Political participation of the poor might increase, leading to heightened political tensions and social interest—or the reverse might occur. Changes in the structure and spatial distribution of economic activity might be widespread and substantial, particularly in the key areas of housing, education, and health services. Existing institutions geared to the amelioration of poverty might wane or disappear and new institutions might arise. The list is endless. Yet we really have no coherent theory of community which would allow rigorous formulation of hypotheses for experimental testing of these questions. We don't know which policy parameters would be crucial to any given effects and, therefore, should be varied experimentally, and—perhaps more importantly—we do not know which nonpolicy variables must be controlled in order to assure valid inference.

By contrast, underlying the investigation of work effort response in the New Jersey experiment is a well-developed body of economic theory relating labor supply to wage rates, income, and other family characteristics. Where even the rudiments of such a theory are lacking, the wisest strategy is probably to devote our research effort to developing the basic theory before proceeding to experimentation.

Closely related to the theoretical underpinnings of experimentation is our ability to measure behavioral responses quantitatively. Our ability to pose meaningful, testable hypotheses and to generalize experimental results is severely constrained by the sophistication with which we can measure responses. Returning to the example of community effects, we face the difficult problem of defining and measuring institutional change. Can we really define appropriate indices of political participation and tension, social adjustment or alienation, or adequacy of social services? If not, the results of experimentation are likely to be ambiguous at best.

The requirement of an adequate theoretical and measurement capability is especially important for the specification of an efficient sample design. The question of adequate sample size will be discussed later in this section; at this point, suffice it to say that efficient determination of sample size depends upon our ability to predict the "normal" variability of the response variable, given the values of relevant nonexperimental variables (which must be specified by our theory or empirical data). The sample must be sufficiently large to distinguish the impact of the experimental variables from this residual noise in the response variable.

The criteria just presented bear upon the selection of hypotheses for experimental testing. Once it has been decided that a particular hypothesis requires, and is amenable to, experimentation, the question of optimal experimental design arises. This is a complex question, and this is not the place for a detailed discussion of the statistical intricacies involved. However, it seems useful to establish certain guidelines for design which are relevant to the development of a comprehensive research strategy involving a number of separate experiments; the following include some of the more important considerations.

D. Experimental Objectives

While the information obtained from any one experiment may be useful in analyzing a wide variety of questions, it seems most efficient to focus each experiment upon a single dominant response variable. This limitation is imposed by the necessity of defining a single experimental objective function which is to be maximized through the sample design. Maximization of the objective function is roughly equivalent to minimizing the error of estimate in the predicted response variable; it is, essentially, the efficiency criterion for the sample design. If an experiment attempts to focus on more than one objective, it is not at all clear what the criterion of efficiency in response estimation should be.

This should not be construed to rule out the collection of data relating to a wide range of behavioral responses in each experiment. Indeed, one of the great virtues of experimentation is that it provides a rich source of longitudinal survey data on low-income households. Still, it seems most efficient to focus upon a single overriding objective in setting the sample design. For example, the design model for the New Jersey experiment is based on the estimation of work effort response, even though the quarterly interviews are designed to elicit additional information on a wide variety of attitudes and behavior, ranging from family expenditures to political participation and social integration.

Selection of a single objective variable for each experiment has the additional advantage of permitting the selection of a relatively homogenous sample population comprised of those households which seem most appropriate to the hypothesis being tested or which are most relevant to policy considerations. Homogeneity of the sample is desirable on several grounds. First, given financial constraints on sample size, it seems wisest to concentrate on that type of family for which a significant response seems most likely and/or important on policy grounds. Second, in many cases, it is not clear that a single functional form of the response function would be appropriate to the behavior of diverse family types.

As noted earlier, a sample of households headed by males in their working years was chosen for the New Jersey experiment because the work effort of that population seemed to pose the greatest uncertainties for policy formulation. For other response variables, other populations would obviously be more appropriate. A study of the impact of income maintenance on fertility would require a sample of households with females in their childbearing years; a study of the effect on marital stability would probably best be carried out with newlywed couples, and so on.

Finally, concentration on a single objective allows the duration of the experiment to be tailored to the particular response variable under investigation. Most of the experiments currently underway or being contemplated entail payments over three to five years. A time horizon of this length is probably quite sufficient for the investigation of, say, work effort, which may be expected to respond to fairly short-term changes in income and wage rates. Other behavioral responses, however, may be determined by much longer-run income concepts; the retirement decision of older workers and family planning decisions are cases in point. To obtain valid estimates of these responses, a much longer payment period is probably required.

E. Comparability among Experiments

One of the greatest potential assets to be secured from a coordinated, national approach to experimentation in income maintenance is the ability to ensure comparability of the data collected in the various individual experiments. As noted above, experimentation can provide a rich source of cross-sectional and longitudinal data on the poor—a group for which existing data are notably meager. To be of greatest value, however, it is important that data from each of the projects be gathered on a comparable basis, so that they can be pooled for analysis. In some cases (e.g., in the measurement of attitudes, motivations, aspirations, and the like), this will simply mean that the same interview questions should be asked in each experiment. More importantly, however, it means that the basic economic concepts, program features, and administrative arrangements should be held constant over all experiments, unless there are explicit reasons to the contrary. In essence, I am suggesting that a uniform set of "rules of operation" (the experimental equivalent of the statute governing a national plan) should be applied to all experiments. These rules would cover such things as the definition of the family unit and family income, filing and administrative procedures, and the timing of payments. Uniformity of operating rules would not, of course, preclude variation either within or between experiments of those policy parameters, such as tax rates and income guarantees, whose effects are to be studied experimentally. Uniformity would simply control for unwanted variation in those program features which are not of experimental interest, but which might act to confound the experimental results.

It should be emphasized that any one of the rules of operation might be selected as an experimental policy parameter. For example, one might wish to study the effect of variations in administrative arrangements (filing requirements, handling of claims, agency-beneficiary contacts, etc.), or of variations in the frequency of payments. The point is that any variation either within or between experiments should serve some well-defined experimental purpose.

F. Sample Size

Income maintenance experiments are an extremely expensive undertaking, relative to traditional social science research techniques. In the New Jersey experiment, the payments to households in the experimental group are averaging over $1,000 per year, and even the control group families must be compensated for their time and trouble. Obviously, there is a premium on selecting as small a sample as is consistent with reasonably accurate response estimation, in order to maximize the information obtained from limited research funds.[3] As indicated above, a priori theory and empirical knowledge are extremely important in determining the minimum required sample size.

The approach which has been developed for solving the sample size problem for the rural negative income tax project is essentially an analysis of variance framework. The analysis requires an a priori estimate of the "normal" variance of the response variable (i.e., the variance in the absence of the transfer program), given the values of other relevant characteristics of the response unit. For example, if the response variable is earned family income, one would want to control for such family attributes as education, occupation, family composition, etc., in estimating the year-to-year variance in family earned income.

Suppose we wish to ask whether the transfer has any significant effect on the response variable. One way of posing this question is to ask whether the difference between the mean response of the experimental group and the mean response of the control group is significantly different from zero, at some specified confidence level. For any given size of control and experimental groups, one can compute the "normal" variance of this difference and estimate the range of the response variable which falls

---

[3] An alternative method of reducing costs is, of course, to concentrate on less generous transfer plans. Given our degree of ignorance about the magnitude and functional form of the response, however, it seems preferable to stick to plans which seem generous enough to elicit a significant response.

within the specified confidence interval—i.e., the minimum response differential which can be detected with control and experimental samples of this size. If, for example, the standard error of earned family income, given family characteristics, is $600 per year, the standard error of the difference between control and experimental samples of 300 families each would be $69. This means that an observed difference of $136 per year would be significant at the 95 percent confidence level. Alternatively, this means that, if average family income in the sample is $4,000 per year, a total sample of 600 families would be sufficient to detect a difference in earned income of about 3.4 percent.[4]

Of course, much of the analysis of the experimental results will be by multiple regression, rather than by simple comparison of means, and the measurement accuracy of regression coefficients will, in general, differ from the accuracy of measurement of mean differences just considered. However, the approach described here can probably be expected to serve as a reasonably accurate guide to sample size. In any case, this technique illustrates the crucial elements of the sample size decision. The prime requirement is, again, adequate a priori theory and empirical knowledge. The more accurately we are able to estimate the response variable in the absence of the experimental treatment, i.e., the smaller the residual error variance, the smaller will be the sample size required for any desired degree of estimation precision. Second, given the best available estimates of the normal variation of the response variable, a decision must be made as to the precision with which we wish to estimate the response. This latter decision is obviously conditional upon the importance of the response for policy formulation; the smaller the sensitivity of policy considerations (program cost, for example) to the response variable, the larger will be the minimum level of response detection which can be tolerated and, therefore, the smaller the required sample size.

III. PRIORITIES FOR EXPERIMENTATION

Taking as our starting point the OEO work incentive experiments in New Jersey and the rural areas of Iowa and North Carolina, a number of possibilities for further experimentation suggest themselves. In this sec-

---

[4] These calculations were made by Professors D. Lee Bawden and Charles Metcalf of the Institute for Research on Poverty, University of Wisconsin, in preliminary design work for the OEO rural negative income tax experiment.

tion, I shall apply the selection and design criteria presented above to obtain a priority ranking of those hypotheses which seem most amenable to experimental research. Heading the list of experimental objectives are a variety of issues in the broad areas of work effort response and changes in family size and structure. The experimental possibilities in these areas seem well within our current capabilities. A lower priority is assigned to experimentation focused on the effects of income maintenance on community structure because, although there are a number of important issues in this area, experimental resolution of these issues does not seem feasible at this time.

In discussing experimental priorities, it is important to define the major program features, or policy parameters, which characterize any income maintenance plan. The characteristics which I consider most basic include:

a) The income guarantee; i.e., the payment which a family would receive if it had no other income. In general, this payment may be adjusted for family size and composition, and the schedule of guarantee adjustments will be an important factor in assessing certain behavioral responses.

b) The implicit tax rate; i.e., the rate at which the basic guaranteed payment is reduced as family income from other sources rises.

c) The definition of the family unit in terms of who may be included as dependents, who must be included as dependents, and who may qualify as a head of household.

d) The definition of the family income and the accounting period over which income is measured for purposes of determining current payments.

e) Coordinate programs which do not involve cash transfers (e.g., in-kind transfers such as job training, day-care facilities, and social services).

It is felt that the policy parameters listed here are general enough to characterize nearly any of the income maintenance programs currently receiving serious consideration. In general, there are three basic types of programs which have been widely advocated: negative income tax plans, children's allowances, and various modifications of the existing categorical welfare programs. Each embodies a particular guarantee schedule and tax rate, defines the family unit and family income in a particular way, and may be coupled with various coordinate programs. Therefore, rather than focusing upon program types per se, it seems preferable to analyze behavioral responses to these more general policy parameters. Proceeding in this manner, the hypotheses which should receive highest experimental priority are as follows.

A. Work Effort Response

The crucial dependence of program cost and the possibilities for the eventual eradication of poverty through income maintenance make the work effort response of recipients a question of highest research priority on grounds of policy relevance. Moreover, the crucial policy parameters of any national program which may be expected to influence work effort (guarantee schedules and tax rates) are features which are readily amenable to replication in the experimental setting. Finally, the existing theory and empirical knowledge of labor supply provide a sound basis for the design of experiments in this area.

1) The labor supply of families headed by nonaged males would seem to be adequately covered in the existing OEO experiments. Further experimentation should focus on the work effort of the two other principal types of poor families, those with female and aged heads. The OEO rural experiment will, of course, include some female and aged heads, but these small subsamples should be augmented with further experimental observations, especially in urban areas. These experiments would be closely patterned after the New Jersey design, in terms of treatments, sample size, sample allocation, and duration of payments. Since the normal work effort of such families is likely to be lower than for male-headed households, however, the cost of these experiments may well be somewhat greater than in New Jersey.

2) The work effort response of the aged (and near-aged) raises a unique problem which may not be amenable to the kind of experiment developed in New Jersey. Since an income maintenance program of the negative income tax type would constitute an assured retirement income which would be available at any time, such a plan might have a significant effect upon the age of retirement, especially for relatively low-income workers. Unfortunately, payments over a period as short as three years are probably not a sufficient inducement to elicit a reliable measure of the retirement response. It may be necessary, therefore, to select a sample of older workers who would be guaranteed income maintenance payments over the rest of their lives, to obtain a valid estimate of the effect of a permanent national program. A preliminary analysis of the response could be made after a fairly short interval—say, three or four years—although the experiment would continue to yield useful data for a much longer period of time.

Such an experiment would obviously be relatively expensive. However, costs could be reduced by sampling heavily at earned income levels near the breakeven point, so that substantial payments would be made only to those workers who actually do curtail their work effort significantly; this would be entirely consistent with the dominant policy interest, since the majority of the retired poor presumably had incomes above the poverty line before retirement. Moreover, at age 65, Social Security benefits could be offset dollar-for-dollar against the transfers. Thus, if the sample consisted of workers in the 55–60 age bracket, one might expect to make large payments in only, say, six or seven years to each household.

In addition to considerations of cost, the long time horizon of this type of experiment might raise some difficult administrative problems, to which careful attention should be given. If the retirement age response is viewed as an important question, however, then this experimental approach would seem to be the most promising means of obtaining valid estimates of the effect of a permanent national program.

3) A third type of experiment would focus on the interaction of income maintenance with manpower, job training, and other work-related programs. It has long been argued that income maintenance programs which seek to preserve work incentive should be accompanied by programs which act to enhance the employability of the poor. The President's proposals for welfare reform, now pending in Congress, which explicitly tie job training, employment counseling, and day-care services to income maintenance, illustrate the concern of policymakers with this issue. The underlying hypothesis for experimentation in this area would be that there are important interactions between these two types of programs; i.e., that their combined effect would be different from the simple additive effects of income maintenance and work-related programs taken separately. One might hypothesize that the existence of income maintenance with work incentive features increases the attractiveness of job training, while the availability of job training or day care serves to reduce the disincentive effects which remain in the income maintenance program.

An income maintenance experiment to test these hypotheses is already in the planning stage. It is proposed that a variety of job training, counseling services, and day-care arrangements be made available to families receiving negative income tax payments, with their response to be compared to a group for whom manpower programs, but not income maintenance, are available, and families receiving only income maintenance. Varying rates of subsidy will be applied to the costs of these manpower programs, in order to ascertain the effective demand for job training on the part of experimental families. This experiment is being carried out by the Department of Health, Education, and Welfare in the city of Seattle. It is anticipated that experimental payments will begin in late 1970.

4) A fourth experimental possibility in the area of work effort is the replication of the New Jersey model with a dispersed nationwide sample.[5] This would provide a check on the generality of the results obtained in New Jersey and other experiments, by drawing observations from a variety of different environments and labor markets. In particular, by including observations from areas with high unemployment rates, one might obtain information on how work effort under a national program would vary with the level of economic activity. Moreover, such an experiment would provide observations in communities which fall between the small towns of the rural experiment and the large industrial cities of New Jersey and other urban experiments currently being contemplated, in terms of population size.

This undertaking would present some difficult administrative problems in maintaining contact with a widely dispersed sample. This might be reduced by cluster sampling in a number of carefully selected areas, and/or contracting with a private survey organization which already has a national sampling capability. In any case, given these problems, this experiment probably should receive somewhat lower priority than some others proposed below, particularly those relating to the effects of income maintenance on family structure. Nevertheless, it has the potential for important contributions to our empirical knowledge of work effort response.

B. Effects on Family Size and Structure

Virtually all of the income maintenance programs now receiving serious consideration provide potentially significant incentives for changes in the basic family structure of the recipients. In terms of policy relevance, these effects may well rival in importance the effects of the program on work effort. I would propose, therefore, that these effects receive an experimental priority just below the investigation of work effort response. Fortunately, experimentation appears to be feasible for at least the more important potential effects on family structure; the relevant policy parameters are readily identifiable and (at least approximately) replicable in the experimental setting, the response variables are easily quantified, and there is a substantial body of a priori empirical information upon which to base the experimental design. The following behavioral responses seem to be the best candidates for experimentation in this area.

---

[5] Such an experiment was originally advocated by Guy Orcutt, of the University of Wisconsin Department of Economics, now at the Urban Institute.

1. Fertility.   To the extent that fertility is influenced by the level
or uncertainty of family income, any income maintenance program will
be likely to affect family size. Perhaps more importantly, any program
which adjusts payments by family size creates financial incentives to
bear children. In the extreme, plans which determine payments solely on
the basis of family size, such as a children's allowance, would seem to
create a maximum incentive for increased fertility. The importance of
the fertility response is highlighted by the recent Presidential address on
birth control and the long-standing (but virtually unsubstantiated)
criticism of AFDC on the grounds that it fosters illegitimacy.

At first glance, it would seem that existing data might be sufficient
to answer this question. A number of countries have adopted children's
allowances, some (such as France) at very substantial benefit levels.
The evidence from these "natural experiments" is, however, ambiguous
at best. The resulting birth rate patterns are rendered virtually unin-
telligible by the absence of any meaningful control group. Hence, experimentation would seem to be called for.

As noted earlier, short-term experiments in this area are unlikely to
produce valid inferences as to the effects of a permanent national program. On the one hand, payments over three or five years provide a much
weaker incentive to increase family size than would a national program
providing payments over the entire eighteen years of a child's minority.
On the other hand, experimental families might be induced to shorten
the spacing of their children in order to qualify for payments during the
course of the experiment. It would be impossible to analytically untangle
these countervailing effects upon birth rates in the experimental group.

To avoid these analytical hazards, it would be necessary to guarantee payments over a much longer period. For example, payments might
be made over a period of fifteen to twenty years, with adjustments in payments for any children born within that time. Analysis of results could
be made after four or five years, although the experiment would continue
to yield useful data for many years. This would substantially reduce, if
not eliminate, both of the biases of a short-term experiment just mentioned.

The primary response rate of interest would be the birth rate, since
increased family size may be expected to result in close spacing of children. Since it is conceivable that an increase in completed family size
might result with no change in spacing, however, one would also want to
gather data on such indicators as desired and expected family size. These
would allow prediction of completed family size in the first years of the
experiment, before most of the families reach their ultimate size.

The payments themselves might be structured in one of several
ways. The obvious approach would be to provide treatments consisting

of various negative income tax plans, patterned after the New Jersey treatments, over the entire course of the experiment. Although this would provide a valid simulation of all the major features of a corresponding national plan, it would be a terribly expensive undertaking.[6] This approach would also raise difficult administrative problems, since the income of the recipients would have to be monitored over the entire course of the experiment. Moreover, current funding of the entire experiment would be complicated by the unpredictability of income streams, and therefore payments, over such a long time horizon.

A second approach, which would substantially reduce these problems, would involve simulating only the features of a national program most relevant to the central issue at hand. One could create the "price effect" implicit in a negative income tax with family size adjustments by simply extending a flat annual payment (again, say, for fifteen to twenty years) to each child born during the experiment. This payment plan would be in effect a children's allowance for additional children born to the sample families.

Although children's allowances and negative income taxation are very different in many respects, the "price" each places on additional children is very similar, at least over a wide range of family income. This may be readily seen in Figure 1, which shows total family income under a negative income tax as a function of earned income. Line *ab* is the schedule of total income (earned income plus transfers) up to the break-even income Y_b under the initial guarantee before the birth of a child. Line *cd* is the total income schedule after the birth of an additional child; the vertical distance between the two up to Y_b is equal to the guarantee adjustment for the child. Thus, the marginal increment to payments resulting from an increase in family size is a constant annual amount, regardless of the level of family income, *as long as earned income remains below the initial break-even level* Y_b. Over this income range, then, a negative income tax is indistinguishable, in terms of this price effect, from a children's allowance equal to the marginal guarantee.

Unfortunately, adoption of this payment scheme would preclude experimental analysis of the "income effect" of income maintenance on fertility, since payments would be generally lower than under a full-fledged negative income tax. I would argue, however, that this question could be adequately analyzed from existing data and is therefore not worth the added experimental cost of a negative income tax.

The cost of payments of this type could be markedly less than under

---

[6] If payments average $1,000 per year, as in New Jersey, the present discounted cost *per family* for a fifteen-year program, discounting at 6 percent, would be about $9,700.

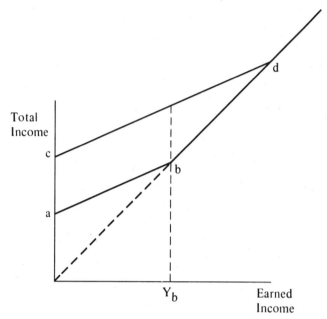

Figure 1. Total and earned income, before and after an additional child

a long-term negative income tax. Suppose, for example, that a sample of families with two children were selected and guaranteed allowances of $400 per year for each additional child.[7] The present discounted cost of a fifteen-year allowance, then, would be about $3,000, discounting at 6 percent. The average expected completed family size of families at these income levels is probably about 3.8 children;[8] let us therefore assume that, on the average, each family has two children, spaced, say, one and three years after the beginning of the experiment. The present discounted cost per family would then be approximately $5,500.[9]

---

[7] Of course, experimentally, one would want to vary the payment among families, in order to estimate a continuous response function, but $400 ought to be a reasonable average guarantee. A negative income tax which guarantees the poverty line income would carry a marginal guarantee of about $400 for a third child.

[8] N. B. Ryder and C. F. Westoff, "Relationship Among Intended, Expected, Desired, and Ideal Family Size: United States, 1965," *Population Research* (March 1969).

[9] In addition, it might be necessary to pay a flat annual allowance on the order of $150 to all families in the experiment to secure their cooperation in keeping in touch with the research organization during the early years when most families are receiving no payments. This payment could be terminated

The children's allowance approach would also greatly simplify administration, as compared to a negative tax plan. The research organization could simply contract with a private firm, say an insurance company, to provide contingent annuities to the sample families, in return for a lump-sum payment at the outset. There would be no need to monitor income or family composition, other than checking the validity of claims of births.

A third payment mechanism which might be considered is the possibility of utilizing the Family Assistance Plan (FAP), once it is enacted, as the basis for this analysis. A sample of families receiving FAP payments could be selected as an experimental group with supplemental payments to obtain sufficient experimental variation in payment levels and to secure the cooperation of recipients. The control group, obviously, would have to be composed of families who are ineligible for FAP. Finding such families at income levels comparable to those in the experimental group may be difficult. This, however, is a problem which will confront any experiment in this area if it is assumed that there is a high probability that FAP will be enacted before the completion of the experimental analysis; eligible families would become useless as controls once they begin receiving FAP payments. The best hope for obtaining a meaningful control group would appear to be by selection of families whose assets exceed the "resource test" under FAP. This procedure would raise the possibility of noncomparability between the experimental and control populations, but it is probable that family planning decisions are not materially affected by asset positions at this relatively low level (especially since the FAP resource test will apparently apply only to liquid assets, with homes and business capital excluded). This assumption could, and should, be tested before a decision is made to structure the experiment along these lines.

"Piggybacking" the experiment on FAP in this manner would greatly reduce the cost of the experiment, and it might provide a more realistic guarantee of permanence (in the view of the recipients) than would an experiment divorced from the national welfare system. The major disadvantage of this approach is, of course, that it is impossible to predict just when—or, indeed, if—FAP will be enacted. This uncertainty might delay the experiment and complicate its planning. However, as noted above, any experiment in this area must be sensitive to the timing

---

after four or five years when the analysis of results is undertaken, so that it would add only about $600 to the discounted cost. Such a payment would probably also be necessary under a negative income tax (in fact, this is being done in New Jersey), so it would not materially affect the comparison of costs under the two modes of payment.

of FAP. Perhaps the best strategy would be to keep this option open throughout the planning phase of the experiment, in the expectation that the outlook for FAP will be clearer at the end of the planning phase, at which time a decision could be made.

2. *Marital stability.* A second aspect of family structure which merits experimentation is the question of the effect of income maintenance on marital stability, in terms of divorce, desertion, and separation. Several policy parameters may be of significance here. First, to the extent that marital instability stems from economic stresses within the family, the sheer effect of additional income, i.e., the income guarantee, may serve to reduce instability. It has also been widely suggested that the schedules of adjustments of the guarantee for family size and structure which have been proposed under most negative income tax plans will create incentives for family breakup.[10] Typically, a spouse receives a smaller marginal guarantee than the head of household. Thus the family's total guarantee can be increased if the couple separates and forms two households, with two head-of-household guarantees. This incentive is analogous to the incentives for family breakup embodied in the AFDC program. Under AFDC a family is eligible for payments only if the father is not present, and it is often alleged that this promotes desertion and separation. Of course, for that group of women currently on AFDC (or those who would become eligible at some time in the future), a change to a system which provides income maintenance for intact families would *reduce* the incentives for separation.

Perhaps more importantly, because of the discontinuity of tax rates at the break-even level of income, a family may be able to increase its total payments by forming two households, one with income above its break-even point and one with income below.[11] This kind of incentive would also be present in any plan which involved a nonlinear tax rate, even if both of the new households remained below their break-even points. This effect is identical in principle to the incentive to file joint returns under the positive income tax, with its nonlinear progressive rate structure.

---

[10] For a typical discussion, see Editors, "A Model Negative Income Tax Statute," *Yale Law Journal,* Vol. 78 (1968), pp. 276–278.

[11] For example, a couple with a $3,000 income, a $2,000 guarantee, and a 50 percent tax rate would receive a transfer of $500 if they live together. Suppose now they split up, with the husband retaining the $3,000 income and the wife none. If each is entitled to a $1,000 guarantee (to maintain the same total guarantee in this example), the husband would now receive no transfer, but the wife would receive $1,000, increasing their total payment by $500.

The effect of income maintenance on marital stability may also interact with the effects on fertility discussed above. To the extent that women in their childbearing years spend less time in a married state, their fertility may be decreased. Conversely, for the AFDC population, for whom incentives for separation would diminish, fertility might rise.

We have only begun to consider the problems of sample design for such an experiment. Since nearly one-third of all divorces occur in the first four years of marriage,[12] it seems reasonable to select a sample of newlywed couples. It is also probable that economic considerations play a larger role in marital instability early in marriage than in later years.

While we have not undertaken a detailed analysis of the required sample size for such an experiment, a rough idea of the requisite sample size can be obtained if we assume that divorce is a stochastic binomial process with each family in the sample having an equal probability of divorce within the experimental period. If, for example, the incidence of divorce among couples of the type selected would be 20 percent in the first four years of marriage in the absence of income maintenance, a sample of 900 couples would be sufficient to detect a change of 2.7 percentage points in the divorce rate at the 96 percent confidence level.[13] In relative terms, this is a rather wide confidence interval; it allows significant detection of changes no smaller than 13 percent of the initial divorce rate, with a fairly large sample. Even a sample of 2,000 couples would allow detection of a relative change no smaller than about 9 percent of the normal divorce rate. Of course, estimation accuracy would be improved if one were able to predict the probability of divorce for individual couples more accurately than by simply applying the mean rate to all couples. Even so, it appears that a large sample will be required if we hope to detect even moderately small changes. It should be noted, though, that payments to couples with no children (or only one or two) under any given plan would be much less expensive than the average payment levels in New Jersey, where the families are fairly large. Thus, cost considerations are less restrictive with respect to sample size.

3. Split-off of dependents. Very similar to the incentives for marital instability are the incentives that may be provided for dependents

---

[12] *Vital Statistics of the United States: 1964*, Tables 2–5, pp. 2–8, Vol. III—Marriage and Divorce, U.S. Department of Health, Education and Welfare, Public Health Service (Washington, D.C.: U.S. GPO, 1968).

[13] This calculation was made in the following manner. The sample variance is given by $\sigma^2 = p(1-p)/N$, where p is the probability of divorce for any one couple and N is sample size. For N = 900 and $p = .2$, $\sigma = .0134$, and the 96 percent confidence interval is $2\sigma = .0268$.

to leave the family and set up new households. Again, the total family guarantee can be increased and payments may rise if the split alters the marginal tax rate facing either the original family or the new unit. The latter effect may be especially important if a dependent of a relatively well-to-do family can set up a new household with an income below the break-even point; this would be the case, for example, for teenage youths leaving families with incomes above the break-even point. A variety of other dependents now living with families (grandparents, in-laws, un-married relatives, etc.) might also be encouraged to set up households of their own if afforded an income guarantee. The fact that these poten-tial income maintenance recipients currently reside in families throughout the income distribution means that the aggregate effect, in terms of program cost, could potentially be very significant. Of course, to the ex-tent that these dependents continue to receive support from their families after leaving, this would count as income and reduce their payments.

While it would seem to be very desirable to attempt to estimate experimentally the impact of these incentives, the design of an experi-ment focused on this question which would constitute a valid replication of a national program poses serious difficulties. The logical experimental approach would seem to be to select a sample of families to receive in-come maintenance payments, and to allow any individual who leaves a sample family, and any dependents he may acquire, to qualify for pay-ments as a separate household. This approach, however, would over-state the incentives for splitting off embodied in the corresponding na-tional plan, especially among young adults, because it creates a "dowry effect." In the experimental setting, a young man or woman would become a differentially attractive marriage partner because he or she would be eligible for income maintenance payments while his or her compatriots would not be. Under a national plan, all single individuals would be equally eligible for income maintenance, so that all would com-pete for marriage partners on an equal footing. This asymmetry be-tween experiment and national program, then, creates an artificial in-centive for others to "marry into" the sample, which would tend to bias upward our estimates of the impact of the plan on marriage of dependents.

An alternative way of defining guarantees for individuals who leave the family to marry, which introduces a downward bias, might be in-corporated into the experimental design in an attempt to bracket the true response under a national plan. This would involve allowing only the individual from the original sample family, but not his dependents, to receive payments; thus, again because of the asymmetry between ex-periment and national program, there would be an artificial scarcity of marriage partners eligible for payments, introducing a downward bias in rates of split-off. The dowry effect would still be present (in a weaker form), but if it is felt that this "scarcity" effect would outweigh the dowry effect, this subsample would provide a lower bound for the estimate of the true effect. The subsample where individuals are allowed to bring in new dependents would provide an upper bound.

For individuals or subfamilies leaving the family to live on their own, there is no problem with the acquisition of dependents. Thus, the experimental results in these cases would be relatively reliable.

C. Community Effects

The experimental possibilities discussed so far relate to essentially individual responses of the income maintenance recipient. These can be estimated from the behavior of families in dispersed experimental samples with little or no interaction among recipients. One might also, however, expect an income maintenance program to have a variety of effects upon social, political, and economic institutions within the community as the result of interactions among recipients and between recipients and nonrecipients, under a national program. To name only a few possibilities, there might be changes in the political power balance, governmental tax and expenditure patterns, attitudes toward the poor and aspirations of the poor, and location of economic activity and the economic opportunity structure facing the poor.

To attempt to induce these effects experimentally, one would have to adopt a strategy of "saturation sampling," giving income maintenance transfers to all households in a given area who would be eligible under a national plan. Moreover, the experimental area would have to be sufficiently large to encompass the geographical extent of the particular institution or activity being studied.

Such an experiment would obviously be very expensive. There are also several reasons to question the validity of the results that would be obtained. For one thing, as mentioned near the outset, we have very little in the way of a theory of community or of institutional change upon which to base the experimental design. Moreover, it is difficult to define measures of institutional change which would serve as response variables, or even to select the policy parameters which should be varied experimentally. More fundamentally, perhaps, an experiment in a single area, measuring the program's impact on one set of institutions, would, in essence, yield a sample of only a single observation. To constitute anything more than a demonstration (albeit, perhaps, a useful demonstration), experiments would have to be performed in a number of communities. Unfortunately, in the absence of an adequate theoretical foundation, it is impossible to say just how many community observations would be required for valid inference.

Given the design problems involved in saturation experiments and the range of other important questions more amenable to experimentation, it seems best to defer experimentation in this area, and to concentrate our research efforts instead upon developing the theoretical prerequisites to experimentation focused on community effects.

IV. EXPERIMENTATION AND THE FAMILY ASSISTANCE PLAN

The enactment of the proposed Family Assistance Plan (FAP) will significantly alter the context within which income maintenance experimentation must operate, although it will by no means eliminate the need for further experimentation. FAP will inevitably be modified, extended, and liberalized in years to come; carefully designed experiments can provide valuable guidance in making these changes.

The most likely changes in FAP over the near future will take the form of liberalization of benefits. The two principal options here are increased guarantees with unchanged tax rates and a lowering of tax rates with or without higher guarantees. The former approach has the advantage of concentrating additional benefits on the poorest families, while the latter serves to further reduce work disincentives at the expense of a less regressive benefit structure. The choice between these options will hinge crucially upon the work incentive effects at different levels of the tax rate. Of particular importance will be the work response of female-headed families, who constitute an increasing proportion of the poverty population and who will face a relatively high tax rate—at least 67 percent—under FAP. Increases in the FAP guarantee will also raise the incentive for increased fertility.

Also quite likely, although not in the immediate future, is the extension of income maintenance benefits to single individuals and childless couples. Many of the family structure responses discussed here will become much more important under a universal plan than they are under a plan restricted to families with children. This is especially true of the incentives for marital breakup and the splitting off of dependents.

Finally, one may expect numerous changes in the as yet ill-defined relationship between income maintenance, job training, and day care. Experiments in this area can point the way toward an optimal combination of these types of support, with the long-run goal of enhancing the self-sufficiency of the poor.

Given the long lead time required for experimentation, it is essential that planning in these areas proceed as rapidly as possible. Our experience indicates that the advance planning for an experiment requires a year to a year and a half, and that another two years are required before even tentative results are available.

Of course, such lags also mean that experimental plans must attempt to anticipate the enactment and future course of FAP. The principal change in the experimental context upon the enactment of FAP will be simply that FAP becomes the new status quo, the base upon which experimental treatments are built. This means that the control families will no longer be families with no income maintenance, but families receiving FAP benefits. Experimental payments will have to be raised accordingly.

At the same time, the enactment of FAP will present unique opportunities for income maintenance research. Careful longitudinal studies initiated before enactment of FAP can provide large bodies of data relevant to the experimental objectives discussed here. It may even be possible to study some of the responses, such as community effects, which do not now appear amenable to experimentation.

V. A BRIEF PREVIEW

To date, two experiments in income maintenance funded by the Office of Economic Opportunity are already in operation; the New Jersey experiment and the rural experiment about to begin transfers in Iowa and North Carolina. Since these have been described elsewhere in some detail, I will simply note that in terms of the priorities proposed here, they focus primarily upon the work effort response of male-headed families under a negative income tax. The rural experiment will also include some families with female and aged heads, but these samples will be small and the results not necessarily applicable to similar families in an urban setting. Finally, several variants of the accounting period will be tested in both experiments but, again, the samples are small and the alternative plans are not exhaustive. These experiments may generate some useful data with respect to other questions on my priority list, but they are not designed for this purpose, so such results will probably be only suggestive at best.

To expand our knowledge in those areas of high priority not covered by these projects, the Department of Health, Education, and Welfare is now considering the initiation of a small number of carefully selected and controlled income maintenance experiments, and it has already given planning grants for the design phase of two experiments. The focus in these two experiments will be upon issues which rank high on the list of priorities presented here.

The first, located in Seattle, will consider the interaction of income maintenance with various manpower and work-related programs. The cash transfer plans will be closely patterned after the New Jersey treatments to ensure comparability of the data obtained. The sample will include a substantial proportion of female heads of households, however, so that we can begin to obtain estimates of the work effort response of females. The manpower programs to be associated with the transfer payments, for at least a subsample of the recipients, will include job training, employment counseling and referral services, and day-care facilities for female heads and wives with pre-school children.

The second experiment for which a planning grant has been made is to be carried out in Gary, Indiana. The experimental focus there will be on the work effort response under several variations in the income accounting period. Again, the sample will include a large proportion of female heads of households, and it is expected that a high proportion of the families will be nonwhite. This experiment will also conform closely to the New Jersey experiment. It is hoped that the transfer phase of both the Seattle and Gary experiments can begin by the end of 1970.

HEW has received requests for support of income maintenance experiments in a number of cities and will undoubtedly solicit additional proposals for experimentation in several of the areas proposed here. The outlook for a fairly ambitious experimental attack on the large remaining areas of ignorance of the effects of income maintenance is quite promising.

INCOME MAINTENANCE REFORM ISSUES WITH RESPECT TO THE AGED

Robinson Hollister

Limitations on the ability of the aged to earn a reasonable living in the labor market make them particularly vulnerable to poverty and social isolation, and this has been widely understood for some time. Still, awareness has not been followed by totally effective action and, therefore, the incidence of poverty among the aged in the United States remains disproportionately high. In this paper I will try to highlight some of the features of the economic status of the aged and indicate those issues which seem particularly important for this segment of the population with respect to potential reform of the income maintenance system in this country.

In what follows, my commentary will be based upon an assumption that the type of income maintenance reform being considered will fall in the general category of plans which have been called "negative income tax" programs; I will not attempt to touch upon the whole range of potential types of reform, both because such a complete survey would be exhausting and because there is an extensive literature on many of these issues elsewhere.[1]

---

[1] See, for example, J. Pechman, H. Aaron, and M. Taussig, *Social Security: Perspective for Reform* (Brookings, 1968) and works cited in their bibliography.

I. RELEVANT DIMENSIONS OF THE ECONOMIC STATUS OF THE AGED[2]

The incidence of poverty among the aged is nearly twice that found among the population of the United States as a whole. The details of this extensive poverty could be spelled out with a variety of statistics. It is most useful, for the purposes of this paper, to examine the sources of income of the aged population. The mean income per household for the aged poor in the United States in 1965 was estimated as $1,106. This compared with a mean household income for those aged who were not poor of $5,350. It is most instructive to look at the major sources of income for these two aged groups (Table 1). The fact which emerges most clearly from an inspection of Table 1—and one which is most surprising in light of the usual stereotypes about all the aged living on fixed pension incomes—is that the major difference in the income of the aged poor and the aged nonpoor is the amount derived from earnings. For families headed by an aged person, the difference in income from earnings accounted for about 60 percent of the difference in income between those poor and those nonpoor. For aged unrelated individuals, had the poor on average been able to earn as much as the nonpoor, they would have lifted their average income above the poverty line. Thus, it can be seen that the common tendency to think of the problems of unemployment as irrelevant for the aged population is quite mistaken. Further implications of this point will be taken up below.

It can be seen that the aged poor at present receive considerably less in income from pensions and social security. I will discuss social security in some detail below, but something can be said here with respect to private pension income. It has been estimated that 40 percent of all families in the United States with the family head working are covered by some sort of private pension; however, of all poor families, only 11 percent have private pension coverage. Thus it can be expected that differences between poor and nonpoor aged in terms of private pension income will persist into the future.

As shown in Table 1, the aged poor received very little in income from assets. Some have argued, however, that looking simply at *current* income from assets may be somewhat misleading as to the relative well-being of particular groups. It is suggested that, particularly with respect to the aged, it is important to take into account the entire net worth

---

[2] In drawing together the material for this section I have relied heavily on A. Craig, "Economic Problems of the Aged" (University of Wisconsin, Institute for Research on Poverty, 1969 [unpublished]).

Table 1. Mean Income of the Aged from Major Source, 1965, by Income Level

	Above poverty level		Below poverty level	
	Mean for those receiving income, this source	Mean for all in this income level	Mean for those receiving income, this source	Mean for all in this income level
Income from assets:				
Families headed by aged person	$1,316	$ 858	$ 232	$ 75
Aged unrelated individuals	1,143	786	245	84
Income from earnings:				
Families headed by aged person	5,282	3,385	574	211
Aged unrelated individuals	2,765	1,033	392	44
Pensions and Social Security:				
Families headed by aged person	2,177	1,875	1,205	897
Aged unrelated individuals	1,526	1,289	843	611
Welfare, public and private:				
Families headed by aged person	1,093	45	809	176
Aged unrelated individuals	1,147	81	741	158

Source: Preliminary tables, CPS Survey of Economic Opportunity, 1966, as reported in R. Munts, "Minimum Income As a Retirement Policy Objective," in *The Aged Population and Retirement Income Programs, Part II*, Joint Economic Committee, Subcommittee on Fiscal Policy, 90th Congress, 1st session, December 1967, p. 292.

position of the household. This is because it is possible, at least in theory, for people not only to live on the income from assets but, as they reach the later part of the life cycle, to sell off some of their assets in order to augment their current income. In one study in which an income-net-worth measure was used,[3] it was found that, whereas the aged comprised 33 percent of the total poverty population when income alone was used as a measure of poverty, when an income-net-worth measure was used the aged accounted for only 28 percent. This reduction is a result both of the higher net worth of the aged and their shorter life-span over which to annuitize that net worth. Thus it would seem that taking into account the asset position of the aged would reduce the burden of

---

[3] An income-net-worth measure is one in which assets are annuitized over the remaining lifetime of the head of the household and added to current income (see B. Weisbrod and W. L. Hansen, "An Income-Net-Worth Approach to Measuring Economic Welfare," *American Economic Review,* December 1968).

poverty in this group as compared to other age groups in the population. It should be noted, however (as the authors of the study cited do) that this picture may be somewhat distorted by the inclusion of the value of owned housing in the net worth measure used. It may be inferred from other studies which calculated such measures with and without housing that when one goes from just current income to an income-net-worth measure of poverty about two-thirds of the reduction of poverty among the aged which occurs is due to the inclusion of housing in the measure. Since about 63 percent of the aged who are poor by a current income measure live in housing which they own, the question of how one is going to assess the contribution of such housing to the well-being of the aged poor is clearly an important question, and it will be examined in more detail below.

The final aspect of the data provided in Table 1 which deserves some comment is the role of current public income maintenance programs in raising the incomes of the aged. Welfare payments are greater for the aged poor than for the aged nonpoor, but the size and coverage of welfare payments is such that on average they do not substantially reduce the gap in income between the poor and the nonpoor aged. Public welfare programs (as distinct from Social Security) covered a limited portion of the aged population; only about 16 percent of the aged poor in the United States in 1965 received public assistance. Of those aged persons who did receive public assistance, 87 percent were poor before receiving such payments, but 70 percent were *still poor* after receiving payments. Thus the coverage is limited and the payments are inadequate.

Social Security is the largest program of income maintenance in the United States. About 80 percent of aged poor families and aged poor unrelated individuals receive Social Security benefits; however, 35 percent of those who received benefits were still poor after such payments were included in their income. The inadequacy of Social Security as a safeguard against poverty among the aged is clear from the 20 percent of the aged poor not covered by the program and the additional 35 percent of those who receive benefits who remain poor in spite of the benefit income.

The major reason for the inadequacy of Social Security payments is that payments are related to past earnings. The relationship to past earnings is not simple since there are minimum and maximum levels set for benefits. Table 2 indicates the character of the relationship for various groups.

The benefit schedules are set so that benefits are a higher portion of past earnings levels for low income workers than for higher income workers; the system works to redistribute income somewhat toward the

Table 2. Social Security Benefits as a Percentage of
Earnings, by Income Level

Average recent earnings	Benefits as a percentage of earnings
Low wage earner ($2,600)	
Individual	40
Worker and wife	60
Medium wage earner ($6,000)	
Individual	25
Worker and wife	37
Salaried employee ($15,000)	
Individual	10
Worker and wife	15

Source: R. Munts, *op. cit.*, Table 1.

low income class. In spite of this redistribution, the benefits do not fully replace the low income worker's already very low income from earnings. Thus workers at or near poverty levels of income before age 65 are likely to face even more severe poverty in their old age because their low earnings in the past have not allowed asset accumulation or qualification for adequate private pensions, and will be reflected in inadequate old age benefits.

One other Social Security-related program deserves mention: Medicare. Prior to the instigation of the Medicare program, medical care was the third most important expenditure, after food and housing, of the aged poor. One early estimate[4] of the effect of the Medicare legislation indicates that it resulted in a decline in private per capita expenditure for those over 65 of 10 percent for hospital care and 31 percent for physicians' services. This legislation improves the well-being of the aged not only because of this once and for all decline in medical expenditures, but also because it minimizes the effects of rising prices of medical services on the aged. Furthermore, to the extent that medical disasters had seriously eroded the meager assets of the aged and caused those originally nonpoor to fall into poverty this program should reduce the incidence of poverty among the aged and free the aged from the need to maintain asset balances in anticipation of meeting the high costs of such medical incidents.

[4] R. Hollister and J. Palmer, "The Impact of Inflation on the Poor" (University of Wisconsin, Institute for Research on Poverty, Discussion Paper 40, 1969).

II. WORK AND THE RETIREMENT DECISION

It should be clear from the previous section that the work experience of the aged poor is central to their condition of poverty, both because current earnings of the aged make a major difference in the extent of vulnerability to poverty and because past work experience affects the amount of Social Security benefits they can receive. The importance of current working opportunities for the aged can be further underlined by comparing the incidence of poverty of the aged and the non-aged who have similar current work status. It can be seen that for all male-headed families, the incidence of poverty among those with heads over 65 was nearly triple that for those with heads below 55 (Table 3). However, when rates for those male-headed families in which the head worked part of the year are compared, the incidence of poverty for heads over 65 is about the same as those with heads under 55. For those male heads who worked all year, the poverty incidence of those over 65 is double that of those under 55. Thus the observed overall incidence rate of male heads over 65 triple that of those under 55 is primarily due to the fact that a considerably larger proportion of the aged male heads are found in those work categories in which incidence of poverty is high, i.e., not working or working part of the year.

For female-headed families, it is not surprising that the incidence of poverty is lower among the aged, since many of these families became female-headed when the male head died after a long work career. How-

Table 3. Percent of Families in Poverty in 1966
by Work Experience of Head

Age and sex of head	Total	Work experience of head		
		Did not work	Worked part of year	Worked all year
Male head				
Total	9.8	30.9	17.1	5.1
Under 55	7.5	39.6	17.3	5.1
55–64	9.2	37.0	15.4	3.9
65 and over	22.5	28.4	18.5	9.8
Female head				
Total	35.0	44.3	43.8	18.4
Under 55	43.3	69.1	50.7	21.4
55–64	21.0	35.6	22.2	8.2
65 and over	20.9	22.5	16.5	8.4

Source: M. Orshansky, "The Shape of Poverty in 1966," *Social Security Bulletin*, March 1968.

ever, even for female heads, part-year and full-year work substantially reduced the incidence of poverty.

In general, then, a substantial part of the difference in the incidence of poverty among the aged, as opposed to families with younger heads, is due to the difference in their current work experience.

In spite of these facts, the picture which many people have of the work status of the aged seems to be one in which the increasing affluence of society has provided ever greater opportunities for the aged to retire to a life of comfort and leisure. This view is often substantiated by pointing to the declining labor force participation rates of elderly and aged males: whereas in the United States in 1948 males 65 and over had a labor force participation rate of 47 percent, this rate has declined so that in 1967 it was 28 percent; for males 55 to 64, the rate of participation has declined from 89 to 84 percent over the same period.

This view has led some people to conclude that, in spite of the fact that the effect of particular features on work effort is the central issue in the current controversy over income maintenance reform with respect to other age groups, the impact of income maintenance programs on the work status of the aged is not of great importance. If this were correct, the problems of reform with respect to this group would be significantly reduced. Therefore, it is important to look more carefully at the factors which may be affecting the work and retirement status of the aged.

First, it is useful to take a closer look at the labor force participation trends cited above. Though the labor force participation rates did decline over the period, it was not a steady downward trend. The period with the greatest decline was 1957 to 1963 and during this period the unemployment rate was on average quite high. In contrast, during the period 1964 to 1967 when unemployment was dropping significantly, the participation rate for males over 65 declined very slightly. Thus it can be suggested that workers in the older age groups become discouraged during periods in which the labor market is slack. In this sense, withdrawal of older workers from the labor force is not entirely voluntary; the cyclical effects of economic activity seem to worsen the relative position of the older worker. Furthermore, there is some suggestion that the decline in labor force participation rates of older workers (55–64) and aged workers (65+) is related to level of educational attainment, the less educated workers having experienced greater declines in labor force participation rates.[5]

---

[5] D. F. Johnston, "Education and the Labor Force," *The Monthly Labor Review,* September 1968.

In surveys which seek to determine the reasons for retirement, the reason most often given by retirees is poor health. It is likely, however, that such an answer is a rationalization of more fundamental causes since labor force withdrawal has been increasing but there is no reason to believe that the health status of older workers has declined precipitously in the last few decades.

In the most complete study to date of questions of employment of older and aged workers,[6] it was concluded that declining relative productivity, combined with technological change which moves against occupations in which older and aged workers are more concentrated, is the most important factor in determining the decreased employability of such workers. The lesser educational attainment and flexibility of older workers limits their ability to adjust to such changes over time.

These factors are accentuated by the lower geographic mobility of older and aged workers; as job locations shift, the older and the aged are not as quick to respond—partly because the remaining working life over which they can hope to regain the costs of moving is shorter and partly because family, social, and other economic ties are stronger for the aged.

One further piece of evidence casts some doubt on the extent to which the trend toward reduced work effort on the part of the aged is entirely voluntary. In 1956 (for women) and 1961 (for men) the Social Security legislation was amended to allow those covered to retire "early," i.e., at the age of 62 rather than 65, and to begin to receive benefits at that time—but to have their benefits permanently reduced if they retire prior to age 65.[7] Analysis of the work history and characteristics of those who choose to retire early suggests that they have had lower earnings, greater than average unemployment and bad health relative to those beneficiaries who retire after 65.[8] Thus it would seem to be limited work opportunities which led to retirement for this group, rather than increasing affluence making voluntary retirement more feasible.

Some analysts have attempted to use data on the response of older workers to public transfer program eligibility requirements in order to estimate the extent to which increase in income made available through

---

[6] M. Brennan, P. Taft, and M. Schupack, *The Economics of Age* (New York: W. W. Norton and Co., 1967).

[7] See Pechman et al., *op. cit.,* pp. 130–48, for a complete discussion of the effects of the early retirement provisions.

[8] Lenore Epstein, "Early Retirement and Work-Life Experience," *Social Security Bulletin,* March 1966.

income maintenance reforms would result in voluntary reductions in work effort.[9] It has been shown, however, such data simply cannot yield information which can be expected to predict behavior under proposed reforms with much degree of accuracy.[10]

It would seem, looking over the range of evidence, that there remains a great deal of uncertainty about the factors which are affecting the work and retirement status of older and aged persons. Though there has been a downward trend in labor force participation of such persons, one cannot be sure whether this is primarily a matter of voluntary reduction in work effort by such persons or whether it is a matter of economic and social forces which are reducing the range of work opportunities open to them.

If it were true that older workers were in fact already voluntarily withdrawing from the labor force in large numbers, then one might well conclude that further reduction in work effort as a result of reforms in income maintenance programs would not be of great concern. If, however, older workers are being forced out of the labor market by limited opportunities, then one is forced to ask whether those income maintenance reforms which might add substantially to such forces are socially (or economically) desirable.

Thus far, I have discussed the work and retirement status of the aged largely in economic terms. I would also like to consider the predominance of work as a social integrative force in most societies. Lower rates of labor force participation mean increasing social, as well as economic, isolation of the aged poor from the rest of the community. In a cross-national study[11] results indicated that old people in Denmark were consistently more cheerful in assessing their relative position in society than old people in the United States and that the aged in Great Britain were least cheerful in making such an assessment. Denmark was found to be the lowest of the three countries in the percentage of the aged com-

[9] L. E. Gallaway, "Negative Income Tax Rates and the Elimination of Poverty," *National Tax Journal,* September 1966.

[10] M. Taussig, "Negative Income Taxes and the Elimination of Poverty: Comment," *National Tax Journal,* September 1967; H. Kasper, "Welfare Payments and Work Incentive: Some Determinants of the Rates of General Assistance," *Journal of Human Resources,* Winter 1968.

[11] Dorothy Wedderburn, "A Cross-National Study of Standards of Living of the Aged in Three Countries," mimeo., University of Essex, International Seminar on Poverty, 1967.

pletely retired, and their economic position relative to the rest of society was the highest; Britain had the highest percentage completely retired and their income was the lowest of the three. Obviously, there is a complex interaction of many factors which determines the relative economic position of the aged in each society and the seemingly related attitudes, but the role of work opportunities in determining both position and attitudes deserves serious consideration when one contemplates program reforms which are likely to affect the work status of the aged.

The effects of reforms on geographical migration by the aged poor should also be mentioned. The geographical location of the aged will be to some degree determined by the character of their current work status and work opportunities. I have already mentioned that the aged tend to be less geographically mobile than the nonaged. However, changes in the strength of ties to work, or dependence on work income, may change the propensities of the aged to locate in one place or another. On the one hand, to the extent income maintenance reforms weaken work effort incentives of the aged, they may be encouraged to move to an area in which they prefer to live but to which they have not gone in the past because of the lack of work opportunities, e.g., return to rural areas of their youth. On the other hand, if income maintenance reforms provided them with a higher income guarantee and/or lower reduction in benefits as a result of earnings, they might be encouraged to take a chance on moving to areas which held promise of better work opportunities (or potential loss on their investment in their own home in their present location might seem less serious to them).

I have argued at length that the work and retirement issue is central for the aged poor. Review of existing research leaves us uncertain as to the extent to which changing work status of the aged poor over time has resulted from voluntary actions on their part (a changing labor supply function) or from changes in opportunities (a changing labor demand function). Furthermore, existing data will not allow a reasonably accurate estimate of the probable work response of the aged poor to changes in income maintenance provisions. It is important to note that the retirement decision has long-term implications for the individual involved—particularly so in light of the difficulties which older persons face in getting rehired. This means that a short-term experiment is not likely to provide reliable estimates of their response to income maintenance reforms, since the time horizon relevant to their decision is likely to be considerably longer than the time horizon of a two- or three-year experiment (and the same may be true for the time horizon relevant for migration decisions). For this reason, even though the aged are included in the Rural Negative Tax Experiment, it would seem that estimation of their work effort and migration response will require an experiment which takes account of the longer time horizon of these sorts of decisions.

III. ISSUES CONCERNING SPECIFIC PROGRAM FEATURES

In this section I would like to touch upon various specific features of income maintenance reforms which could affect the aged. My review of specific issues will not be exhaustive; the number of behavioral responses, both intended and unintended, to the variety of program features which might be incorporated is almost limitless. However, I do wish to use the case of the aged to illustrate the fashion in which, for any given area, a variety of program implications were discussed as the various stages of the project to which this volume is devoted were worked through.

Since Social Security is the most extensive form of income maintenance in the United States, it is clear that a major issue is: What role might Social Security play in any sort of reformed income maintenance system? There has been, during the current national debate on income maintenance reform, surprisingly little discussion of the adequacy of income maintenance for the aged. Discussions related to the proposed Family Assistance Program have limited the consideration of the aged to improvements in Old Age Assistance, ignoring the question of the role of Social Security. FAP will not do much for the aged, so it is important to bring this issue to light.

The current Social Security system has been designed to serve two basic functions: first, to ensure that those who have had adequate earned income prior to retirement will have reasonable benefits to replace those earnings and second, to provide basic income support for those who have had very low income before retirement. To meet both of these objectives within one program has necessitated certain compromises. Some of these compromises are reflected in the benefit schedules shown in Table 2. As I noted there, the benefit system does provide some income support by virtue of the higher ratio of benefits to past earnings for low-income workers, but the fact that the system remains strictly related to past earnings experience handicaps it in providing basic income support for many of the aged.

A negative income tax program which applied to the aged would provide an important opportunity to separate these two functions which the Social Security system currently attempts to perform and thereby to allow the elimination of some of the compromised features of the system.[12] Basic income support could be achieved through the negative income tax program and earnings replacement could be dealt with through Social Security. Without going into a detailed discussion of the issues, I would like to suggest several features which seem to me to be desirable to incorporate in such a combined system. First, it would be possible to remove the redistributive features from Social Security and make the ratio of Social Security benefits to past earnings the same regardless of the level of past earnings, because the negative income tax program would remove the necessity for this feature in Social Security. Second, it would seem desirable to make the Social Security benefits no longer subject to an earnings test. It has been very roughly estimated that removal of the earnings test would raise the budgetary costs of the Social Security system by 10 percent. However, this estimate included only the initial direct budgetary costs. With the removal of the earnings test we would expect work effort of the aged to increase, and this would mean some reduction in net budgetary costs due to the higher income tax receipts associated with the increased effort. Furthermore, we should surely take into account the total social gain from the increased work effort of the aged, not just that reflected in somewhat lower budgetary costs. I think the removal of the earnings test would be useful both because it would simplify the Social Security system and because it would remove any adverse work incentive effects.[13] This would leave the Social Security system as basically a federal aged pension transfer system, and would remove at least one of the forces working for involuntary withdrawal from the labor force.

Second, in order to further equity among low-income individuals it would be important to make Social Security benefits subject to the income test under the negative income tax. If they were not, those low-income persons who happened to be eligible for Social Security would be made better off than those who had the same level of income but from other sources. This is simply an extension of the general argument for equity in

---

[12] For further discussion of these issues see Pechman et al., *op. cit.*, chap. 9.

[13] Pechman et al. (*op. cit.*, pp. 143–48) argue that a provision which would permanently increase benefits for later retirement would be preferable to removal of the earnings test and might be designed so as to have similar effects in removing work disincentives. The choice seems arguable to me. Retention of earnings tests in a system with a negative income tax complicates the system requiring either, as they note on p. 216, a choice between benefits from one system or the other for those eligible for both, or toleration of higher marginal tax rates on earnings for those eligible for both. Without deep analysis, I would opt for the simplicity of the removal of the earnings test, at the cost of somewhat higher incomes for those working aged with high earnings.

taxation and the same grounds upon which others have argued for treating Social Security just like earned income for the purposes of the positive income tax. Of course, making Social Security benefits taxable in the positive income tax system would lower the costs of the removal of the earnings test for benefits suggested above.

Third, I would propose that payroll taxes for Social Security be treated like federal income tax payments in the negative income tax. It has been argued that the continuation of a separate payroll tax for Social Security is in any case both regressive and anachronistic and that it should simply be integrated with the general payroll withholding for the positive income tax.[14] The arguments for treating the Social Security payroll tax like the federal income tax under the negative income tax would be the same as those for integrating it with positive tax withholding in general.

If the effects of payroll taxes are not "neutralized," then the marginal tax rates under the negative income tax can be lowered for very large size families when the earner's income exceeds the maximum cut-off point for Social Security payroll taxes, and the intended marginal rate of taxation will not be preserved.[15]

The same sort of problem arises if positive income taxes are not "neutralized" by allowing a double[16] deduction of federal (and state and local) income taxes.[17] Unless such a deduction is allowed, families with incomes low enough to qualify for the negative income tax but high enough to be subject to the positive income tax (these would again be large size families with a high income cut-off for the negative tax) will face a marginal tax rate equal to the sum of the negative tax rate and the positive tax rate.

Both on the same grounds that one can argue for the integration of the Social Security payroll tax and federal income tax withholding and for the purpose of preserving the intended marginal rate of taxation, it

---

[14] Pechman et al., *op. cit.*, chap. 4.

[15] Some might argue, however, that since the Social Security payroll tax has such high cut-off point and applies only to earned income the number of families having a lower marginal tax rate under the negative income tax as a result of passing the payroll tax cut-off point might be small and therefore this inequity could be ignored.

[16] The double deduction would only be appropriate if the marginal tax rate (rate of reduction of negative tax benefits with a dollar increase in income) is 50 percent; for marginal tax rates other than 50 percent the "neutralized" deduction would be 1/marginal tax rate.

[17] See W. A. Klein and Michael Asimow, "Accounting Alternative for a Negative Income Tax," University of Wisconsin, Institute for Research on Poverty, Discussion Paper 60 (1970), p. 14, for a discussion of this issue.

seems reasonable to treat the Social Security tax and the federal income tax equivalently under the negative income tax.[18]

This review of the issues for reform of Social Security has been largely a statement of my opinions. I do not wish to pretend this is adequate. The importance of further discussion of this issue is illustrated by the fact that some "expert groups" have been advocating improving the income maintenance of the aged poor by raising benefit levels in the existing Social Security framework while pressing for public programs to improve the work opportunities of the aged. Not only is Social Security an inefficient instrument for improving the income support of the aged poor but it has important features which discourage work effort which would become even more serious at higher benefit levels. The "experts" seem unaware of the inconsistency of increasing Social Security benefits at the same time as trying to improve work opportunities for the aged.

There are several problems that would arise under a negative income tax reform because income would probably be more inclusively defined than it is under the federal positive income tax. In particular, the inclusion of what amounts to some sort of wealth test in determining negative income tax benefits has some implications for the aged. I would like to touch on three issues related to this provision.

a) It has been suggested (and incorporated in the New Jersey and Rural experiments) that income from owner-occupied housing be imputed in the determination of a family's taxable income, i.e., an estimated rental value of the housing would be added to the family's income for determination of their benefits. As I indicated above, 63 percent of the aged poor (as measured by current income) live in housing which they own. Thus the issue of whether and how such income is imputed can be important in determining the level of benefits flowing to the aged poor.

On the surface, one might assume that the extensive home ownership among the aged poor contributes to their well-being. Most studies indicate that both the aged and their children prefer that aged people live separately from their children and, since homeownership would seem to facilitate the exercise of that preference, it would seem desirable to encourage it. However, there are several reasons for arguing that the contribution of an owned home to the welfare of the aged poor is not well measured by its market value. At the end of the life cycle, as children leave the home, the aged may find themselves with quarters which ex-

---

[18] I wish to mention one other problem: the treatment of medical costs under Social Security and a negative income tax. The treatment of medical costs under the negative income tax is an area which deserves careful consideration and carries the discussion into new realms of potential major social reform.

ceed their needs. However, limitations on the market for their home may make it difficult for them to realize the value of their equity in the home and the availability of smaller suitable quarters at reasonable rates may be limited. There are some indications that the owned housing of the aged may be something of a burden on them. Although it has been estimated that homeownership reduces shelter costs by approximately 5 percent relative to rented quarters,[19] and relatively more of the aged than the nonaged own their own homes, housing expenditures as a percentage of total expenditure is considerably *higher* for the aged poor than it is for the nonaged poor.[20] It is not clear whether the propensity of the poor to put such savings as they are able to accumulate into homeownership serves in later years to alleviate their poverty or to exacerbate it.

It would seem that imputation of rent from owner-occupied houses would tend in general to discourage investment in homeownership by low-income people. The discouragement of homeownership through rent imputation could occur either early in the life cycle when low-income people currently eligible, or anticipating their later eligibility, for negative income tax benefits have reduced incentive to do this particular form of saving or when aged people become eligible for a negative income benefit because of declining income and are thereby more encouraged to divest themselves of the home they own. In the past, our national policies seem to have had a strong bias toward encouragement of homeownership. It may be that the discouragement of homeownership among the aged is, in light of this seeming national preference, to be considered an undesirable feature and imputation of rent could be argued against on these grounds. One might also argue against imputation of rent for the aged on the basis of the sort of data cited above which suggest that owned housing of the aged poor actually constitutes a special burden on them; since it is unlikely that the housing market will operate adequately to allow them to recover their equity special relief for them should be provided by *not* imputing rent for homeownership.

I have no strongly formed views on this issue, but given the extent of homeownership among the aged poor it seems important to highlight this issue for more careful study and consideration.

b) In addition to the imputation of rent from owner-occupied housing, it is likely that a negative income tax would have some form of

---

[19] M. Orshansky, "Living in Retirement," *Social Security Bulletin,* October 1968.

[20] It is estimated that the aged poor, in 1960, spent about 42 percent of their income on housing, while the poor as a whole (aged plus nonaged) spent 36 percent of their income on housing. See R. Hollister and J. Palmer, *op. cit.,* Table 4.

capital consumption imputation (e.g., 20 percent of capital assets not used in business would be imputed to income in any year) or an assets limitation provision (e.g., anyone with $2,000 of assets would be ineligible for negative income tax benefits). One dimension of such a test, which must be considered from the point of view of the aged, is the extent to which such a provision would provide a strong incentive for intergenerational transfers. If aged people with incomes close to the eligibility line have assets that will make them ineligible, or will significantly reduce their benefits, then they will have a strong incentive to transfer those assets to their children, relatives or friends in order to enhance benefits coming to them under a negative income tax.

c) In a similar and more general way, the various forms of the wealth test may tend to discourage saving among low-income people in general. If they know that their benefits under a negative income tax may be lower because of assets accumulated through saving, their incentive to save may be considerably weakened. In the past, similar arguments have been put forward about the effects of Social Security on personal savings, but there does not seem to be any clear evidence that such effects have occurred.[21] On the one hand, it would seem that any discouragement of saving due to negative income tax provisions would apply to a relatively more limited range of the population (those who could increase their lifetime satisfaction by consuming at higher rates in earlier life and then living entirely on negative tax benefits in later years) than those whose saving might have been affected by the availability of Social Security. On the other hand, the savings discouragement for that group would be considerably stronger than that caused by Social Security since Social Security does not have a wealth test which affects benefits. Thus it is not clear, a priori, to what extent savings motives within this group may be weakened.

There are several issues which arise when one views the aged as a group which is strictly separable from the rest of the population. First, it should be noted that the fact that the negative income tax is likely to use the family as the unit determining eligibility for and levels of benefits could have some affect on the relations of the aged to second and third generations of their family. To the extent that the adjustment of benefits for size of family are large there will be a greater incentive for families to maintain the aged as part of their household. Thus the rate at which aged parents separate from their children could be affected, among low-income households, by the character of the negative income tax regula-

---

[21] See Pechman et al., *op. cit.,* pp. 61–67 and 186–87, for a discussion of this issue and the evidence.

tions defining the family unit and the size of benefit adjustments to family size.

Second, some people have suggested that some of the negative income tax regulations might be different for the aged than for the rest of the low-income population. One idea has been that it might be possible to make benefits higher for the very low-income aged by making the basic income guarantee higher but offsetting that by also making the marginal tax rate on income higher (thus the break-even level of income—the point at which benefits become zero—could be the same as for the rest of the population, but benefits would be higher for the aged at the lowest part of the income range). Any such differentiation of regulations is likely to create secondary incentives which could affect behavior (and therefore both economic and social costs). For example, if there were such differential levels there might be incentives for the switching of dependents among generations of a family. If aged people had higher benefit levels, then it might well pay to have grandchildren counted as being in the aged parent's household. This is just another illustration of the principle that the creation of special categories in which there will be differential treatment of individuals is likely to encourage individuals to attempt to change their behavior in order to fit into the category which is most beneficial to them (thus the infamy of the "man in the house" rule under AFDC).

This principle has particularly serious implications for the aged. Aging is really a continuous process; it does not occur when a person is exactly 65 years old. Yet if, as a society, we create regulations which treat everyone who has reached a particular age as having a special set of characteristics, we will find that our institutions are essentially forcing those characteristics on those individuals.[22] Thus, for example, to the extent it is assumed that persons over 65 prefer not to work and we create regulations on that assumption, we will tend to create behavior that will seem to conform to that assumption. In my discussion above, I indicated that there is some evidence that this sort of process is at work. As social legislation developed, based on the assumption that aged persons would retire at 65, private company regulations and informal practices have tended to grow up which enforce this assumption. It may be that this social process has fostered a substantial reduction in work opportunities made available to older and aged low-income persons.

This consideration applies to the suggestion of different guarantee and marginal tax rates for the aged under a negative income tax. This suggestion has been based upon the view that labor-force attachment of

---

[22] This point is dramatically made in R. A. Scott, *Making of Blind Men* (Russell Sage, 1969).

the aged is very weak and that therefore higher work disincentives created by the higher marginal tax rate would be of little importance as far as the aged are concerned. I feel this assumption is unproven and has serious economic and social implications. It is important that before we build assumptions of this sort into social legislation we carefully examine both their validity and the incentives, both intended and unintended, which might be created by their institution.

THE WORK EFFORT RESPONSE OF WOMEN TO INCOME MAINTENANCE

Leonard J. Hausman and Hirschel Kasper

I. THEORETICAL RESPONSE TO PROGRAM PARAMETERS

It is important to establish theoretically what the work effort response of female heads of families will be to a universal income maintenance program. This theorizing will be done on the assumptions that the new program guarantees a certain amount of income in the absence of adequate earnings and that benefits from the new program are "taxed" away as earnings and other income increase. We will also consider the fact that any new program will supplant AFDC, an on-going program for poor female-headed families. Wherever possible, contrasts will be drawn between the expected behavior of female and male heads.

The central work response issues are: what are the elasticities of work effort with respect to level of income guaranteed and with respect to the implicit tax rate on earned income? Theoretically, poor female heads should have a higher elasticity of work effort with respect to the guarantee level than male heads on two grounds.[1] First, the services of the female heads, unlike those of the males, are customarily heavily de-

---

[1] The two basic theoretical and empirical studies on the work effort of women are: Jacob Mincer, "Labor Force Participation of Married Women," in *Aspects of Labor Economics,* National Bureau of Economic Research (Princeton: Princeton University Press, 1962); and Glen G. Cain, *Married Women in the Labor Force* (Chicago: University of Chicago Press, 1966).

manded in the home. To the extent that the females have large families and/or young children, the females may prefer to remain at home rather than accept outside employment. Because the "freeing effect" of an income guarantee enables women to pursue an option usually closed to men, one would expect women to be more sensitive than men to the guarantee. Second, it is more socially acceptable for women not to work; and thus the provision of an income guarantee might mean that they are more apt than men to substitute "leisure" for work as the guarantee rises. How sizable this effect is likely to be remains, of course, an open question.

It is more difficult to predict the direction of change in work effort with respect to a change in the implicit tax rate on earnings. The income effect of the guarantee level is going to be negative, even if its size remains unknown. But the tax rate, like any tax on income, is going to have both an income and a substitution effect. The former effect is likely to be positive and the latter negative; for example, a rise in the tax rate means that a given amount of work effort yields less income, thus inducing more work, and also reduces the price of leisure, thus inducing a decrease in work effort. Previous research, as will be noted below, indicates that the (negative) substitution effect outweighs the (positive) income effect, but that does not fully resolve the question. How the tax rate effect differs by the sex of the family head is even more difficult to predict. A priori, we would expect the income-effect part of the tax rate change to be larger for women. Even if the substitution effect carries for both male and female heads, it is not easy to predict how the net effects of a change in the tax rate will compare.

In addition, if income-leisure preferences change as a result of receiving income maintenance, the ex ante relative elasticities of male and female heads may be different than the ex post elasticities.

In anticipating the response of female heads of poor families to a new universal income maintenance scheme, it is first of all important to realize that, for most female heads (compared to only a small proportion of male heads), the scheme will replace a current program, i.e., AFDC. Roughly 75 percent of all poor female heads now receive AFDC.[2] For some small proportion of these female heads, the guarantee level will undoubtedly rise under a new program; for most AFDC mothers, those concentrated in the larger industrial states, the guarantee level will probably not change at all. We would guess that the guarantee, by itself, in any likely new scheme will influence the behavior of no more than two-fifths

---

[2] Irene Lurie, "An Economic Evaluation of Aid to Families With Dependent Children," (unpublished monograph; Washington, D.C.: Brookings Institution, Sept. 1968), pp. 151–52.

of poor female heads and perhaps that of some near-poor female heads. By the time the tax rate in a new scheme comes into effect, the new "30-and-⅓ rule"[3] will be in effect universally. This probably means, given the inescapable relation of reduced implicit tax rates to break-even levels of income, that the tax rates on earnings in a new scheme will not go much lower. Thus a new universal plan may not, of itself, sharply change the work effort of presently covered AFDC mothers. By contrast, the work effort of the newly incorporated female heads may be sharply influenced by a new universal plan.

A second consideration in anticipating the response of female heads is that of the relationship between nominal and effective tax rates in in AFDC. Joseph Heffernan, in an early draft of a staff paper for the Income Maintenance Commission, and Joel Handler, in another recent paper,[4] have contended that effective rates are far below nominal ones because of caseworker treatment of increased earnings. If this is generally the case, and if nonemployed recipients are generally aware of this, then the effective rate under a well-policed new scheme might actually rise. This would imply, quite obviously, that work effort would not increase in response to what is only a nominal cut in the tax rate on earnings.

A third consideration in theorizing about the work response of female heads to a new scheme is the fact that many such persons would continue to receive transfer payments under one or more other programs in which earnings would be implicitly taxed at some positive rate. If the female heads face high marginal rates in other programs, this may reduce the work effort response to the observed change in the cash program's tax rate—because the total marginal tax rate on earnings may actually be cut by relatively less than it *appears* to be cut.[5] Since the new scheme will not be the first or only remaining transfer program for female heads of poor families, predicted responses will be to changes from non-zero and, in some cases, unknown values of important program parameters. We might also indicate that long-term recipients may have a more accurate "feel" for the net implicit marginal tax rate than families who were just brought into the program.

---

[3] For an expanded discussion of the new "30-and-⅓ rule," see Hausman, "The Marginal Tax Rates on Earnings in Existing Transfer Programs for the Poor," in this volume.

[4] Joel F. Handler and Ellen Jane Hollingsworth, "Work and Welfare" (unpublished paper, University of Wisconsin, Institute for Research on Poverty, August 1969).

[5] For a discussion of the "total marginal rate on earnings" when a recipient's earnings are implicitly taxed under two or more transfer programs, see Hausman, *supra* n. 3.

Lastly, it should be noted that a new universal income maintenance program may affect not only the quantity of work effort, but also the type of work that beneficiaries do. It may encourage persons to enter jobs in which they have greater control over their hours of work; such jobs would be in seasonal and marginal industries, as well as part-time work (domestics, repair service) of all sorts.[6]

II. THE NATURE OF THE LABOR MARKET

A. The Structure of Job Opportunities

The effect of income maintenance programs on work effort depends upon the relation between (1) the wage rate opportunities of persons in poor and near-poor families and (2) both the level of welfare benefits and the implicit tax rate on their earnings. Almost by definition, most of the healthy poor have low wage rate prospects and the ratio of allowable welfare payments to potential earned income is high. Although the expected wage rate is low for many of the poor and nonpoor, a wide range of wage opportunities are apparently available even to persons with seemingly little human capital.

Occupational wage rates, after all, vary with location (both regional and urban-rural differences are substantial), age, industry, frequency of unemployment, sex, race, unionization, and length of residence, etc.[7] Good file clerks, for example, earned $84.50 per week in firms in the utilities and transportation industry, but only $67.00 in the retail industry in metropolitan areas in February 1967, a 26 percent difference. Similar relations hold for other jobs which require little or no training or skill. Male janitors earn $2.37 per hour in manufacturing, but only $1.77 in service industries, about 33 percent less. Indeed, although it is possible to make useful statements about the average effects of different variables on earnings, the suspicion remains that luck and other random elements play a large role in the determination of an individual's earnings.[8]

The implications of this are twofold: First, low education attainment does not necessarily imply low wages for each worker; second, job shifts

---

[6] James O'Conner, "Seasonal Unemployment and Unemployment Insurance," *American Economic Review,* Vol. 52 (June 1962), pp. 460–71.

[7] Leonard W. Weiss, "Concentration and Labor Earnings," *American Economic Review,* Vol. 56, (March 1966), pp. 96–117.

[8] Weiss explains just over one-third of the variance in annual incomes of male semiskilled workers, using a model which contains more than 40 independent variables. *Ibid.*

to another industry or another firm may be a more efficient way to raise a person's earnings than to enroll him in a program designed to improve his skills or work habits.[9]

None of this discussion, however, should imply that there is a simple one-to-one relation between low wage rates and low family income or poverty. Families with multiple earners at steady employment may escape poverty and the need for welfare even though their wages are low. It would be important to know precisely how many families have escaped poverty because their jobs are steady and/or there are secondary workers. Unfortunately, such data have not yet been published, although they are available from the recent Census survey of the poor population. The other side of the coin is the number of families who are poor in spite of the fact that there are multiple earners. Orshansky estimates that more than one-third of the nonwhite and one-fourth of all the 1966 poor families had two or more wage earners sometime during the year.[10]

Data on the labor force experience of families receiving public assistance (excluding Old Age Assistance) is even more difficult to obtain. Some local agencies have attempted studies, but the coverage was neither complete nor sufficiently detailed to allow rigorous analysis. In addition, such surveys are somewhat misleading with regard to occupational skills, if the work histories of welfare recipients reflect recurring underemployment. Casual impressions from the growth and stamina of welfare rights organizations suggest that substantial organizational and managerial talents have been lying fallow until recently.

In sum, the average wage rate facing most households now receiving welfare is very low, and inadequate to remove their families from poverty, but it is important to bear in mind the normal dispersion of wages for given occupations and educational achievements as well as the possible danger in assuming that one's skills and talents are necessarily or adequately measured by previous occupational experience.

B. Low Wage Occupations

The job experience of welfare recipients and the poverty population in general is concentrated in the unskilled, semiskilled, and service occupations, if they worked at all. The female heads, of course, tend to work in service occupations, particularly domestic service, while the men tend

---

[9] Although horizontal shifts may raise wages at relatively small social costs, we do not know how many workers could be benefited by such programs.

[10] Mollie Orshansky, "The Shape of Poverty in 1966," *Social Security Bulletin,* Vol. 31 (March 1968), Table 6, pp. 12–13.

Table 1. Frequency of Low Earnings of Year-Round Full-Time Workers,
by Selected Occupations, 1965

Occupation	Total	Percent distribution by earnings			Median
		Less than $1,999	$2,000–$2,499	More than $2,500	
Male	100%	6.0%	2.7%	91.3%	$6,388
Professional and technical	100	4.9	1.0	94.1	8,459
Salaried medical workers	100	5.3	1.8	92.9	7,388
Farmers and farm managers	100	34.6	7.7	57.7	3,098
Managers	100	5.4	1.1	93.5	7,895
Self-employed	100	10.5	1.9	87.7	6,765
Salaried	100	2.8	0.7	96.5	8,531
Clerical	100	2.0	1.1	96.9	6,280
Sales, retail	100	4.0	3.1	92.9	6,077
Skilled	100	1.6	1.5	96.9	6,751
Semiskilled	100	3.7	2.8	93.5	5,782
Manufacturing	100	2.7	2.1	95.2	5,967
Nonmanufacturing	100	4.9	3.5	91.6	5,543
Waiters, etc.	100	3.7	5.9	90.4	4,880
Other service	100	6.4	7.0	86.6	4,853
Farm laborers	100	42.7	13.3	44.0	2,274
Unskilled	100	9.1	6.7	84.2	4,651
Female	100%	13.3%	7.8%	78.9%	$3,828
Professional and technical	100	5.8	1.7	92.5	5,514
Salaried medical workers	100	4.2	3.1	92.7	5,079
Clerical	100	5.0	3.6	91.4	4,223
Secretaries, etc.	100	3.7	3.3	93.0	4,436
Other clerical	100	5.7	3.9	90.4	4,094
Sales, retail	100	14.5	23.0	62.5	2,814
Semiskilled	100	9.0	13.0	78.0	3,273
Manufacturing	100	5.7	12.3	82.0	3,360
Nonmanufacturing	100	23.4	16.5	60.1	2,746
Service	100	39.5	13.8	46.7	2,380
Private household	100	69.9	10.2	19.9	1,238
Waitresses, etc.	100	35.9	23.3	40.8	2,301
Other service	100	29.2	12.5	58.3	2,878

Source: Vera C. Perulla, "Low Earners and Their Incomes," *Monthly Labor Review*, Vol. 90 (May 1967), Special Labor Force Report No. 82, Table A.

to be semiskilled operatives, although many of the nonwhite men work as unskilled laborers.[11] Except for domestics, these jobs have shown little or no tendency to shrink during the past half dozen years, although the movement of many firms out of the city and the further sprawl of the suburbs have made it more difficult and costly for the welfare recipients to travel to and obtain such employment. To the extent that locally owned retail stores, hotels, and restaurants are giving way to national firms, the

---

[11] *Ibid.*

wages of clerks, janitors, orderlies, cleaning women, and waitresses may tend to rise. Continued economic stabilization may keep rates of unemployment low and increase the annual earnings of low-wage jobs and thereby may make work somewhat more attractive to those on welfare.

Table 1 provides a rough indication of the occupations which pay low wages. Approximately 5.5 million persons (3 million aged 25–54) worked full time but could not earn more than $2,500 for the whole year 1965. About 1.8–2.0 million men and 300,000 women were trying to support their families on those low earnings. Annual earnings of $2,000 for a fully employed person means generally a job at $1 per hour. Note that there is a heavy concentration of earners in jobs which not only pay low wages, but where chances for promotion are slim and where little premium is paid for experience.

Women are twice as likely as men to be working in low wage occupations; 9.7 percent of the men and 21.1 percent of the women were fully employed in 1965 but received less than $2,500 for the year. We do not know how many of these received public assistance, nor how many of those who received public assistance could have earned (or even did earn) as much as $2,500 for the year. Yet it is worth noting that, in the same year, 2.9 million households received public assistance, suggesting that even when faced with very low wages many people seemed to work rather than rely entirely on welfare.[12] Apparently a significant but unknown number of persons are likely to work at low wages even though they could increase their total income by seeking relief.[13] Equally important, there are no data on the number of poorly paid full-time year-round earners who, for various reasons, could not pass the eligibility for welfare and, therefore, had to work. Nor do we know why some persons eligible for assistance have not sought it, which may be an increasingly important issue, even if the "taste" for welfare declines as family income rises.

C. Low Wage Industries

Table 2 presents the same information as in Table 1, only by industry classification. It indicates that, at the current implicit tax rates, jobs in trade, service, and agricultural industries seem barely worth taking for anyone who has an opportunity for a transfer income. One additional item, given interest in the government as the employer of last resort, is that

---

[12] Data for this and the next paragraph are from Vera C. Perulla, "Low Earners and Their Incomes," *Monthly Labor Review* (May 1969), Special Labor Force Report No. 82 (U.S. Department of Labor).

[13] Of course, a small but unknown proportion of the welfare recipients needed welfare to supplement their inadequate earnings.

Table 2. Frequency of Low Earnings of Year-Round Full-Time Workers,
by Selected Industries, 1965

| | | Percent distribution by earnings | | | |
	Total	Less than $1,999	$2,000–$2,499	More than $2,500	Median
Male	100%	6.0%	2.7%	91.3%	$6,388
Agriculture, fishing	100	34.6	8.8	56.6	3,026
Construction	100	4.8	3.0	92.2	6,276
Manufacturing	100	2.6	1.5	95.7	6,788
Trade, retail	100	6.4	3.2	90.4	5,734
Trade, wholesale	100	4.0	1.7	94.3	6,564
Personal service	100	9.8	7.5	82.7	5,025
Entertainment, etc.	100	5.8	5.2	89.0	5,886
Public administration	100	0.8	0.9	98.3	6,934
Female	100%	13.3%	7.8%	78.9%	$3,828
Manufacturing, durable	100	3.3	5.4	91.3	4,177
Manufacturing, nondurable	100	6.6	10.3	83.1	3,502
Trade, retail	100	18.9	14.9	66.2	3,097
Trade, wholesale	100	4.8	4.0	91.2	4,102
Personal service	100	27.1	10.8	62.1	3,100
Public administration	100	4.2	2.0	93.8	5,055

Source: Vera Perulla, *op. cit.*, Table B.

relatively fewer men and women are employed in public administration
at low wages than any other broad industry classification. In fact there
is some evidence that in large cities public employment has been an important factor in reducing the welfare rolls.

The characteristic rapid turnover and employment instability of jobs
in the low wage industries which appear available to welfare recipients
causes two problems. First, accepting employment can be risky if it means
submitting to another lengthy eligibility examination for welfare whenever
one is laid off, especially if a demonstrated ability to obtain employment
increases the possibility of welfare disqualification. Second, continuous
instability of employment tends to cause the welfare recipient to always
apply for "entry" jobs at the lowest wages because of an inability to
accumulate seniority and experience. Thus the relevant comparison for
each relief recipient is always the welfare payment against the entry wage,
and he or she is unable to share in the normal pattern of earnings growth.

D. Low Wage Areas

There are some important similarities between the areas of low-wage
opportunities and the bulk of the welfare population. The South generally
pays lower wages than the rest of the country and the industries in the

South tend to have more than their share of low-wage industries. That region also has many welfare recipients and nearly 50 percent of the poverty population. As expected, with so many people to support from a relatively poor region, the average welfare payment tends to be very low, although the variation from one poor southern state to another is much larger than among the northern industrialized states.

The low levels of welfare assistance in the South, together with the seemingly harsh eligibility requirements, may have encouraged some families to move North to improve their economic chances. Much of this movement may have been to the inner cities of the North where relatives and friends live, but where the new wage opportunities may not be very attractive relative to the available welfare benefits. As a result, migration may have made the population of the inner cities poorer and increased the proportion of the population which is supported by welfare payments.[14] The residential concentration of the poor serves to limit knowledge of good job opportunities since much job information passes from one friend or neighbor to the next.

E. Unemployment

Until recently there was widespread agreement that unemployment was an important cause of the demand for public assistance. However, the continuing rise in welfare cases together with the decline in unemployment rates has stimulated concern about the relation between labor market conditions and the welfare population. Moynihan has indicated that many of those on welfare may be no longer connected to the job market and just dependent on the charity of society.[15]

It may have gone unrealized that there has been no tightening of the labor market from fall 1966 to late 1968 and early 1969. The unemployment rates for women have not been declining. For a number of reasons, inflation and migration among them, there may have been an increase in the number of poor people in the northern urban areas, where welfare payments tend to be higher and eligibility easier to establish.

The proper consideration of unemployment as a cause of welfare requires the appropriate measure of job opportunities based on age, sex, regional specifications, etc. Evidence indicates that changes in unemployment are more relevant than the current levels in determining the wel-

---

[14] For example, see Herman D. Stein (ed.), *The Crisis in Welfare in Cleveland* (Cleveland: Case–Western Reserve University, 1969).

[15] Daniel P. Moynihan, "The Crises in Welfare," *The Public Interest,* No. 10 (Winter 1968), pp. 3–29.

fare rates; that total unemployment is more relevant than the insured unemployment rates;[16] and that the AFDC rolls respond more to the unemployment rate for women than for men.

Until we have more labor market information on the welfare and low-income populations, it will be impossible to make any judgments about whether they are more or less attached to the labor market than formerly.

F. The Appropriate Use of Demand and Supply Factors

Public policy may improve the market opportunities of welfare recipients by increasing the demand for workers in general or specific welfare recipients by expansionary macroeconomic policy or more microoriented programs such as wage subsidies to employers, respectively. Market opportunities for recipients may also be improved by changing the skills and talents which they bring to their prospective employers by training and retraining programs or by providing more and better knowledge about job opportunities to the people. Neither demand nor supply policies are costless or foolproof. Increasing the national demand for labor may tend to raise all wages and prices while providing more and somewhat better jobs; improving the supply of labor may tend to depress wages slightly and, unless there are appropriate job openings, may be a fruitless exercise.[17]

Increases in aggregate demand have historically had high benefit/cost ratios, but differences in the economic climate of various areas and differences in the skills of welfare recipients often render it inappropriate as the sole national policy. Policies of creating jobs for local areas have not been adopted frequently, aside from some small or temporary programs.

Although there is substantial evidence that job retraining programs generally improve the well-being of the trainees, there is no evidence that the level of total employment is higher or the well-being of the entire community improved.

The achievement of a full employment goal may reduce the welfare population in two ways; first, by increasing the number of job oppor-

---

[16] Hirschel Kasper, "Welfare Payments and Work Incentive: Some Determinants of the Rates of General Assistance Payments," *Journal of Human Resources,* Vol. 3 (Winter 1968), pp. 86–110.

[17] For a discussion of the effect of expansionary fiscal and monetary policy on the low-income population see Hirschel Kasper, "The War on Poverty: A Program for the Taxpayers or the Poor," *Quarterly Review of Economics and Business,* Vol. 8 (Autumn 1968), pp. 15–28.

tunities available and, second, by creating upward pressure on (particularly low) wages so that jobs are even more attractive to welfare recipients than before.

The commitment to reducing the welfare rolls by changing the talents and skills of the welfare population necessarily requires a much more flexible approach. Individual communities will select different means depending upon the nature of their local industries, the welfare population, and their tastes for the economic and social behavior of those who may be supported by the public. Unfortunately, there is no guarantee that, just because a community has people on welfare, it will also have abundant administrative talents to successfully operate individualistic programs.

III. AN EVALUATION OF OUR UNDERSTANDING OF THE WORK EFFORT RESPONSE OF FEMALE HEADS OF FAMILIES

A. The Nature of the Evidence

There have been a few studies in which attempts were made to estimate the impact of the guarantee level and/or the implicit tax rate in a cash transfer program on the work effort of female heads of poor families. Hausman,[18] in a study for the President's Commission on Income Maintenance Programs, estimated the impact of AFDC by using data on AFDC recipients in three states from the 1967 SRS survey of the AFDC rolls. The study was done with data from Alabama, Kentucky, and Mississippi, because these three states have AFDC programs in which the implicit tax rates on earnings are constant, non-zero and non-100 percent ones over the entire range of earnings.

Before its results are summarized, a number of limitations in the study ought to be noted. First, the data may have been poor because caseworkers completed the questionnaires on the basis of information obtained in their last regular (and possibly long-past) meetings with the clients; and because AFDC data on employment and earnings are often inaccurately kept by caseworkers, although in these states record keeping may be far better than average. Second, two of the three states have a reputation for coercing recipients to work; thus the AFDC mothers may

---

[18] Leonard J. Hausman, "The Impact of Welfare on the Work Effort of AFDC Mothers," *Report of the President's Commission on Income Maintenance Program—Appendix* (Washington, D.C.: U.S. GPO, forthcoming).

not have been freely responding to the financial aspects of the transfer program in making their work-welfare decisions. Third, one must question whether recipients are in fact aware of the tax rates that face them, since program administrators often seem to be unaware. Fourth, it was unfortunately the case that the critical independent variables were highly correlated: the guarantee level, the implicit tax rate on earnings, and the (presumed) degree of coercion moved together. Last, the dependent variable in the regressions had to be categorical, since no data on hours worked were available.

The key results are still of interest and tend to support the hypotheses about the work effort effects of a cash transfer program that were suggested above. The income effect of the guarantee level was negative; and the elasticity of labor force participation with respect to the guarantee level was slightly under .4. Thus, for example, in those three states a 50 percent increase in the guarantee level—which averaged $50 per month in the three states in 1967—would have resulted in a roughly 20 percent decline in labor-force participation of AFDC mothers, from about 30 percent. The net effect of the implicit tax rate was also negative; and the elasticity of labor force participation with respect to the tax rate varied beween .3 and .4. Thus, for example, in the three states, a 16 percent cut in the mean tax rate (from 60 percent to 50 percent) would have resulted in a 7 percent increase in labor-force participation among these mothers. The results seem plausible and indicate only a minor degree of sensitivity to the key program parameters. At other guarantee levels and in different administrative contexts, of course, the results might be very different.

There have been two instances in which the effects of alternative welfare tax rates were studied in a somewhat controlled setting: first, between July 1959 and July 1961 the Denver Department of Public Welfare conducted The Incentive Budgeting Demonstration Project;[19] second, between July 1964 and June 1965 the Cuyahoga County (Cleveland) Welfare Department conducted the Employment Incentives Demonstration Program.[20] In both projects the sensitivity of work effort to changes in the implicit tax was found to be slight. Whatever measures were used in measuring the effects of a reduction in the implicit tax rate indicated that work effort was negatively related to the tax rate, but to a (statistically) insignificant degree. Both projects, however, were defective in

---

[19] Denver Department of Public Welfare, "The Incentive Budgeting Demonstration Project" (December 1961).

[20] Cuyahoga County Welfare Department [Cleveland], "Employment Incentives and Social Services: A Demonstration Program in Public Welfare" (1966).

design and in implementation. For example, unmeasured tax rate reductions also applied to control group cases; and caseworkers who administered the experimental caseloads were not fully committed to allowing the AFDC mothers to make their own work-leisure choices: in Cleveland it was frequently the case that caseworkers did not inform the mothers of the reduced tax rates; and, further, many mothers believed that to reveal any employability was to run the risk of being denied all assistance payments.[21] The projects, if anything, did suggest the value of future experimentation with alternative implicit tax rates.

Two other studies suggest that, since the guarantee level in AFDC has been rising far more rapidly than have average or minimum wages, and given the fact that there has been an implicit 100 percent tax rate on earnings for most recipients, the high AFDC guarantee has induced more and more persons to leave work and go on AFDC.[22] Durbin has noted, for example, that in New York City welfare allowances rose by almost 40 percent between 1962 and 1966, whereas average wages rose by 13 percent and minimum wages rose by 30 percent over the same time interval; so that by 1966, a 2,000 hours per year "minimum wage income" was less than the welfare allowance for a family of four in that city. Gordon has noted that between January 1964 and January 1968 average welfare grant levels rose by about 45 percent in New York State. Similar, although not nearly so marked, trends probably exist nationally; given the confiscatory tax that often prevailed until recent legislation took effect, these have made welfare more competitive with work.

B. Determinants of the Supply of Public Assistance

We may assume that the government agency has an implicit utility function which describes the programs which it wants to support (for whatever reason). It is restrained from doing all that it wants because of (a) a lack of public and legislative unanimity on public goals and ends, (b) restricted tax collections, and (c) a desire to perpetuate one's own administration. Thus the quantity and quality of welfare which will be offered in a jurisdiction will be greater the more sympathetic the public

---

[21] U.S. Commission on Civil Rights, "Children in Need: A Study of a Federally Assisted Program of Aid to Needy Families with Children in Cleveland and Cuyahoga County, Ohio" (Washington, D.C.: U.S. GPO, 1966), pp. 19–21.

[22] Elizabeth F. Durbin, "The Effect of Welfare Programs on the Decision to Work" (New York University Graduate School of Business Administration, August 1968); and David M. Gordon, "Income and Welfare in New York City," *The Public Interest,* No. 16 (Summer 1969).

and the agency, the greater the budget, and the more politically inclined the welfare recipients and their "lobbyists." There is no reason to believe that agency tastes are equally important in all situations, since there is some evidence that agency tastes are less relevant to program variables in areas where there is strong competition between political parties.[23]

IV. A STRATEGY FOR GREATER KNOWLEDGE

Data on the work effort response of female heads of families to the guarantees and tax rates built into income maintenance programs can be gathered from a number of ongoing transfer programs. These sources and their deficiencies will be discussed in order of their expected payoffs.

First, and least promising as a source of data, is the survivors' part of OASDHI, the benefits of which flow largely to female-headed families in which there are one or more orphaned children. Maternal orphans and paternal orphans whose mothers have remarried also receive aid under this program.[24] Benefits received by paternal orphan families are a function of the previous earnings of the deceased father—which determine the family's "primary insurance amount" (PIA)—family size, and the earnings of the surviving mother. Generally, surviving mothers face either a constant zero tax rate on earnings or a tax schedule that combines zero, 50 percent, and 100 percent rates. Mothers in families in which the maximum family benefit can be reached when the mother is excluded from the group—generally, all families which have three or more eligible children and two-children families with very low PIA's—face a zero rate on earnings. Mothers in other eligible families face a zero rate on the first $1,680 of annual earnings, a 50 percent rate on earnings between $1,681 and $2,880, and a 100 percent rate on earnings above $2,880, until only the mother's part of the family's benefit is reduced to zero.

There are three serious statistical problems that arise with the available data from a 1963 survey[25] of beneficiaries in this program. (1) The guarantee to families is determined by the PIA, but the mother's

---

[23] See Hirschel Kasper, "On Political Competition, Economic Policy, and Income Maintenance Programs" (unpublished paper, September 1969).

[24] In maternal orphan families the surviving father cannot receive any aid for himself. His children do receive benefits, if their deceased mother was covered under OASDHI.

[25] U.S. Department of Health, Education, and Welfare, Social Security Administration, *Widows with Children under Social Security: The 1963 National Survey of Widows with Children under OASDHI* (Washington, D.C.: U.S. GPO, 1966).

potential wage rate is likely to be highly correlated with her family's PIA because the latter is a function of the deceased father's earnings; thus two important independent variables, the guarantee and the mother's potential market wage, are likely to be highly correlated. (2) There is no information in the 1963 survey data on the mother's potential or actual market wage rate, although it may be possible to obtain information indirectly from somewhat crude hours and earnings data. (3) As may be obvious from the discussion in the previous paragraph, the tax rate on earnings and the number of children within a family are two other highly correlated independent variables. Since about 8 percent of the OASDHI families received public assistance, and since roughly 20 percent received veteran's benefits, both of which are transfer programs in which there are implicit tax rates on earnings, there is a small possibility that, holding family size constant by stratifying the sample, there would be enough variation in the tax rate variable to measure the response to it. Since the Social Security Administration possesses the tape with the data from this program and survey, some manipulation of the data may be inexpensive and worthwhile.

Second, a study is about to be launched on the impact of the "30-and-1/3 rule," i.e., the new AFDC tax rates, on the work effort of AFDC mothers in twenty cities. Since the researchers will not be allowed to manipulate guarantee levels and tax rates within a given welfare jurisdiction, they will have to rely on two means of obtaining variation in the tax rate and guarantee level variables: (1) they may be able to get an entire welfare jurisdiction to adopt tax rates other than those built into the 30-and-1/3 rule; (2) as discussed at some length elsewhere in this book,[26] there will be some variation among welfare jurisdictions in the implicit tax rates on earnings, even after the 30-and-1/3 rule comes into effect, because of the fact that many states do not pay 100 percent of family needs; also, there is always considerable variation among states in the level of payments guaranteed to given types of families. The use of experimental groups in different welfare jurisdictions presents serious problems. First, the researchers will have to get cities which are closely matched with respect to industrial structure and labor market conditions. Second, the researchers will have to match cities with respect to general AFDC policies, like the degree of coercion experienced by recipients on the question of employment. If they fail to come up with experimental and control groups, the researchers will be forced to rely on before-and-after comparisons, which may be especially poor in a time of deteriorating labor market conditions.

The third source of data on the work response of female heads is the

---

[26] See Hausman, *supra* n. 3.

most promising. The experiments with the negative income tax in North Carolina, Iowa, Indiana, and Washington (state) will probably contain female-headed families in the experimental groups. If these experiments are able to overcome the problems created by working with families who can or do receive aid under other cash transfer programs, like AFDC and OASDHI, they should provide the most meaningful results.

The substantial expansion of coverage of any new income maintenance program means that the work incentive issue will be relevant to many more people. While we have a few studies of the demand for various welfare programs and the work incentive response of current welfare recipients, we have no reason to think that any of those results can be extrapolated to the larger population. It is important that we develop new research on the work incentives of the population at large, especially for all female family heads and the adult members of poor and near-poor families.

A sample of such families, together with detailed information on the experience of welfare recipients in the sample, may prove the only way to estimate the work effort response of those expected to be affected by the extended coverage. It is imperative that information on wage rate opportunities be obtained from the sample as well as recent history of labor force participation. It may also be necessary to investigate the benefits of other welfare programs, such as public housing, food stamps, and youth opportunities.

Additional information must be obtained on the nature of the welfare agencies, the way programs are administered, their formal and informal rules, and the relations among various social welfare organizations. We must understand the behavior of government agencies, as the recipients do, if we are to understand the response of recipients to the various policy variables.

MARITAL STABILITY

Myron J. Lefcowitz

The apparent relation between economic position and family stability was first raised as an issue for public discussion by the Moynihan Report in the summer of 1965. Without getting into the controversy about the Negro family, the possible effects of changing the cash transfer system for marital stability is a relevant issue. In this paper three aspects of that question are discussed:

1. Is marital stability a social policy objective?
2. What are the consequences of marital instability?
3. What seems to be a fruitful line for experimentation in this area?

I. SOCIAL POLICY OBJECTIVE

Whether keeping two people together in a marital state ought to be the objective of social policy is certainly a moot point. It is quite clear, however, that the once-married couple is the statistical norm at any given point in time. In 1960, of the 44 million males who had ever been married and not widowed, 35 million had been married only once and were living with their spouse. To obtain some idea of the marital stability history, a look at the 55–64-year-old category is instructive. Among the 6.5 million males in this age category who had ever been married and non-widowed, 4.9 million had been married once and were living with their spouse (0.4 million had been widowed).

Talking about the statistical norms, however, only obscures the deeper meaning of the described modal marital situation. The desired state in our society is for a man and woman, once wedded, to remain

105

Table 1. Percentage Married Once with Spouse Present
among Ever-married and Nonwidowed Males in 1960[a]

	All incomes	*Income under $3,000*
All ages	80(44)[b]	66(13.7)
55–64 years	74(6.6)	61(2.3)

[a] Derived from Table 6, *Marital Status*, Report PC (2)—4E, U.S. Census of Population 1960, U.S. Department of Commerce, Bureau of the Census.

[b] The numbers in parentheses are the total in millions of ever-married and nonwidowed for that category.

together "until death do us part." There has been some question whether the lower classes share this so called middle-class value system. Most researchers agree, however, "that one learns that lower class life styles are pursued not because they are viewed as intrinsically desirable, but because the people involved feel constrained to act in those ways given the deprivations and threats to which they find themselves subject. The lower class does not have a separate system of ultimate values. Lower class people do not really 'reject middle class values.' It is simply that their whole experience of life teaches them that it is impossible to achieve a viable sense of self esteem in terms of those values. . . ."[1]

If Lee Rainwater is correct in his assessment, an examination of the marital stability for the population in 1960 with less than $3,000 income should show that the majority of the nonwidowed and ever married had been married only once and were still living with their spouse but that the proportion will be less than in the general population because of the strains induced in their way of life by their deprived economic situation. That is indeed the case, as we can see in Table 1. Eighty percent of all ever-married nonwidowed males were married only once and still with the same wife compared to 66 percent of the same category of males with less than $3,000 income in 1960. Among the men who were 55–64 years old, the comparable figures were 74 and 61 percent.

Given the apparent normative definition of marriage to a single spouse with whom one lives over a lifetime, any social policy which has as its direct objective, or indirect aim, the encouragement of marital stability is consistent with the values of our society. Nevertheless, it is also part of our value system that persons who find that situation unrewarding are permitted to separate and to form new unions. At least

[1] Lee Rainwater, "Poverty and Deprivation in the Crisis of the American City," statement presented to the U.S. Senate Committee on Government Operation, Subcommittee on Executive Reorganization, December 6, 1966.

25 percent of the population have not stayed with the spouse to whom they were first married (see Table 1 for those 55–64 years of age). Thus social policies directed to the maintenance of marital stability should be designed to encourage but not to constrain individuals to what might be an intolerable situation.

Moreover, these policies might best be directed to persons with low income since the evidence suggests that the stresses and strains of their economic situation make difficult their behaving in directions consistent with the values of a larger society which they accept.

II. MARITAL STABILITY AND HUMAN CAPITAL

To a large extent, the interest in marital stability has been stimulated by concern with the consequences of broken homes for children. Systematic investigation of the available research raises questions about whether there are any such consequences.[2] Unfortunately—for our purposes—most of the discussion has focused around the differences between black and white family structures.

Data are available, however, that indicate growing up in a broken family may have visible effects upon one's educational achievement. The most persuasive evidence comes from the analysis done by Duncan of data obtained from a study of intergenerational occupational mobility.[3] Whether one grew up in an intact family or not can result in more than three-fifths of a year difference in school attainment; that is, growing up in a broken family depresses educational achievement (see Table 2). Since the major direct influence on occupational achievement is educational attainment and the major direct influence on income is occupational achievement,[4] it appears that family stability bears in some relevant degree on the locomotion of individuals into the opportunity structure. Caution should be exercised, however, not to place undue emphasis on the relevance of family stability for educational and occu-

---

[2] Elizabeth Herzog and Celia E. Sudia, "Fatherless Homes: A Review of Research," *Children,* Vol. 15 (1968), pp. 177–182; and Elizabeth Herzog and Celia E. Sudia, "Family Structure and Composition: Research Considerations," in *Race, Research, and Reason: Social Work Perspectives* (New York: National Association of Social Workers, 1969), pp. 145–164.

[3] Peter M. Blau and Otis Dudley Duncan, *The American Occupational Structure* (New York: John Wiley and Sons, 1967).

[4] Otis Dudley Duncan, David L. Featherman, and Beverly Duncan, *Socio-Economic Background and Occupational Achievement,* Final Report to Bureau of Research Office of Education, HEW, May 1968, unpublished, p. 52.

Table 2. Regression of Number of School Years Completed of Family-Background
Variables, by Color, for Selected Age Groups of U.S. Native Males
(March 1962)

Color and age in 1962	Color	Education of family head	Occupation of family head[a]	Intact family	Number of siblings	Coefficient of de-termination
			Independent variables			
		Partial regression coefficients, raw form				
Total						
27–36	0.843	0.197	0.040	0.744	−0.199	.277
37–46	1.956	0.196	0.042	0.659	−0.222	.312
47–61	2.061	0.229	0.047	1.116	−0.213	.325
White						
27–36	–	0.192	0.040	0.671	−0.225	.267
37–46	–	0.195	0.041	0.626	−0.223	.281
47–61	–	0.217	0.047	1.203	−0.222	.283
Nonwhite						
27–36	–	0.220	0.034	0.763	−0.043	.136
37–46	–	0.199	0.055	0.718	−0.246	.137
47–61	–	0.329	0.051	0.435	−0.168	.167

[a] Occupations scored on Duncan's socioeconomic index, which has a range of 0 to 96 and a standard deviation of about 24 points in the United States male population aged 25–64 in 1962.

Source: Otis Dudley Duncan, "Discrimination against Negroes," *The Annals*, Vol. 37 (May 1967), p. 100. Reproduced by permission.

pational achievement since its increment is marginal relative to other background factors such as father's occupation, father's educational level, and race.[5]

In summary, then, any social policy which encourages marital stability will, it appears, have some net positive consequences for the achievement of the children of those families—albeit marginal.

III. AN EXPERIMENT IN MARITAL STABILITY

Given that marital stability is apparently normatively desirable in our society and has positive intergenerational effects, an experiment to assess the consequences of a cash transfer program for marital stability appears to be in order. Moreover, marital stability is less in the low-income

[5] Blau and Duncan, *Id.*, pp. 331–336; Duncan, *et. al., Id.*, p. 79.

Table 3. Percentage Distribution of Divorces and Annulments in 1961 and in 1964, by Duration of Marriage

Years of marriage	1961	1964
Under 1	5.6%	5.3%
1	9.4	8.8
2	8.0	8.4
3	7.7	7.3
4	7.3	6.8
(Under 5)	(38.0)	(36.6)
5–9	24.7	24.8
10–14	15.5	14.6
15–19	9.7	11.4
20 and over	12.2	12.6

Source: *Vital Statistics*, 1964, Vol. III, Marriage and Divorce, Section 2, p. 8, Tables 2–5; and *Vital Statistics*, 1961, Vol. III, Marriage and Divorce, Section 3, p. 19, Table 3-E.

population than among the nonpoor (see Table 1). Hence, insofar as low income is not conducive to marital stability, it might be expected that an increase in the income of the poverty population would increase the marital stability rate.

A major problem for experimentation in this area is that the breaking of a marital union is a relatively rare event. Although less rare over the lifetime of an age cohort, experimentation, to be useful for policy, ought to provide results within a three to five year period. Of the 5.8 million ever-married males who in 1960 had their first marriage no earlier than 1955, 79 percent had been married only once and were still living with the same wife.[6] In any given year, more than one-fifth of the divorces and annulments take place before the third wedding anniversary (see Table 3). Any short-run experiment, then, which selects from newly and first married has a probability of at least 20 percent incidence in marital instability, all other things being equal.

Since 83 percent of the males in 1960 had married at least once by the time they are 34 years of age, the experimental group will undoubtedly come from the younger age population. Although the sensitivity of marital stability to income has already been noted in Table 1, it is more directly relevant to look at the relationship among the younger aged groups. We can see in Table 4 that marital stability, as it has been indexed in this paper, is particularly sensitive to the $3,000 income level.

[6] See Table 2, U.S. Census of the Population, *Marital Status,* Report PC (2)—4E (U.S. Dept. of Commerce: 1960).

Table 4. Marital Status of Males under 35,
by Income and Race[a]

	Ever married (thousands)	Percent married once spouse present
Under 25		
All	2,700	85
Under $3,000	1,298	77
$3,000–$4,999	961	91
$5,000–$6,999	396	93
$7,000 and over	87	92
Nonwhites		
All	297	75
Under $3,000	220	72
$3,000–$4,999	62	84
$5,000–$6,999	12	82
$7,000 and over	–	–
Age 25–34		
All	9,372	85
Under $3,000	1,846	73
$3,000–$4,999	2,859	89
$5,000–$6,999	2,917	90
$7,000 and over	1,750	91
Nonwhites		
All	961	73
Under $3,000	486	66
$3,000–$4,999	322	78
$5,000–$6,999	123	82
$7,000 and over	30	80

[a] Derived from Table 6, *Marital Status, op. cit.*

In that category, 77 percent of all ever-married males under the age of 25 have been married once and are with spouse present. Above the $3,000 income level comparable figures are slightly over 90 percent and do not vary. The same pattern can be found for the 25–40 age group and for nonwhites in both age categories.

There is evidence, moreover, that marital instability is higher in large cities and in the slums. In any case it is a reasonable hypothesis that the higher the break-even point in any cash transfer system, the more maritally stable the population will be.

It is suggested, therefore, that an experiment be designed with newly married and first-married families as the unit of analysis. Given the high incidence of marital stability in the first four to five years of marriage and sensitivity of that rate to the approximate poverty line, it would be anticipated that a small sample—say 125–150 couples in one community—subjected to relatively few combinations of guarantees and tax rates could provide some insight within three years of the consequences of negative income tax for marital stability.

SOME DEMOGRAPHIC ASPECTS OF INCOME MAINTENANCE POLICY

James A. Sweet

Orshansky[1] has shown that families with several children are more likely to be in poverty than families with fewer children.

Number of children under 18	Percent of families with incomes below	
	"Economy level"	"Low-cost level"
1	12.1	17.7
2	11.3	17.5
3	17.4	26.8
4	22.8	34.8
5	35.8	53.0
6 or more	49.3	63.5

These data and the well-known historical association between fertility and socioeconomic status have led persons concerned with poverty policy to begin to take an interest in fertility and family planning programs.

The fertility of the poverty population is relevant to income maintenance policy in at least two ways: (1) we need to be able to anticipate the effects of proposed income maintenance programs on fertility, and (2) we need to be able to anticipate the fertility of the population (even if it is not modified by the program) in order to estimate the cost of the

---

[1] Mollie Orshansky, "The Shape of Poverty, 1966," *Social Security Bulletin* (March 1968).

program (assuming the cost is somehow tied to family size and the resultant need for income).

This paper deals with two issues: a brief description of the fertility patterns of the poor; and a discussion of some potential consequences of income maintenance programs on fertility, marriage, and marital disruption. Before we deal directly with these issues, several problems need mentioning.

The data that are now available may be out of date and misleading. There are two major sources of data on the fertility of the United States population which are of large enough scale to permit discussion of the fertility of the poverty population: the 1960 United States Census and a 1960 sample survey study on "The Growth of American Families."[2] To the extent that there has been any major change in fertility patterns of the poor since 1960, our estimates will be in error. (The results of the 1965 Fertility Survey were published in 1970, and 1970 Census information should be available by 1972.)

In addition, however, there is another problem having to do with the currency of information: for any given birth cohort (group of women born at the same time), fertility is spread over a period of some twenty-five or thirty years. We do not know precisely what the completed fertility of a cohort will be until it reaches the age of 35–39 or 40–44. The completed fertility of younger women who are still reproducing is always an unknown. Thus, in order to have an adequate indication of completed fertility, it is often necessary to wait until a cohort has reached its fortieth or forty-fifth birthday. Some of the data we will be using refer to women aged 40–44 in 1960—women whose fertility experience occurred between 1935 or so, and 1960. Inferences drawn from the experience of this age cohort may therefore be misleading when applied to women currently in their child-bearing years if fertility patterns have changed significantly in the intervening years. Finally, it should be noted that analysis of completed family size by income level for this cohort is based on *current* income, rather than income during the years of family formation; the latter relationship would be conceptually superior, but such data are unavailable.

Most of what is known about fertility concerns the fertility experience of women who are currently married at the time of observation. We tend to think that that is not a serious bias in general because most people in the reproductive ages who have ever been married are currently

---

[2] The recently completed Survey of Economic Opportunity constitutes an important addition to the data in this area. These data were not available for analysis at the time this paper was written, however.

married at any point in their reproductive lives, since those whose marriages are disrupted tend to remarry quickly. For the poverty population, the analysis of fertility may be seriously biased by the inclusion of only the currently married—particularly since one major source of poverty is marital disruption and nonremarriage. Related to this, we know virtually nothing about the incidence of illegitimate fertility, nor of its determinants and consequences.

The data that are available refer only roughly to the poverty population as it is now conceptualized and measured. Available fertility data classify the population by education (of the woman, and/or of her husband, if she is currently married), by husband's income, by family income, and by husband's occupation. No study that I am aware of has ever classified the population in terms of a poverty index relating income to family size and composition. Indeed, for most purposes this would be circular. The poverty population as classified by an Orshansky-type poverty index is selective of the more fertile and more fecund population (fecundity referring to the physiological capacity to bear children).

An additional problem has to do with the discrepancy between the dynamic questions that we are interested in and the static nature of information that is available. With very few exceptions fertility studies are cross-sectional. We know very little about the sources of change in fertility behavior or the responses of fertility to changes in economic and social environment.

I. COMPLETED FERTILITY

A. Education Differentials

In the United States in 1960 only the very small segment of the urban female population with less than five years of education had a mean completed family size of more than three children per married woman. Women with five to seven and eight years of education had marital fertility levels that were only slightly higher than fertility of high school graduates (see Table 1).

B. Rural-Urban Differentials

A comparison of the rural with the urban education specific mean family sizes reveals a wide difference between rural and urban fertility, particularly among the poorly educated and nonwhite population (see

Table 1. Children Ever Born per 1,000 Women Age 40–44, by Education for the Population Residing in Urbanized Areas and on Farms

| | White | | | | Nonwhite | | | |
| | Urbanized areas | | Rural farm | | Urbanized areas | | Rural farm | |
Education	Per 1,000 women	Per 1,000 ever married women	Per 1,000 women	Per 1,000 ever married women	Per 1,000 women	Per 1,000 ever married women	Per 1,000 women	Per 1,000 ever married women
0	2,850	3,567	4,291	5,671	2,371	2,725	4,813	5,578
1–4	2,891	3,219	4,436	4,737	2,320	2,487	5,679	5,986
5–7	2,478	2,650	3,782	3,919	2,413	2,593	5,910	6,177
8	2,229	2,370	3,401	3,520	2,293	2,439	5,336	5,466
9–11	2,226	2,341	3,106	3,167	2,339	2,482	5,211	5,304
12	1,985	2,132	2,853	2,937	1,957	2,080	3,609	3,738
13–15	1,965	2,146	2,856	2,925	1,821	1,971		
16	1,968	2,244	2,460	2,583	1,627	1,789		
17+	1,404	1,933	1,611	1,892	1,105	1,261		
Total	2,103	2,270	3,165	3,270	2,207	2,361	5,357	5,618

Note: The columns of Table 1 refer to total fertility and total marital fertility. The difference between the figures in each set of columns reflects the degree to which the group of women marry.

Source: 1960 Census of Population, *Women by Number of Children Ever Born* (PC(2)3A), Table 26.

Table 1). Implicitly, these comparisons indicate the degree to which the fertility of the poorly educated urban population is restricted from what it might be.

C. Occupational Differentials

Table 2 presents similar data for currently married women classified by the occupation of husband. In addition to comparing means, we can also examine the distribution of completed family sizes among the various occupations. The distributions for laborers, farm laborers, farmers, unemployed, and not in the labor force are presented in this table, along with those for operatives and professionals for comparison. Apart from farm laborers, occupations and labor-force statuses characterized by a high incidence of poverty do not seem to have very high proportions of very large families (four or more children): laborers, 19.6 percent; farm laborers, 36.6 percent; farmers, 21.8 percent; NILF, 21.6 percent; unemployed, 19.8 percent; in comparison to 7.9 percent for professionals and 15.0 percent for operatives.

D. Income Differentials

Similar figures are shown for completed family size in relation to 1960 family income and 1960 husband's income in Table 3. There is no relationship worth talking about. If the farm population were included, however, a spurious association between income and fertility would appear. Farm couples are disproportionately included in the low-income categories and also tend to high fertility.

II. SPACING PATTERNS

First-birth intervals are somewhat shorter for women with lower education than for women with moderate or high education (a mean of 21.6 months for less than eight years' education, and 29.5 for women with twelve years). For higher-order intervals the differences are very small (Table 4). Among women who go on to have large families, mean intervals between births beyond the first birth are *longer* for the poorly educated than the well educated.

Table 2. Children Ever Born per 1,000 Women Age 40–44 (distribution and mean), by Husband's Occupation in 1960 (percentage distribution)

	Children ever born							Mean	
	0	1	2	3	4	5–6	7+	Total	Per mother
Professional and technical	12.9%	15.9%	31.2%	21.6%	10.7%	6.4%	1.5%	2.31	2.65
Operatives	11.3	16.2	26.7	19.1	11.7	10.0	5.0	2.69	3.03
Laborers	12.1	14.8	23.4	17.8	12.4	11.4	8.2	2.97	3.38
Farm laborers	9.3	10.9	15.4	16.2	11.6	17.4	19.2	4.01	4.89
Farmers	8.8	11.9	23.0	20.2	14.2	14.1	7.7	3.16	4.23
Not in labor force	19.2	16.9	18.6	14.3	9.3	10.8	10.8	2.88	3.57
Unemployed	14.8	15.4	22.5	16.2	11.2	11.8	8.0	2.97	3.37

Source: 1960 Census of Population, *Women by Number of Children Ever Born* (PC(2)3A), Table 31.

Table 3. Children Ever Born per 1,000 Women
Age 40–44, by 1959 Family Income and 1959
Husband's Income, for Residents
of Urbanized Areas, by Race

	White	Nonwhite
Family income		
< $2,000	2,446	2,421
$2,000–$3,999	2,398	2,456
$4,000–4,999	2,285	2,400
$5,000–5,999	2,343	2,503
$6,000–6,999	2,330	2,505
$7,000–9,999	2,301	2,418
$10,000–14,999	2,266	2,566
$15,000+	2,385	2,475
Husband's income		
None	2,330	2,236
< $2,000	2,380	2,513
$2,000–$2,999	2,438	2,576
$3,000–3,999	2,322	2,434
$4,000–4,999	2,250	2,398
$5,000–6,999	2,277	2,419
$7,000–9,999	2,317	2,342
$10,000–14,999	2,351	2,186
$15,000+	2,402	2,225

Source: 1960 Census of Population, *Women by Number of Children Ever Born* (PC(2)3A), Table 37 and 38.

Table 4. Mean Birth Intervals (in Months) for Women
Age 35–39 in 1960, by Education

	Birth interval from:							
	Marriage to first child		First to second child		Second to third child		N + 0 (N + 1) for fourth and higher intervals	
Education	A	B	A	B	A	B	A	B
0–7	21.6	16.4	36.8	29.5	37.1	29.8	39.2	40.1
8	23.7	15.6	41.1	28.9	40.2	29.5	40.8	40.5
9–11	26.1	17.0	43.3	30.2	42.9	30.4	42.4	40.2
12	29.5	16.9	41.9	27.7	43.0	30.4	39.7	36.9
13–15	30.7	17.1	38.8	26.6	40.3	28.5	38.0	34.7
16+	32.7	18.2	35.3	23.2	37.2	26.3	35.2	32.5
Total	27.8	16.8	41.1	28.4	41.5	29.8	40.0	38.3

A = all women.
B = women who had borne 5–6 children by 1960.
Source: 1960 Census of Population, *Childspacing* (PC(2)3B), Table 75.

III. EXPECTED COMPLETED FAMILY SIZE

One way that some demographers have devised for studying differential fertility prior to the time when families are complete is to ask women how many children they expect to have. There is a certain amount of evidence that expectations have some stability and meaning, at least in the short run. There is, however, no consensus among demographers on the utility of birth expectation data.

Grade-school-educated women expect about half a child more on the average than do high school graduates (they have already had 1.1 child more, largely because they are somewhat older and have married at younger ages). There are no large differences by husband's income, family income, or husband's occupation. Wives of farm workers expect to have 3.5 children and blue-collar workers 3.2, in comparison to 3.0 for white-collar workers (see Table 5).

The fertility of different groups in the population may differ for a variety of reasons, including: (1) Differentials in contraceptive practice,

Table 5. Expected Completed Family Size for Married Women,
Age 18–39, 1960 by Education, Husband's Income,
Family Income and Husband's Occupation

Wife's education	Current 1960	Total expected	Husband's occupation	Total expected
13+	2.0	3.0	Upper white collar	3.0
12	2.1	3.0	Lower white collar	3.0
9–11	2.6	3.3	Upper blue collar	3.2
<9	3.1	3.7	Lower blue collar	3.2
Total	2.3	3.1	Farmer	3.5
			NA, not in labor force	3.0

Income	Family Size, by Husband's Income		Family Size, by Family's Income (Total expected)
	Current 1960	Total expected	
$10,000+	2.5	3.1	2.8
$7,000–$9,999	2.3	3.0	2.9
$6,000–6,999	2.4	3.1	3.2
$5,000–5,999	2.3	3.1	3.3
$4,000–4,999	2.3	3.2	3.4
$3,000–3,999	2.2	3.3	3.3
<$3,000	2.1	3.2	3.2

Source: P. V. Whelpton, A. Campbell, and J. Patterson, *Fertility and Family Planning in the United States* (Princeton: Princeton University Press, 1966), chap. 3.

in type of contraception used, consistency of use, use of abortion, and sexual patterns. (2) Differentials in the pattern of marriage including age at first marriage, proportion ever marrying, and proportion of child-bearing years spent in an unmarried state as a result of marital disruption. (3) Differentials in fecundity and in the probability of fetal loss. (4) Differentials in fertility goals and ideals. We will summarize some of what is known about these.

IV. FAMILY SIZE GOALS—IDEAL FAMILY SIZE

Low-income families may have a slightly higher ideal family size than higher-income families (see Table 6). Unfortunately the data available make the lowest income cut at $5,000 or less, and we do not know anything about the lower-income groups. Also, we cannot with available data assess the degree of rationalization of already larger families.

Table 6. Ideal Family Size (married women, age 18–39, 1960)

Husband's income	Ideal for average american family	Want if life could be relived	Wanted at time of interview	Most likely expected
$7,000+	3.3	3.7	3.3	3.0
$5,000–6,999	3.4	3.6	3.3	3.1
< $5,000[a]	3.5	3.7	3.3	3.2

[a] Data for lower income categories not available.
Source: Whelpton et al., Table 60.

V. CONTRACEPTIVE USE

Smaller proportions of low-status than higher-status women have ever used contraception (see Table 7). However, about 70 percent of women with husbands earning less than $3,000, or with less than nine years of schooling, have used contraception. Data are also presented in Table 7 on planned use by those women who have never used contraception. About two-thirds of the women who have never used and do not plan to use contraception are probably sterile. Women with low levels of education begin to use contraception later in their reproductive lives than do the better educated. Table 8 presents illustrative data for women who by 1960 had had two and six pregnancies.

Table 7. Contraceptive Use by Married Women
Aged 18–39, 1960, by Wife's Education
and Husband's Income

	Have used	Expect to use	Total
Wife's education			
College	88%	5%	93%
High school–12	83	7	90
High school 9–11	78	7	85
Grade school	66	6	72
Husband's income			
$10,000+	89	2	91
$7,000–$9,999	84	5	89
$6,000–6,999	85	4	89
$5,000–5,999	80	8	88
$4,000–4,999	81	7	88
$3,000–3,999	77	8	85
< $3,000	70	11	81

Source: Whelpton et al., Table 120.

Table 8. First Use of Contraception

Education	3 Pregnancies		
	Before 1st	Before 2nd	Before 3rd
College	68%	83%	94%
High school–4	45	75	90
High school 1–3	25	55	76
Grade school	18	57	78

Education	6+ Pregnancies					
	Before 1st	Before 2nd	Before 3rd	Before 4th	Before 5th	Ever
College	–	–	–	–	–	–
High school–4	19%	38%	54%	65%	73%	89%
High school 1–3	7	25	44	51	61	77
Grade school	0	9	21	23	33	51

Source: Whelpton et al., Table 114.

VI. EXCESS FERTILITY

Thirty-two percent of the women with less than nine years of education
reported that their most recent conception was unwanted (this does not
include those women who regarded their last pregnancy as too soon), as

against 14 percent of the women with twelve years of education. These cases were distributed in relation to contraceptive status as follows:[3]

	Education	
	Less than 9 Years	12 Years
Conceived prior to beginning contraception	15%	2%
Attributed to irregular use, etc.	10	6
Contraceptive failure	8	6
	32	14

The poorly educated contraception users are probably less likely to use effective methods and less likely to use whatever method they use as consistently as the better educated. Few data, however, are available. We do know that the pill has diffused somewhat faster among the better than the poorly educated. At the younger ages, however, the differences are not consistently large (see Table 9).

Table 9. Pill Use—1965

	Age					
	<20	20–24	25–29	30–34	35–39	40–44
Currently Using						
Grade School	27%	15%	21%	7%	3%	2%
High School–12	31	31	20	14	7	6
Ever used or may use						
Grade school	73%	52%	53%	20%	20%	11%
High school–12	70	67	60	45	36	23

Source: N. B. Ryder and C. F. Westoff, "Use of Oral Contraception in the United States, 1965," *Science* 153 (9 September 1966) 1199–1205.

VII. CONCLUSION

The poor as classified by income alone have a somewhat higher level of fertility than the nonpoor, although it would not be accurate to say that their fertility is uncontrolled. The rural poor seem to have very high fertility.

The poor as measured by a poverty index incorporating family size and composition along with income selects families with high fertility

---

[3] P. K. Whelpton et al., *Fertility and Family Planning in the United States* (Princeton, N.J.: Princeton University Press, 1966), Table 138.

into the poverty population. The high concentration of families with many children in the poverty population apparently results less from the fact that poor people have more children, than from the fact that large families need a higher income in order to get along adequately.

VIII. EFFECTS OF INCOME MAINTENANCE PROGRAMS ON FERTILITY

There are a wide variety of ways in which income maintenance programs may influence fertility. We will enumerate several of these, speculate on them, and consider whether it is feasible to learn more about their effects in an income maintenance experiment.

1) Fertility goals—i.e., the number of children wanted—may change. To the extent that couples reduce their fertility from what it might otherwise be because either (a) they feel that they cannot afford as many children as they would like to have, or (b) because of economic instability and insecurity, an income maintenance program might result in an *increase* in marital fertility. Some economists who view children as a consumption good have argued that it is reasonable to expect a positive correlation between income and family size, and indeed there is some indication that such a pattern is emerging among some groups in the population—e.g., Roman Catholics. In the 1960 Growth of American Families survey, most respondents gave economic reasons in response to why they did not want to have more children.[4]

It is also commonly supposed that income maintenance payments which are adjusted for family size would increase intended fertility by lowering the "price" of children relative to other consumption goods. That is, part of the cost of bearing and raising an additional child would be offset by an increase in the income maintenance payments received by the family. There is no evidence to support this assertion. The general feeling in countries with family allowances is that the family allowance has had only a minimal effect on fertility. However, it is most difficult to measure the effect of these national programs since fertility in the West has been changing continually for many decades—differentially from time to time and place to place. Also, in most cases, the family allowance has been a small proportion of family income.

2) Income maintenance programs might change marriage rates at young ages. There are two ways of speculating here—(a) early marriages might be encouraged by reducing the need for economic self-sufficiency

---

[4] Ibid., p. 93.

of the marriage, or (b) early marriages might also be discouraged by increasing the high school retention rate among girls. I know of no way to assess the magnitude of either of these effects.

3) An income maintenance program might increase the proportion of the poor practicing contraception, or increase the efficiency with which contraception is practiced. Increased income may be spent on contraception, or on more expensive (and more effective) contraception such as the pill (which normally requires the expense of a physician's visit). I know of no data to support this argument.

4) Increased income might result in increased fecundity. There appears to be a considerably higher rate of fecundity impairment for poorly educated women than for women with high school or college education at every age.[5] There may be several reasons for this. A high proportion of couples who want to have children and have difficulty conceiving can be helped by medical attention. With higher incomes more poor couples could avail themselves of these services. In addition, it is believed that fecundity has something to do with diet and nutrition. I know of few documented causal connections. However, Farley has speculated that particularly high rates of childlessness among Negroes in the United States were a result, in part, of the high incidence of pellagra, a disease caused by dietary deficiency.[6]

5) Income maintenance might have an effect on marital stability, reducing the rate of marital disruption. This argument is well known in the case of AFDC where eligibility depends on disruption and nonsupport by the father. We do not really know the degree to which low and unstable income (and often low earning potential of the husband in relation to the wife) leads to marital tensions and marital disruption. (Actually, we do not even know the incidence of marital disruption in the United States.)

The effect of reduced marital disruption ought to be to increase fertility by increasing the risk of conception. This conclusion supposes that the risk of conception is greater in a married than a nonmarried state, and makes assumptions about the frequency of intercourse and the conditional probability of conception. Nonmarital intercourse may be more or less likely to involve contraception than marital intercourse. There are, of course, no data or even speculative evidence. With greater marital stability (and happiness?), it is possible that contraceptive use might increase (or that more children might be desired?). Again there is no real basis for speculation.

---

[5] R. Freedman et al., *Family Planning, Sterility, and Population Growth* (New York: McGraw-Hill, 1959), p. 39.

[6] R. Farley, *Growth of the Black Population* (Chicago: Markham, 1970), p. 217.

6) The rate of illegitimate fertility might change as a result of an income maintenance program. The most likely outcome might be to cause an increase in the proportion of premarital conceptions resulting in marriage and thus a decline in illegitimate births. This assumes that some premarital pregnancies become illegitimate births because the couple feels that they cannot afford to marry. Again, little is known about this.

Welfare programs are frequently attacked as encouraging unmarried women to become pregnant and bear illegitimate children. The argument is that, in the absence of welfare, the costs of bearing illegitimate children would be sufficiently high to discourage nonmarital sex (or encourage women to take care not to get pregnant?). I know of little research on this matter.

7) One of the most important demographic effects of income maintenance may be to increase the rate of remarriage after marital disruption. According to Orshansky's figures for 1963, 6.7 million of the 34.6 million poor persons in the United States were in families with children headed by women.[7] While we know almost nothing about the process of remarriage, it seems reasonable to expect that one important reason that it is not more common than it is among the poor is because it is not economically advantageous for the man. An income maintenance program should reduce the costs of marrying a woman with children and raise the rate of remarriage. What effect the increase in remarriage would have on fertility is unknown. We might expect it to increase fertility by increasing the proportion of a woman's life spent in marriage. To my knowledge, no research has been done on the fertility of second and subsequent marriages.

The responses discussed here vary greatly in their amenability to experimental analysis of the type developed in the area of work effort response. An experiment to assess fertility goals would involve fairly long-term payment guarantees to avoid the biases (with respect to fertility decision) inherent in the short-term (three-year) experiments currently underway. Effects on contraceptive practices and fecundity could probably be adequately studied within the context of such an experiment.

Experimental investigation of the effect of income maintenance on marriage, remarriage, and resultant changes in fertility would be much more difficult. Any small-scale experiment in this area faces the apparently insurmountable problem of bias introduced by the "dowry ef-

---

[7] Mollie Orshansky, "Counting the Poor: Another Look at the Poverty Profile," *Social Security Bulletin* (January 1965).

fect": to the extent that such payments are not universally available, recipients (or potential recipients) become differentially attractive marriage partners. Thus, the marriage and remarriage rates in the experimental population would tend to overstate, to an unknown degree, the response to be expected from a national program.

Serious problems also arise in any experimental attempt to analyze the impact of income maintenance on illegitimacy. Since illegitimate births are a relatively rare event in the population at large (25 illegitimate births per year per 1,000 unmarried women under the age of 45), reliable estimation would undoubtedly require an extremely large sample.

EXPERIMENTAL INCOME MAINTENANCE PROGRAMS TO ASSESS THE EFFECT ON FERTILITY

Glen G. Cain

This paper discusses a fairly concrete proposal for experimenting with the effects of an income maintenance program on fertility. The proposal is suggested after first noting some of the special constraints on or obstacles to assessing fertility effects.

I. CHARACTERISTICS OF FERTILITY WHICH CONSTRAIN AN EXPERIMENTAL PROGRAM

When fertility is defined as the number of children ever born (or the number of surviving children), it is clear that the variable is defined over the total number of years in which the female is fecund. This fact constrains an experiment to use some short-run proxy measures of this "lifetime" fertility concept.

Fertility is not only defined over a relatively long time span, say 20 or 25 years, but even short-term fertility (for example, the number of children born over a 1–3 year period) is believed to be based on long-run considerations, such as the standard of living expected or desired and attainable over the years of parental responsibility. Because of this constraint, experimental payments will have to be made over a fairly long time period, say over the entire eighteen years of each child's minority. Such a plan would obviously cost a lot more per participant than the three-year payment plan in the New Jersey experiment. The cost factor leads to the need to keep the number of recipients low.

Fertility is a discrete variable, unlike income, work, and expenditure behavior, and births occur relatively infrequently. Moreover, our a priori notions suggest a relatively minor effect of income maintenance programs on fertility.

This combination of outcome and treatment variables calls for a large sample size and/or a sample in which the variability of the outcome variable is sharply limited. Otherwise we would not be able to detect any treatment effects (if they exist) at acceptable levels of statistical significance. The cost constraint imposed by the second obstacle above leads to an emphasis on a sample from a population with a relatively small variance in fertility. At the same time, the population should represent a relatively large share of the national population of potential eligible recipients and should, of course, be one whose fertility behavior *can* be affected. (A group of sterile couples could be found whose fertility rate would have a zero mean and zero variance, but we could hardly expect to learn much from an experiment with this group.)

II. PROPOSED STRATEGY IN LIGHT OF THE CONSTRAINTS

A. Sample Design

Select a relatively small number, say 100 families, who are similar with respect to the parity and birth interval; e.g., couples who have had two children only, the second child being born 5–7 months before the first interview (this design is copied after "Family Growth in Metropolitan America," hereafter referred to as "the Princeton Study").[1] This design is desirable not only because there is intrinsic interest in this family-size type, but also because there is a vast amount of a priori information available to the experimental investigation as a result of the Princeton Study. Two waves of interviews were conducted in this study, the second three years after the first, and further follow-ups are also planned.

The Princeton sample was confined to white couples who were living in seven of the eight largest metropolitan areas in the United States. In an

---

[1] C. F. Westoff, R. G. Potter, P. C. Sagi, and E. G. Mishler, *Family Growth in Metropolitan America* (Princeton University Press, 1961); (hereinafter cited as FGIMA) and C. F. Westoff, R. G. Potter, and P. C. Sagi, *The Third Child* (Princeton University Press, 1963) (hereinafter cited as TC).

experimental program blacks would be included, but the restriction to the same seven cities (or fewer) would facilitate close comparisons as well as ease the administrative burden of carrying out the experiment. It might be useful to limit the age of the respondents to, say, 18–30, again in the interest of getting a relatively homogeneous group whose fertility is more likely to be influenced by an income maintenance program.

The justifications for two-parity families in an experimental program (aside from the comparative information available from the Princeton Study) are several. First, there would be virtually no sterile couples and even sub-fecundity would be less prevalent than among one-child families. Sub-fecundity not only is a source of variability in fertility, but also implies that fertility will be relatively unresponsive to effects of economic changes. Second, both the average *desired* and *expected* family size in the United States today is around three or four children. The poor probably expect closer to four children, and there is some controversy about whether they desire more or less than nonpoor families.[2] Thus the selection of two-parity families permits a focus on movements toward completed family formation in a relatively short period of time. (From the Princeton Study, over half the wives wanted the third child in two and one-half years or less, and 85 percent wanted the child in four years or less.)[3] Furthermore, families preferring four or more children will tend to space their children at shorter intervals. Nearly all children are born in the first ten years of marriage.[4] Finally, the question of whether the experimental families are exceeding their own first opinions about desired

---

[2] Ryder and Westoff report on the basis on their 1965 survey that, for the total sample of married women under 45 living with their husbands, the mean numbers of children intended, desired, and ideal were 3.24, 3.29, and 3.29, respectively. For Negroes, the means are 3.79, 3.21, and 3.61. They also report a generally inverse relationship of the means with respect to education, although the education relationship differs for white Catholics. N. B. Ryder and C. F. Westoff, "Relationship Among Intended, Expected, Desired and Ideal Family Size: United States, 1965," *Population Research* (March 1969). Judith Blake Davis argues vigorously that the poor want more children and offers several studies in evidence: "Population Policy for Americans: Is the Government Being Misled?" *Science*, Vol. 164 (May 2, 1969), pp. 522–29. She reports a 1968 survey (of 539 respondents) which indicates that the mean number of children desired is 3.2, 3.0, 3.4, and 3.6 for upper, upper-middle, lower-middle, and lower economic status groups, respectively (p. 529). However, Davis's evidence was subsequently challenged, and the argument was that, although the poor expect more children than the nonpoor, they desire no more (and perhaps fewer) children. O. Harkavy et al., "Family Planning and Public Policy: Who Is Misleading Whom?" *Science*, Vol. 165 (July 25, 1969).

[3] FGIMA, p. 126.

[4] TC, p. 17.

or intended numbers of children, or whether they are exceeding "national" averages of three or four, can be observed more quickly if we start with two-children families.

The Princeton Study offers some limited information on ways of stratifying the sample to get more efficient sample design. For example, the two variables most successful in predicting fertility were religion (Catholic, Jewish, Protestant) and, understandably, statements about desired family size.[5] Race would be another important stratifying variable, and oversampling of black couples would be necessary to ensure comparably reliable statistical results in the face of the probably larger variances in fertility behavior in comparison with white couples. Other variables can be used to predict fertility and these would be used to reduce the residual or unexplained variance of the dependent variable; for example, age at marriage, age at interview, sex composition of the two children, etc.

B. Choice of Dependent Variables

A number of dependent variables could be used during the course of the experiment—some of which would provide short-run indicators of the critical lifetime fertility variable.

1. Fertility—actual number of births (or pregnancies) over time
2. Total number of children desired, as expressed by the parents at various stages of the study
3. Total number of children intended (or expected), as measured at various stages
4. Desired interval between second, third, and further children
5. Actual intervals between second, third, and further children
6. Various measures of the use of contraception

The total number of children desired is obviously one proxy for the actual number of children that will be born. The Princeton Study made extensive use of this variable, and, as indicated, the expressed number desired at the first interview was one of the best predictors of the actual number born three years later. If we accept the desired number of children as representing the actual number that will be born over the

---

[5] "Wife's desired family size 6 months after the second birth [i.e., the time of the first interview] has proved to be the strongest predictor of fertility over the next three years of all the data collected in the first interview. Several reasons for this are: her desired family size is found to remain rather stable . . . and finally, contraception becomes more effective once desired family size is attained, so that relatively few of those desiring two have an unwanted birth" (TC, p. 236).

parents' lifetime, we can use the Princeton Study to illustrate the sample distribution of desired numbers, and on this basis estimate the mean and variance of the actual fertility rate. These calculations are shown in the tables in the next section.

The total number of children intended or expected was, unfortunately, not used in the Princeton Study. However, extensive use of this variable was made in three nationwide surveys in 1955, 1960, and 1965.[6]

The fourth and fifth proxy variables listed refer to the *spacing* of children. This variable is interesting not only because it can be used as a proxy for the number of births—the closer the spacing the larger the desired and expected number—but also because a number of speculations about the causes of poverty concern the birth of too many children too soon. Ronald Freedman makes this point in the following terms: "In the West, we are beginning to learn that the most significant differentials in family growth are no longer in the total number of children born but in their spacing. The poor and the disadvantaged are not so much distinguished by large families as by the fact that they have children so quickly after (or even before) marriage. This goes along with the fact that almost everyone in the U.S. uses some form of family planning sometime in married life but the poor start late and use it much less effectively."[7]

The same reasons that justify our interest in the spacing variables apply also to the sixth item in the list of dependent variables, the use of contraception. Generally speaking, data about nonuse or "careless" use of contraception can be used to predict fertility, can supplement the information about desired family size, and has particular relevance to the poverty population. There are a large number of ways in which the use of contraception can be measured, of course. Suffice to say that both the

---

[6] The 1955 survey is reported in R. Freedman, P. K. Whelpton, and A. A. Campbell, *Family Planning, Sterility, and Population Growth* (New York: McGraw-Hill, 1959). The 1960 survey is reported in P. K. Whelpton, A. A. Campbell, and J. E. Patterson, *Fertility and Family Planning in the United States* (Princeton University Press, 1966). The 1960 survey, incidentally, includes some 250 nonwhite families, whereas the 1955 survey covers whites only. The 1965 survey is mentioned in Ryder and Westoff, *supra* n. 2.

[7] Ronald Freedman, "Applications of the Behavioral Sciences to Family Planning Programs," *Studies in Family Planning,* no. 23 (Oct. 1967), pp. 5–9. For an empirical study of the thesis that "children, too many too quick" cause poverty, see R. Freedman and L. Coombs, "Child-spacing and Family Economic Position," *American Sociological Review,* Vol. 31 (October 1966), pp. 631–48.

Princeton Study and the studies from national surveys have a great deal of information about the type of questions to ask and their interpretation.

C. Selections of Explanatory or Independent Variables

The main independent variable is obviously the income guarantee plan. The payment plans would probably vary in a more limited way than in the New Jersey experiment because there would be fewer experimental units in a fertility study. Information would be gathered on a number of other variables to serve the usual purposes we assign to "control variables": (a) to stratify the sample (or, in other words, to detect possible interaction effects between treatment variables and control variables); (b) to reduce residual variation in the dependent variables; and (c) to avoid obtaining biased measures of the effects of treatment variables as a consequence of intercorrelations between control variables and treatment variables.

In the Princeton Study the explanatory variables were grouped under the following categories: religion, socioeconomic status, social mobility, reactions to change in general economic conditions (specifically the 1958 recession and the 1959 steel strike), residence, migration, family relationships, age, family composition, and sex preferences regarding children. Another group of psychological variables were used in the first interview (and reported in FGIMA) and then dropped from the study because they proved so uninformative.

Only a few comments will be made here about these variables. One is that, by the tests of simple linear correlations, very few variables had much predictive power concerning the various dependent variables used, particularly actual fertility rates over the three-year period. Moreover, the independent variables measuring social mobility and socioeconomic status were characterized by very low correlations, some with the "wrong" sign. We should remember, however, that the variables were not employed in a satisfactory theoretical framework (as the authors, themselves, imply). Remember, also, that the simple linear correlation coefficient (or even a partial correlation, linear or nonlinear) is a poor measure of the policy significance of the variable.[8] Finally, the Princeton Study dealt with a special and restricted sample, so that the performance of various independent variables may have been likewise restricted.

---

[8] This is a point explained at length in Glen Cain and Harold Watts, "Problems in Making Policy Inferences from the Coleman Report," *American Sociological Review,* Vol. 35 (April 1970), pp. 228–42.

In contrast to the economic conditions affecting the families in the Princeton Study, an income guarantee plan can produce sharp changes in the economic status of a family, including virtual elimination of the anxiety about zero income levels and reduction of the concern about financial instability. The effects of income guarantee programs are related in a very direct way to the number of children—in particular, it will no longer be true that a fixed income will have to stretch to accommodate the demands of another child; the child will bring with him a larger family income guarantee (and for low-income families a larger transfer payment).

III. ACHIEVING STATISTICAL SIGNIFICANCE OF TREATMENT EFFECTS

Two sets of data from the Princeton Study permit an estimate to be made of means and variances of birth rates for two-child families. The first set, in Table 1, shows the actual fertility rates of the sample families in the three-year period between the first and follow-up interviews. The second set gives the distribution of the desired, total number of children, which I use as an estimate of the actual number if we were to follow the families for 10–15 years.

Let y = the number of births shown in Table 1 (column 1) and $p(y)$ stand for the relative frequency of that number shown in column 2. Then $E(y)$ = the expected value of $y = \Sigma\ y_i p\ (y_i) = .65$. Thus for 100 wives the expected number of births is 65. Using the definition of the variance: $V(y) = E(y^2) - [E(y)]^2 = \Sigma y_i^2 p(y_i) - (.65)^2 = .4475$.

Table 1. Percent of Families Having 0, 1, or 2
"Births" in the Three-Year Period
(905 White Wives in the Princeton Study)

(1) Number of births[a]	(2) Percent of families
0	46
1	43
2	11

[a] A birth is defined to mean "the number of pregnancies presumably adding to family size. Hence, if the first of two pregnancies ends in wastage, so that the two pregnancies cannot contribute more than one live birth, the two pregnancies are counted as one" (TC, pp. 60–67).

The standard deviation is, then, .6689, so that for a sample of 100 wives, one standard deviation of the number of births is about 6.7. If we assume we can explain 25 percent of the total variance on the basis of such explanatory variables as desired number of children, age of wife, age at marriage, etc.,[9] then .4475 is reduced to about .336 and the resulting standard deviation for 100 wives is about 5.8. *Therefore, the null hypothesis of "no effect" would be rejected at slightly more than a 96 percent confidence level (using the conservative 2-tail test) whenever the number of births was 53 or less or 77 or more over a three-year period.* (Recall that the expected number was 65, although, of course, the number of births in the control group would represent the expected number in an experiment.) Similar calculations show that, for a sample of 300 wives, the 96 percent confidence interval would be 175 to 215 births, with an expected number of 195 during a three-year period. Thus, a sample of 100 would allow detection of a change of about 18 percent in the birth rate, while the minimum change that could be detected (at the same 96 percent level of significance) with a sample of 300 would be about 10 percent.

Let us now turn to the distribution of the desired number of births, which I use to estimate the mean and variance of the total number of births for completed families. It turns out that the relative variance is less for the desired number than for the three-year period actual numbers. Table 2 provides the basic data, and the calculation of $E(y)$ and $V(y)$ follows the same procedures as for Table 1. The expected number of additional births is 127 per 100 wives (who already have two children) in the Princeton Study.[10] The standard deviation is 10.8. If we again assume that 25 percent of the total variance could be explained by all the independent variables in the model, the residual standard deviation would be about 9.4. *Thus the null hypothesis of "no effect" would be rejected at slightly more than a 95 percent confidence level if the number of desired births was 108 or less or 146 or more.* The latter figure implies a fertility rate of 3.46, which is higher by .19 than the expected rate. For a sample of 300, the confidence interval would be 348 to 414 desired

---

[9] The assumption that the "control variables" in our model can explain about 25 percent of the variance should be reasonable. Westoff et al. report that, "Wife's desired family size at first interview accounts for about one-quarter of the variance of fertility since second birth . . ." (TC, p. 67). Other variables could only increase the R^2, although the families in the experimental program would probably have a larger variance of fertility than the Princeton sample, since nonwhite and poor families would be more prevalent.

[10] This implies a fertility rate of 3.27 which is very close to the 3.29 applying to the national sample in 1965 (*supra* n. 2).

Table 2. Percent of Families Desiring the Specified Number
of Children[a] as Stated at the Time of the First Interview
(905 Wives in the Princeton Study)

$Y =$ Number of children desired[a]	Additional number of births	Percent of wives
2	0	23.2
2.5	0.5	9.8
3	1.0	22.0
3.5	1.5	10.3
4	2.0	22.2
4.5	2.5	5.6
5	3.0	2.5
6	4.0	2.6
7	5.0	1.7

[a] There were two questions that were combined to form an index of the wife's total fertility desires. For example, wives who say they want four children but "may want less" are assigned the value 3.5 for their desired fertility. The two questions were: "How many children do you want to have *altogether*, counting the two you have now?" "Do you feel sure that is the number you want or do you feel that you might want more or that you might want fewer children?" (TC, p. 68).

births, with an expected number of 381. This is a range of 1.16 to 1.38 births and a mean of 1.27 per family. Including the two children already born, the desired fertility rates range from 3.16 to 3.38 per family. A sample of 100, then, would allow detection of a minimum change of 5.8 percent in the desired fertility rate, while a sample of 300 would allow detection of a change of 3.3 percent.

IV. FINAL REMARKS

Any proposal to attempt to measure the effects of an income maintenance program on fertility by means of experimental methods has got to be rather presumptuous, but the proposal discussed above is relatively conservative in its focus on the two-parity families. It would be worthwhile to examine other groups which have the characteristics of relative homogeneity and substantive interest. From the remarks of Professor Freedman, quoted above, we can judge that a great deal of interest would center on just-married couples to determine whether income maintenance programs: (a) reinforce for some the tendency to have too many children too soon,[11] or (b) eliminate the alleged poverty-producing consequences of (a) such as terminating education and training. However, to measure (b) calls for a much more elaborate and complicated set of outcome measures. Indeed, given the number of marriages that take place after pregnancy, and the relatively high divorce rates and poverty incidence alleged to be associated with such marriages, there would be interest in couples who are "going steady" for inclusion in an experimental income maintenance program. From the standpoint of effects on the number of births, an important reason for aiming at this group is to measure the effect on marriage rates per se. A lowering of the age of marriage would probably produce an increase in the total fertility rate. It is hard to see how any experiment with unmarried persons could be conducted, however. Even experiments with just-married couples would encounter the difficulties of both large variances in fertility behavior and a long wait (in years) before the number of births resulting in completed family size could be measured.

A number of interesting hypotheses could be tested in an experiment like the one described. Up to now I have not discussed whether the main hypothesis is that birth rates go up or down. Income effects and price effects both ought to work in the direction of raising birth rates. Only a small positive effect of income on the numbers of children is expected, however, since the major impact is expected to be on the amount of expenditure on children. It is in this sense that children have been likened to cars and houses: modest increases in income lead to spending more on cars and houses, but it usually takes a substantial increase (on a more or less permanent basis) to justify buying a larger number. Nevertheless, this point of view does not support the conclusion that the income effect is negative, and, indeed, as long as we make the reasonable assumption that children are not an "inferior good," we should expect that as income rises parents would on average desire no fewer and probably more children than they would in the absence of such a rise in income.[12]

---

[11] It is relevant to note that about 21 percent of the Princeton sample of 1165 wives (the number in their first interview) believed that their first child "came too soon." About 75 percent of these wives said that the birth came too soon from the standpoint of "not having sufficient time to prepare their finances" (41 percent) or not being able "to enjoy things with one's husband before the responsibilities of parenthood." (FGIMA, pp. 117 ff.). The latter point is partly an economic reason, and a possible inference from this is that income maintenance plans would encourage earlier births in the marriage.

[12] The expected positive effect of income on the number of children desired does not necessarily conflict with the evidence cited in n. 2 purporting to show that the poor desire more children than the nonpoor. The poor are more likely to have low educational attainment and live in rural areas (or have rural back-

The price effect is also pro-fertility, in the sense that the cost of children is lowered by income maintenance plans so parents could afford more. This direct price effect is reinforced by an indirect price effect. For all families who were not previously on welfare but who are eligible for positive transfer payments from the income maintenance plan, the plan acts as a tax on earnings, since the amount of transfer payments declines as earnings rise. This tax on market work lowers the opportunity cost of staying at home to raise children.

The basis for expecting negative effects on fertility is considerably more speculative. Perhaps, as a consequence of income transfers, poor parents may change their preferences for material goods and children and begin to aspire to more material possessions. Another unknown is whether birth control usage is positively related to income (or income security) and whether the relation is at all strong. If these forces are operative a net negative effect on fertility might result, but my guess is that this would be unlikely.

Consider, also, the hypothesis that sub-fecundity (even "sterility") is related to psychological factors of anxiety and tension among married people, which interferes both with their frequency of intercourse and/or conception. If income maintenance plans remove this anxiety, another pro-fertility influence results. If there is *any* possibility of the validity of this hypothesis, the sample selection discussed above—two-parity families—would pretty much rule out testing it. Or, even if fecundity is not affected, what about adoption rates among low-income families? (Presumably this would not affect the total number of births in the nation.)

Finally, the issue of a Hawthorne effect deserves mention, but it is difficult to conjecture about how it might operate. On the one hand, fertility behavior involves intercourse and contraception usage—both delicate matters that might be subject to Hawthorne effects. On the other hand, childbirth occurs only a few times in a person's (wife's) life, and the consequences of it are so large that perhaps it would be impervious to Hawthorne effects from the relatively modest income maintenance schemes we have in mind.

---

grounds). Since poor wives are less likely to be able to earn a high wage in the labor market, the opportunity cost of raising children is lower for them. These factors could explain an observed negative gross relation between income and numbers of desired children. Furthermore, if low educational attainment and other factors are responsible for the poor being less effective users of contraceptives, their opinions about desired numbers of children may merely serve to rationalize the fact of having more children.

To summarize, an experimental income maintenance program to assess the effect on fertility is feasible insofar as the measurability of both outcome and treatment variables is concerned. Our theories linking changes in economic status to changes in fertility are not, however, well developed. A good deal of skill and ingenuity would be demanded of the analyst responsible for interpreting the results of such an experiment.

INCOME MAINTENANCE, MARKET IMPERFECTIONS, AND SAVINGS DECISIONS

Donald A. Nichols

I. THE TRADITIONAL THEORY

A useful framework for organizing the theory of saving is the "life-cycle" saving hypothesis developed by Modigliani and Brumberg.[1] Briefly, this theory isolates a few of the major motives for transferring purchasing power from one time period to another. For example, if one wishes to maintain high consumption standards when retired, he should save part of his income before he retires. The framework is useful because it focuses interest on the roles of interest rates, lifetime earnings power, and forecasts of future needs and resources in determining saving.

In its most abstract formulation, an individual is viewed by this hypothesis as maximizing his expected lifetime utility subject to his budget constraint (expected lifetime income) and the prices of goods in different time periods (derived from expected interest rates and credit conditions). Equilibrium is attained when the prospect of future pleasure from an additional dollar of saving is equal to the pleasure yielded by that dollar if spent on current consumption. If such an equilibrium does not obtain,

---

[1] Franco Modigliani and Richard Brumberg, "Utility Analysis and the Consumption Function—An Interpretation of the Cross-Section Data," in Kurihara (ed.), *Post-Keynesian Economics* (New Brunswick, N.J.: Rutgers University Press, 1954).

the consumer can increase his total satisfaction by spending more or less until the equilibrium is reached. Presumably, the effects of any income maintenance program on saving behavior can be predicted from the way the program affects both expected income and capital market conditions. Before examining income maintenance, a further development of the theory as it pertains to credit is in order.

A. Borrowing for Consumption

Borrowing involves the use of future income to buy current goods. Thus, ceteris paribus, a decision to borrow for consumption is a decision to consume less future goods and more present goods. The amount of future goods that must be sacrificed for a specific increase in current consumption depends on the borrowing interest rate. The higher the rate, of course, the more expensive is the current consumption in terms of future goods.

The interest rate at which one can borrow depends on the probability of default on the loan. The more likely a default, the higher must be the interest rate to guarantee the lender the same return on risky loans as on nonrisky loans, and the probability of default depends on how much has already been borrowed. Thus any individual finds that the more he wishes to borrow, the higher the interest rate he faces. At first he can acquire modest loans at low interest rates by using his house or other marketable assets as collateral; then he must pay higher rates using his car and durable goods as collateral; finally, he must obtain personal loans at very high interest rates using his future wages for collateral. Of course, criminal organizations will supply credit at very high rates, even when legitimate institutions refuse to lend, by using the borrower's very life as collateral. Thus the cost of current consumption in terms of future goods increases as one sacrifices more and more future goods in order to increase present consumption.

The optimal amount of borrowing occurs as noted above when the value of the last unit of present goods acquired by borrowing is exactly equal to the current value of the future goods that are implicitly sacrificed by the act of borrowing.

B. Time Preference

A complete knowledge of the determinants of saving requires a knowledge of the values of present and future goods. This is known as time preference. Rigorously, it is derived from a knowledge of the consumer's intertemporal utility function. We must know how much satisfaction is obtained from the prospect of future consumption and be able to compare this with the satisfaction derived from present consumption before we can predict saving or borrowing.

An oft-repeated but untested hypothesis about poor people is that they are unable to postpone satisfaction. Two alternative interpretations of this can be given: (1) They have a great preference for the present over the future, or (2) They are irrational and do not act the way they would like to. It would be very difficult, perhaps impossible, to distinguish between these two hypotheses. Both would imply that individuals would borrow a great deal, in one case to trade away the less desired future goods for the highly desired present goods, and in the other case to acquire present goods despite the awareness of future sorrow that they entail or, at worst, without any conscious knowledge that the decision involves a sacrifice of future goods. While I know of no way to distinguish between the two hypotheses, such a distinction may not be unimportant for policy purposes. The framework outlined above in which an individual rationally allocates his resources to different time periods is consistent only with the first of these two hypotheses. As the hypotheses are operationally indistinguishable, we will assume here that the observed inability to postpone satisfaction is merely a decided preference for present goods.[2] Using data on income, wealth, borrowing, and interest rates, it should be possible to test whether in fact the poor do have different time preferences from the nonpoor. The alternative hypothesis, of course, is that they have the same preference functions but are merely in different circumstances. That is, they differ from you and me because they have less money.

A few complications are necessary before describing such a test.

C. Uncertainty

Uncertainty affects the saving decision in ways that have been outlined elsewhere.[3] We have no idea of the magnitude or direction of the

[2] Of course, when welfare mothers picket in an attempt to obtain credit, one feels that a women carrying a sign that reads "more present goods, less future goods" would get kicked out of line. That feeling is inconsistent with the choice of hypotheses just made.

[3] Edmund S. Phelps, "The Accumulation of Risky Capital: A Sequential Utility Analysis," *Econometrica*, Vol. 30 (October 1962), pp. 729–43; James Tobin, "Notes on Optimal Monetary Growth," *Journal of Political Economy*, Vol. 76, No. 4, Part II (July–August 1968), pp. 833–59; Paul A. Samuelson, "Lifetime Portfolio Selection by Dynamic Stochastic Programming," *Review of Economics and Statistics*, Vol. 51 (August 1969), pp. 239–46.

effect. The uncertainty of future income and prices lowers the utility of a given dollar's worth of expected future consumption. But this has two effects on the saving decision: (1) it lowers the cost of an extra dollar's worth of present consumption in terms of future utility forgone, and (2) it lowers future expected utility for any given allocation of resources. These two effects have opposite implications for saving; effect (1) says that less should be saved since future utility has become more expensive, but effect (2) implies that more should be saved because the lower level of future expected utility makes an additional dollar's worth of future goods worth more.

Empirically, the effects of uncertainty on saving have never been isolated. Thus we do not know if a guaranteed (certain) future income would lead to more or less saving than would occur with the same level of uncertain income.

II. INCOME MAINTENANCE

An income maintenance program would affect saving behavior in three ways: (1) by increasing expected income; (2) by perhaps changing the costs of borrowing to individuals by making them better credit risks; and (3) by making future income more certain. Different programs will have different implications through each of these factors. A knowledge of the magnitude of the three separate factors is necessary if we are to be able to predict the impact of any kind of program on saving behavior.

The intent of an income maintenance program is to increase the incomes of the very poor. With high incomes they may behave differently, and one of the differences may be their views of the relative values of present and future incomes.

If the income is guaranteed, creditors need not fear future unemployment of prospective borrowers. If the future payments can be attached by the creditors, the poor may find themselves able to borrow at much lower rates because they will have become better credit risks. Loans to the poor will be repaid with certainty.

Income maintenance programs partially insure future income. By ruling out the worst of the possible future states of the world, such a program would increase satisfaction on average even if it did not increase expected income. As noted above, we do not know the effect of this factor on saving behavior.

Research should be directed toward isolating the size of these three effects.

III. RESEARCH STRATEGY

Ordinary cross-section data would allow us to estimate income effects and price effects if we were certain that poor and nonpoor had the same preferences on average and if we were able to obtain enough variation in interest rates. Current data would never let us estimate the effect of changes in the certainty of income. This is because the variation that exists concerning the degree of certainty about future income is not independent of other variables that should affect saving behavior such as retirement status.

It appears, therefore, that experimentation would allow us to determine three relationships that could not be determined satisfactorily using ordinary cross-section data. The first is the effect of higher income on saving. When the current poor become better off through a transfer program, will they act as those who are currently better off act? Or are they poor because of the way they act? Such a relationship could not be identified from current data if one thought there were a relationship between actions and poverty as well as vice versa. An experiment with a control group would allow us to determine if the poor are like you and me except that they are poor, or if they are in fact different as far as saving behavior goes.

The second relationship that would be difficult to isolate without experimental data would be the reaction of the poor to a change in interest rates. While cross-section data gives us some variance in interest rates, it does not appear that the range of rates observed includes the rates that would be relevant if the poor became prime lending customers due to attachable future transfer payments.

Third is the effect of the elimination of some uncertainty about future income. The measurement of this effect would require that a sample group be guaranteed a minimum lifetime income. Otherwise the change in uncertainty would not be similar to that which will accompany an income maintenance program.

An experiment designed to test these three effects would, of course, need to be controlled so that different people are confronted with different opportunities. This is necessary in order to gain enough variability in the relevant factors to measure their effects.

A. Credit Markets

The previous analysis focuses on individuals and their response to different opportunities that may confront them. An equally important set of responses is that of the suppliers of credit. Above, we have assumed that borrowing interest rates depend on the credit worthiness of the borrower. They also depend on his awareness of alternative sources of credit and his willingness to drive a bargain. It may well be that the poor will continue to borrow at high rates even after they have become good credit risks simply because they are unaware of the change in their borrowing status.

It would be difficult to construct an experiment to test the response of lenders to an income maintenance program. Currently, the financial market is divided by institutions which specialize in loans of specific qualities. Finance companies, for example, do not make loans at the prime rate to anyone regardless of his credit worthiness. If one wants a loan at the prime rate, he must go to a commercial bank. Each institution makes its own kind of loans at its own interest rates.

Thus today, if the credit worthiness of an individual were to change, the way he would capitalize on this change of status would be to borrow at a different institution. For a small experiment, the knowledge of this fact might not get around or even be discovered. With a large program, however, the discovery would be made and might become common knowledge. If the credit worthiness of a whole segment of the population changed, certain institutions specializing in loans to that group would find that their market had dried up. They would either contract or change the nature of their business. That is, they might lower interest rates and specialize in better loans while keeping their old customers. Such a change would bring lower rates to those who do not drive hard bargains or search the market, as well as those who do. But surely such a change could never be brought about by a small local temporary experiment. I know of no way to gather data to allow us to predict the response of lending institutions to an income maintenance program.

The inability to alter the behavior of the existing lending institutions will limit the range of free market rates that the experimental group faces. Certainly, this group will not observe the same opportunities as they would if the program were nationwide. If greater variability in interest rates is desired—for example, if we wish to observe the response of this group to prime rates of interest—it may be necessary to include borrowing in the program offered to the group. That is, a recipient might choose between two packages, one containing $50 this month and $50 next month, the other containing $95 this month and nothing next month. For a three-year experiment, we might allow some the right to claim all their future payments immediately with a 10 percent per annum penalty. Care would have to be taken to see that they believed the experiment would last for three years, but this could be checked by observing how borrowings are disposed of. Only if the borrowings were saved might we believe that a doubt in the program motivated the borrowing. The experiment, of course, could face different individuals with different packages to choose from implying different rates of interest. Individuals would have the right to switch from one program to another at any time subject to the constraint that all past borrowings count against them on any new program chosen.

The situation just described confronts an individual with a choice that he would face in free credit markets if his future payments could be attached by creditors in the event of default. The whole question of whether the ability to attach payment is desirable or not is an interesting one in its own right. Unfortunately, because of the reasons mentioned above, we will not be able to observe the response of lending institutions to this feature of a program. To guarantee that the potential borrowers were aware of the desirability to lenders of this feature of the program would require a great deal of counseling that might invalidate all of the behavior responses of the test subjects.

It is my feeling, however, that attachability will definitely improve the borrowing prospects of the people in the program. There will be no risk of default and therefore no risk premium must be built into the interest rate. This unambiguously makes the borrowers better off if they intend to repay debts. It makes them worse off if they intend to default, of course. My own preference is to stack the program so as to reward those who intend to repay, not those who would like to default. Assuming that profit rates to lenders are the same under both programs and that borrowing rates are lower with attachability, the addition of this feature to the program leads to a redistribution from those who default to those who repay. A more illuminating way to state this would be that attachability would eliminate the redistribution that now takes place from repayers to defaulters. It all depends on how one feels about the honest poor. I am in favor of attachability.

B. Summary

Thus experimentation would yield us answers to questions about saving behavior that would not be obtained without experiments. In particular, the experiments should be focused toward isolating the separate impacts of three effects of any income maintenance program: (1) the effect of higher incomes on saving; (2) the effect of lower borrowing interest rates on saving; and (3) the effect on saving of the elimination of uncertainty about future income. Some knowledge of the magnitude of these effects will be necessary if we are to be able to predict the impact of an income maintenance program on the macroeconomic variables of employment, interest rates, and price level.

PART THREE

INTRODUCTION: COMMUNITY EFFECTS

Myron J. Lefcowitz

In the previous section the essays focused on problems related to the responses of recipient families and individuals to various types of income maintenance reform. For example, what will be the work effort response; the impact on birth rates; the effects on marital stability? These effects can be estimated from the behavior of individual families in dispersed experimental samples.

While recipient individual behavioral responses must be central to the determination of the ultimate effects of any reform, an exclusive focus on such responses could lead us to overlook a whole realm of other determinants of the effectiveness of various reforms; that is, an income maintenance program could affect and be affected by the social, political, and economic institutions within the community. We have chosen to call these relationships community effects. The papers in this section are devoted to the examination of selected aspects of such effects.

The major theme of this section is the difficulties which must be overcome before a systematic assessment of community effects can be undertaken. These difficulties arise from our lack of theory and of data. Each paper illustrates to some degree one or both of these problems.

I. COMMUNITY AS A CONDITION FOR INDIVIDUAL RESPONSE

In general, considerations of economic and social structures are typically more concerned with the extent to which individual or family effects are constrained by these structures. Work disincentives, for example, would be expected to be in some part a function of available job opportunities. Similar community conditions for other individual and family responses to the various types of income maintenance schemes should be anticipated. For instance, marital stability is affected by predispositions for or against divorce in an economic or social stratum, the alternatives available outside marriage, and pressures from significant social networks.[1]

Thus the preference systems and opportunity structures within a community can constrain or magnify the aggregate response to a change in the income maintenance system. It is precisely this problem which Spilerman and Elesh treat in their paper. They go on to develop specific hypotheses about the constraints imposed by ethnicity on individual responses to an income maintenance program.

Although social scientists have been alert to the effects on behavior of the interaction between situational conditions and frames of reference since at least the time of W. I. Thomas, we know very little about the process; that is, we know enough to be alert to the generalized model (changes in behavior are a function of conditions x frames of reference), but cannot go much beyond this statement. Thus Spilerman and Elesh focus on the correlation between residential homogeneity and homogeneity of culture. Yet we really do not know the extent to which any given subculture is different from or similar to the surrounding main culture; or whatever the similarities or differences, whether it has any real effects on the behavior of ethnic-group members in the dominant economic system. Spilerman and Elesh pose this last question, and they answer it affirmatively, although again very generally; that is, sometimes it makes a difference and sometimes not. These authors at least take us as far as we can go at present and point us in the appropriate research and policy directions. Bonner's paper on migration is another example of the more traditional approach to research on the social constraints for individual behavior. He discusses the function of risk-bearing institutions (family, friends, and public or private agencies) for reducing the uncertainties inherent in relocation. His discussion develops the hypothesis that a national income maintenance program could be a functional alternative to risk-bearing institutions and thus widen the options available to potential migrants, particularly the young. He concludes that this change might lead to an even heavier concentration of young poor in metropolitan communities and of older poor in nonmetropolitan areas. Such dichotomization of the poor could place differential demands on the service structures of the two types of communities.

---

[1] W. J. Goode, *World Revolution and Family Patterns*. New York: Free Press, 1963.

Bonner's conclusion about the possible secondary consequences of income maintenance brings us to our main concern in the community effects area; that is, the ways in which the community will change in response to a changed income maintenance system.

II. COMMUNITY EFFECTS OF AN INCOME MAINTENANCE PROGRAM

Our discussion of community constraints on *individual* responses to an income maintenance program illustrates the difficulties in such analysis because of inadequate theories and data. These difficulties are even greater when the focus is on *community* responses.

A. Economic System

Certain types of economic effects are relatively commonly discussed and dealt with so that concrete examples can be given. When we talk about the level and industrial composition of economic activity, a theory is available according to which we can intelligently estimate the likely "institutional change" in response to changes in income maintenance. While the data are not currently available to make such estimates, Bonner indicates the procedures which have been developed for making such estimates once the proper data are collected.

More concretely, Hugh Nourse has estimated the effect of a 50 percent negative income tax on substandard housing. Using a model to analyze the consequences of changes in income distribution for housing quality, he concludes that a guaranteed income policy could be as influential as current public housing policy. He is careful to point out, however, that the reliability of his estimate is highly dependent on some unverified assumptions and to call for more research.

B. Social Organization

Less discussed is the impact of a changed income maintenance program on the social organizations impinging on the deprived population. Would income maintenance reforms, by raising the aggregate level of income in low-income neighborhoods and/or by reducing the individual family income variance in such areas, cause an increase in the amount of health or transportation services made available? This might be the case, for example, if there is some sort of threshold level of area income below which it becomes difficult to maintain such service networks. We have already noted the possible effects of changes in the migratory scheme on such systems. This type of "institutional change" is again one for which existing theory and means of measurement are somewhat weak, but which seems within the reach of an reasonable research effort.

As a result, some attention has been paid to the consequences of separating the cash transfer system from the service system within the welfare structure. To what extent and in what ways will the welfare departments and caseworkers respond to welfare clients' demands for services? Essential to answering this question is the availability of information on what services are currently being offered, and in what amount, for the present recipients of welfare. These services can fall into two general categories: (1) those that link the welfare recipient to the existing noncash part of the income maintenance system, which can range from the provision of information about services to advocacy for the client until the service demand has been met; and (2) those that function as a "poor man's psychiatrist" by assisting the underprivileged to allocate their own resources for the optimum solution of their individual and family problems. It is not clear whether the beneficiaries of the cash transfer program demand such services; nor is it quite clear what the appropriate structure is for efficiently supplying these services.

These questions are addressed by Piliavin. He first suggests some experimental variations in the structure of the delivery of services. The objective of the experiment is to ascertain (a) whether use of the caseworker by the poor varies with the structure, and (b) whether the services are used and more effective under different structural conditions. Second, he presents an experimental design to assess the impact of the source initiating the service demand on use of services. To predict outcomes, he has introduced the self-concept and internal-external orientation of the client as intervening mechanisms.

What will happen when cash transfers and welfare services are separated, a process already under way? These experiments will help to predict the outcome.

The following studies might also be relevant:

1. A survey of the service market is needed. We need to know more about what services are provided and who uses them with what effects.

2. Experiments could be devised to vary systematically the costs and benefits of services. For example, we could vary out-of-pocket costs, time, personal inconvenience, and psychological costs of services to see how effective demand varies. In somewhat different words, Piliavin's experiments are special cases within this frame.

There is a much broader range of institutional change, however, for which the difficulties prove to be very substantial; that is, the political and social institutions, both formal and informal, which make up the community structure.

Other community institutions may also respond to changes in the existing cash transfer system. In addition to welfare services, there are city services, employment patterns, health resources, prices of goods and services, educational systems, and political structure. Some of these may be seen as responding more directly to the higher incomes of the population, and others somewhat indirectly through the demands created by the changed economic situation of the poverty population.

III. METHODOLOGICAL ISSUES AND DIRECTIONS

Substantial difficulties arise in the pursuit of potentially interesting issues in this broad area because there are neither measurements nor adequate theory with respect to community structure and dynamics. This became abundantly clear to us as we approached these questions in the context of experimentation. Let us suppose that we wished to conduct an experiment in which the entire low-income population of a community is eligible for the proposed type of transfer (as opposed to experiments, like that in New Jersey, which focus on individual response and select experimental and control families at random from the low-income population)—we called this approach a "saturation experiment." It is clear if we are really going to have an *experiment,* rather than just a *demonstration,* we must have more than one such "saturated" community and must face up to the statistical requirements of experimental design. In order to determine how many "saturation" sites one would need in order to actually estimate institutional change due to income maintenance reform, one must have some prior theory about what is "normal" institutional change and some proximate measures of the orders of magnitude of such change. In the absence of such theory and measures one would have no more than a highly intuitive idea whether the changes in institutions observed at a saturation site were the result of the income maintenance reforms or were simply within the range of the normal dynamics of such institutions. Thus one would have at best a demonstration. We found that there was not only no such proximate measurement of institutional change, but there was very little theory about such change which might give guidance to such measurements.

To indicate the difficulty of studying the effects of an income maintenance program on communities, we have put together some

Table 1. Mean Changes in Neighborhood Social Service Agencies, 1964–1968, by Number of People Served in 1964

	Mean change	Standard deviation	Coefficient of variation
Number of people using services:			
All agencies	549	963	175
Large agencies	879	1175	134
Small agencies	131	170	129
Number of referrals made:			
All agencies	135	254	188
Large agencies	180	299	166
Small agencies	55	86	156
Number of volunteers used:			
All agencies	18	47	261
Large agencies	22	50	227
Small agencies	10	40	400
Percent of clients who are unemployed:			
All agencies	−1.1	13.9	1264
Large agencies	0.1	15.4	15400
Small agencies	−2.2	11.9	541

information on changes in neighborhood social service agencies and schools in fifty cities after the advent of community action programs. The data were obtained from interviews by the National Opinion Research Center with the directors of these social service agencies and the presidents of PTA's. No brief is offered for the accuracy of the data. Our intention is merely to illustrate the difficulties inherent in studying community change experimentally. (NORC and OEO provided the basic data tapes. Neither agency is responsible for the present use.)

As mentioned earlier, there is no basis for predicting what changes, if any, will occur in utilization of social services when a more general income maintenance program is instituted. One problem is our lack of knowledge of current use. As we can see in Table 1, the mean change in the number of people using the services of the agencies in neighborhoods with a community action center was 549. However, the standard deviation was 963. Even when the size of the agency is taken into account, the coefficient of variation, although reduced, is still substantial. Moreover, if we look at other indicators of changes in the relationships of social service agencies to the community—number of referrals made, volunteers used, and percentage of unemployed clients—we find similarly large coefficients of variation even when size is taken into account (see Table 1). Similar results are obtained for selected changes in neighborhood schools (Table 2).

Table 2. Mean Changes in Neighborhood Schools, 1964–1968, by
Number of Students in 1964

	Mean change	Standard deviation	Coefficient of variation
Student-teacher ratio			
All schools	−2.02	5.46	270
Large schools	−2.47	6.39	259
Small schools	−1.89	3.80	201
Number of black teachers			
All schools	1.44	6.78	471
Large schools	1.63	3.40	209
Small schools	0.53	1.49	281
Percentage of parents in PTA			
All schools	−0.50	22.39	4478
Large schools	−1.54	14.54	944
Small schools	−2.97	9.61	324

With some further effort, the relative homogeneity of these means could probably be increased. It is problematic, however, that variability would be decreased substantially. For one thing, we know so little about these institutional areas that our effort would be guided largely by intuition. Thus any experimental study designed to investigate such institutional effects would require a large sample of communities to give us statistical confidence in the changes detected if they were anything less than sizable. Therefore, it seems there is a fundamental methodological problem which blocks actual experimentation in this broad area of "community effects." What seems to be required is a major theoretical and empirical effort to specify a theory of institutional change and to gather measures of such changes. On the empirical side, the following list of community dimensions is an attempt to specify the kinds of information measures which we think would be useful.

1. Education
   a. Student/teacher ratio
   b. Per capita expenditures
   c. Facilities
      i. Class size
      ii. Sessions
      iii. Non-classroom facilities, e.g., library
   d. Achievement levels
   e. Attendance
   f. Disciplinary actions
   g. Substitutes or staff
   h. Teacher turnover
2. Consumer market
   a. Prices (goods, medical care, housing, transportation, etc.)
   b. Credit: bank loans/applications
   c. Amount of shoplifting
   d. Commercial insurance costs

e. Store vacancies
f. Commercial profile
3. Family and individual services
   a. Day care
   b. Recreation
   c. Health services
   d. Legal services
4. Public services
   a. Police availability
   b. Sanitation: garbage pickup, rodent control
   c. Welfare: services and eligibility rules
   d. Housing inspection
5. Housing
   a. Persons/room
   b. Condition
   c. Turnover-mover/units
6. Employment
   a. Types of industry by number of jobs and job levels; industry profiles—number of companies
   b. Job vacancies—want ads

c. Unions—membership, organization drives
7. Political
   a. Percent voting
   b. Ethnic control—office holders, party positions
   c. Militancy—civil rights, separatist, welfare, tenants, local school control organizations (existence, membership, activity)
   d. Organizational profile and density
8. Community attitudes
   a. Reactions to income maintenance changes—public leadership
   b. Resources allocation
9. Infrastructures (for small communities)
   a. Thresholds for multiplier effects
   b. Transportation to communities above thresholds

Two types of "community effects" have been of concern here: First, the particular organizational structure and informal networks of communities may condition the response of low-income individuals to income maintenance reforms; second, the income maintenance reforms themselves will certainly have some effects on the organizational structure and informal networks of the communities.

We think this general area of "community effects" is of great potential research interest. Our explorations of the subject can at best be called forays. Some topics appeared to be within reasonable reach of research efforts, while others presented profound methodological problems. In all cases, the lack of data collected at the community level on a systematic basis across communities is an important shortcoming. At this point, we believe that in the area of "community effects" more traditional and basic research methods and data collection should precede any attempts at experimentation. Thus, although very little is known about the subject, we have at least reached the point of appreciating our ignorance.

THE INFLUENCE OF A NATIONAL INCOME MAINTENANCE PROGRAM ON MIGRATION OF THE POOR

Ernest Bonner

I. INTRODUCTION

At issue in this analysis will be the influence of a national income mainte-nance program on migration of the poor. A major problem confronts the analyst in that little specific information is available in published form concerning the migration propensities and patterns of the poor. Thus it is difficult to analyze deviations from these patterns as a result of a national income maintenance program.

The author has attempted to deal with this problem by presenting two sets of hypotheses—one dealing with the migration of the poor in general and a second set dealing with the expected changes in these hypothesized patterns with the introduction of a national income mainte-nance program. Though the first set is based upon relevant information from published data and studies, it has not been subjected to any reasonable test. It is hoped that both experimental (through control group information) and other data might serve as a test of both sets of hypotheses.

II. PRESENT MIGRATION THEORY

Generally speaking, migration is presently understood with reference to characteristics of the regions from which migration originates and to which it is destined, the distance between the two regions, and remarkably consistent empirical observations concerning the characteristics of migrants as a group; for instance, migrants are typically in the younger age groups, and these younger migrants make, on the average, larger moves; males are more mobile than females; the unemployed are more apt to migrate than the employed; migrants exhibit typically higher educational levels than nonmigrants and are relatively concentrated in certain occupational groups; and nonwhites are less mobile than whites.[1]

Everett Lee, in a recent *Demography* article, makes the following four-point classification of the factors affecting migration: (1) factors associated with the area of origin (push factors); (2) factors associated with the area of destination (pull factors); (3) factors associated with obstacles intervening between origin and destination (distance and alternative destinations); and (4) personal factors.

Economists and to a certain extent geographers have largely focused on the first three factors, assuming that migration from one area to another is in response to differential economic opportunity (areas with relatively high average or median income or low unemployment experience net in-migration and areas with relatively low income or high unemployment experience the opposite).[2] This movement is supposedly an outcome of individual decisions made on the basis of expected costs and returns to migration,[3] distance accounting for an important part of

---

[1] For examples of studies devoted to the characteristics of migrants see: Samuel Saben, "Geographic Mobility and Employment Status," *Monthly Labor Review,* Vol. 87 (August 1964); Robert L. Bunting, "Labor Mobility: Sex, Race and Age," *Review of Economics and Statistics,* Vol. 42 (May 1960); John B. Lansing and Eva Mueller, *The Geographic Mobility of Labor* (Ann Arbor: Survey Research Center, University of Michigan, 1967).

[2] See, for example, Robert L. Raimon, "Interstate Migration and Wage Theory," *Review of Economics and Statistics,* Vol. 44 (November 1962), pp. 428–38, where he finds significant association between per capita income and net changes in population with regard to migration for states. Also, George H. Borts, "Returns, Equalization and Regional Growth," *American Economic Review,* Vol. 50 (June 1960), p. 343, where he notes: "interstate migration occurs, as expected, from low to high-wage areas." In addition, see Larry Sjaastad, "Income and Migration in the United States" (unpublished Ph.D. dissertation, University of Chicago, 1961). Also, Phillip Nelson, "Migration, Real Income and Information," *Journal of Regional Science,* Vol. 1 (Spring 1959), Regional Science Research Institute, Philadelphia, pp. 43–74.

[3] Larry Sjaastad, "The Costs and Returns of Human Migration," *Journal of Political Economy,* Vol. 70 (Suppl., October 1962), pp. 80–93. Also, *The Cost of Geographic Mobility,* U.S. Dept. of Commerce, Area Redevelopment Research (Washington, D.C.: U.S. GPO, April 1964). See also Lansing and Mueller, *supra* no. 1, pp. 246–49, where actual returns to migration (higher, same, or lower salaries) are shown for their sample. Most moves permitted

the costs of migration.[4] But the case for migration in response to differential economic opportunity has not been proved. Phillip Nelson reports:

> Perhaps the single most interesting statistical result of our study is the finding that there is no significant relationship between migration and income and unemployment differences. The only significant relations between migration and income and unemployment occur when these latter are destination variables and even in those cases the correlations are low.[5]

In other words, the volume of migration between any two areas did not appear to be influenced by factors associated with the origin (push factors) and only slightly influenced by economic factors associated with the destination (pull factors). Similar findings were recently reported by Lowry[6] and Rogers.[7] Lowry was unable to interpret the relation between

---

higher wages at destination. The chances for financial reward for moving were much higher for the young.

[4] Geographers and sociologists have been most active in this area, particularly in their widespread use of the gravity model. The allegedly competing theory of Stouffer—the intervening opportunities—did not explicitly account for distance. However, see Britton Harris, "A Note on the Probability of Interaction at a Distance," *Journal of Regional Science,* Vol. 5 (Winter 1964), pp. 31–37, where he demonstrates, with assumptions as to the distribution of opportunities over space, that the intervening opportunities model reduces to the gravity model. See Lansing and Mueller, *supra* n. 1, p. 342, for doubt that the cost of moving associated with distance is important. For important findings on the influence of distance on migration, see in particular Theodore R. Anderson, "Intermetropolitan Migration: A Comparison of the Hypotheses of Zipf and Stouffer," *American Sociological Review,* Vol. 20 (June 1955), pp. 287–91, for a concise review of early tests and writings on the two hypotheses, in addition to some estimates of the elasticity of migration with respect to distance; Charles T. Stewart, Jr., "Migration as a Function of Population and Distance," *American Sociological Review,* Vol. 25 (June 1960), pp. 347–56. In general, the *American Sociological Review* is a good source for work on distance and its effects on migration. For studies showing some relationship between distance of move and socioeconomic class, see Melvin Lurie and Elton Rayack, "Racial Differences in Migration and Job Search," *Southern Economic Journal,* Vol. 33 (July 1966), pp. 81–95; and Arnold Rose, "Distance of Migration and Socioeconomic Status of Migrants," *American Sociological Review,* Vol. 23 (August 1958), pp. 420–23.

[5] Nelson, *supra* n. 2.

[6] Ira S. Lowry, *Migration and Metropolitan Growth* (University of California at Los Angeles, Institute of Government and Public Affairs, 1966).

[7] Andrei Rogers, "A Regression Analysis of Interregional Migration in California," *Review of Economics and Statistics,* Vol. 49 (May 1967), pp. 262–67.

the income of a destination region and migration into that region. Rogers found that the unemployment rate at *both* origin and destination inconsistently related to migration flows. Lansing and Mueller agree in general with these conclusions:

> Low levels of employment opportunity or low income levels *in an area* do not stimulate out-migration, nor do high levels of economic activity inhibit out-migration. High levels of employment opportunity do attract in-migration. To a much lesser extent in-migration also varies with area income level. Thus economic conditions do not have a symmetrical effect on in- and out-migration . . .[8]

For instance, Lansing and Mueller survey data do *not* show high rates of out-migration from labor market areas with high unemployment. Indeed, their data suggest the opposite—more of a tendency to migrate out of areas with relatively low unemployment.[9]

But these results are not the same as Saben's,[10] which show that, of those unemployed at the beginning of his one-year survey (March 1962), 11 percent had migrated to another county by March 1963. Only 6 percent of those employed in March 1962 had moved to another county by March 1963. Thus it appears that the unemployment rate of an area is a poor indicator of out-migration from that area, but out-migration is more frequent for the unemployed from any given area.

The foregoing inconsistencies suggest consideration of the characteristics of individual migrants rather than a continuing emphasis on the characteristics of regions as important factors in migration. From this vantage point, accepted propensities to migrate of population subgroups may be compared to the same propensities on the part of income maintenance program participants to test hypotheses concerning the effect of the program on migration of the poor. After a short discussion of the propensity of the poor to migrate (as compared to the nonpoor), we will inquire how the propensity to migrate may vary by certain categories of the poor.

---

[8] Lansing and Mueller, *supra* n. 1, p. 337.

[9] This tendency held for every occupational category. An exception occured when nonwhites were considered alone. In this case, out-migration rates were higher from high unemployment areas in every occupational category save sales workers. Their explanation of this appears valid: "This difference may reflect the particularly acute employment problems which Negroes experience in an area with inadequate labor demand." Lansing and Mueller, ibid., p. 95.

[10] Samuel Saben, *supra* n. 1. p. 873.

III. MIGRATION PROPENSITIES OF THE POOR

Blue-collar, less educated, older, and Negro population groups are relatively immobile.[11] Insofar as these are characteristics of the poor, low-income groups should also be relatively immobile. The Area Redevelopment Association provides more direct evidence of low mobility among the poor, finding that persons with family income over $3,000 are twice as likely to have moved during the year previous to the survey as those with less than $3,000 income.[12] The 1960 census data on migration between 1955 and 1960 shows a positive relationship between migration and income of family heads up to about $5,000, and then a slight negative association.[13] But families with income less than $2,000 had lower rates than any other income group, and families with incomes below $3,000 had rates lower than any other group save the highest ($15,000 and over). The same general result held when migration rates were related to occupation of head of household—the lower-paying and less skilled occupations were significantly less mobile than others. It seems clear, then, that we are dealing with a population which is relatively immobile.

Within the poor population, however, there may be substantial differences in mobility. The literature makes much of the finding that younger, better-educated individuals and heads of families are considerably more prone to migrate than others. These differential propensities appear to be stable and well established when the population as a whole is considered. In the case of the poor, however, education is irrelevant to migration, since differences in migration rates are not significant except between those who have a college education and those who do not, and we will assume the poor are not college graduates. Practically the same considerations apply with respect to occupation. The significant differences in migration rates occur between white-collar and blue-collar workers. If the poor are not represented in the white-collar occupations, this socioeconomic determinant of migration will not be relevant for the poor population. To the extent that race is closely correlated with occupation and education, this variable should also be irrelevant. In sum, an initial premise of this analysis is that out-migration rates of the poor can be considered mainly a function of age.

A modification to this might be labor-force status. Though occu-

---

[11] Lansing and Mueller, ibid., p. 337.

[12] *The Propensity To Move,* U.S. Dept. of Commerce, Area Redevelopment Administration (Washington, D.C.: U.S. GPO, July 1964).

[13] See Lansing and Mueller, ibid., p. 393, for tabulation in general conformance with the census results.

pational categories do not appear relevant, whether the head of household is in the labor force or not (employed or unemployed) may significantly condition migration rates; Saben's study notes that a much higher proportion of the unemployed migrate than the employed.[14]

Another possible modification might be family status. Families tend to be immobile because of the expected costs (both money and psychic) involved in any move. Individuals, not burdened by either dependents or household goods, can move more easily and less expensively. Among the population as a whole, moving costs appear relatively low for almost all moves. Among the poor, however, they may become a more important factor in the moving decision. The higher cost to families may then be a significant deterrent to their move. Further, the difficulties in maintaining a family before, during, and especially after a move are certainly greater for a family than for an individual, particularly if the family has children. Some evidence bearing on this point is furnished by Lansing and Mueller, who report steady and consistent drops in mobility with progression through life cycle stages.[15]

To summarize, then, out-migration of the poor from any origin is presumed to vary significantly only with age, labor-force status, and family status.[16] Hypotheses about the effect of an income maintenance program on this determination of migration rates must then predict direction of change in these specific rates.

Expected changes in the propensity to migrate in the event of a national income maintenance program are not entirely clear. On the one hand, it is conceivable that the availability of subsistence income in their present area of residence may permit some residents to stay who might otherwise have migrated. This would appear to be a logical reaction on the part of large families, where income transfers may be relatively

---

[14] This finding of Saben's is moderated by Lansing; see Lansing and Mueller, ibid., pp. 72–73.

[15] The life-cycle stages used were: young, single; young, married, no children; married with youngest child 4½ or less; married with youngest child 4½–14½ years; married with youngest child 14½ or over; older, married, no children; older, single. Lansing and Mueller, ibid., p. 396.

[16] Because it is not expected that a number of origins will be studied and comparison made, the characteristics of the origin have not been considered as a factor in out-migration. There is some evidence, however, that migration rates may vary among regions on some rural-urban scale. Lansing and Mueller, for example, find that "people are least disposed to leave metropolitan areas [SMSA counties] and most likely to leave smaller cities and towns [not SMSA county and not rural county]. The rural counties [20 percent of employment in agriculture] are in an intermediate position" ibid., p. 120.

significant and for which migration can be especially onerous.[17] It may also be the reaction of certain population groups who labor under a kind of "place inertia."[18] In short, it should reduce the propensity to migrate of all cohorts which heretofore had found migration a necessary but difficult decision.

On the other hand, the availability of a subsistence income, without reference to residence, could permit migration which otherwise would not take place. It might happen that those members of high-propensity-to-migrate cohorts (young, better educated, etc.) who would not ordinarily choose to migrate would, upon assurance of a reasonably steady income no matter where they are located, decide to emulate those more "adventurous" members of the cohort so long as a lesser risk of failure would attend their migration. Also, increased return migration appears plausible, particularly if the initial move was less than successful economically and ties to the old community remain strong.

The net result of these anticipated changes should be a lower propensity to migrate for older and younger members of the origin area and a higher propensity to migrate for members of the teenage to 30- or 35-year-old cohorts. It should increase the propensity to migrate of females relative to males on the theory that many of those in high-propensity-to-migrate cohorts who do not migrate are females. It would be expected that families with school-age children would be less inclined to migrate. It is also expected that the propensity to migrate of the unemployed will be reduced. Though the unemployed appear more likely to migrate than the employed, the unemployed display a rather remarkable reluctance to move, and they seem to be even more reluctant to move if their income loss (through unemployment) is not substantial or if some support is forthcoming locally, through public assistance or relatives.[19] An income maintenance program will bear on both of these

---

[17] Poor families rarely migrate as a unit. Wives are sometimes left at the origin and children frequently left in the care of relatives. This separation of the unit can be difficult for some. See Morton Rubin, "Migration Patterns of Negroes from a Rural Northeastern Mississippi Community," *Social Forces,* Vol. 39 (October 1960), p. 64.

[18] Julian Wolport makes much of this in his paper, "Behavioral Aspects of the Decision to Migrate," *Papers and Proceedings of the Regional Science Association,* Vol. 1 (Philadelphia: Wharton School of Finance, 1965), p. 1661. The strength of this inertia, even among those who migrate, can be inferred from the level of return migration. Return moves, under certain definitions, may be as high as 20 percent of all moves.

[19] See Lansing and Mueller, ibid., p. 77; "unemployment constitutes a 'push' which leads people to move if they are young, well-educated or trained, or live in a small town. In the absence of such characteristics, unemployment

conditions. Unless the accounting period precludes relatively immediate program grants, income losses through unemployment will be less severe and financial assistance through the program guarantees will be available.

In short, migration will be *more* selective with respect to age and family status while becoming *less* selective with respect to sex and labor-force status.

IV. THE DESTINATION OF MIGRANTS

It was presumed in the previous section that the level and composition of poor migrants from any origin is a function of the characteristics of the population at that origin. With some knowledge of these propensities to migrate, along with such modifications as may become clear from experimentation, and an indication of the characteristics of the population at any origin, a prediction of total out-migration from that origin may be obtained.

The destination of these migrants is then the subject of further study. Clearly, if migration is selective, knowledge of the loss (gain) at the origin and gain (loss) at the destination will be important. In fact, much of the concern with rural-urban migration is predicated on the belief that this process leaves the rural areas of the country relatively worse off in terms of productivity and income,[20] and this concern carries over to whole regions.[21] In this section, then, attention will center on the task of predicting the destination of migrants already selected by origin.

is highly unlikely to overcome the reluctance to move, unless the unemployment is prolonged, the income loss substantial, and the family has no alternative local source of support."

[20] Dale E. Hathaway and Brian B. Perkins, "Farm Labor Mobility, Migration and Income Distribution," *American Journal of Agricultural Economics,* Vol. 50 (May 1968), pp. 342–53. See also, President's National Advisory Commission on Rural Poverty, *The People Left Behind* (Washington, D.C.: U.S. GPO, September 1967). Also, Lansing and Mueller, ibid., p. 319: "out-migrants are younger, better-educated, more likely to be in the labor force, and also more likely to be white collar workers than people who remain . . . it follows that net out-migration deprives redevelopment areas of some of their potential business and community leadership as well as some of their more productive people."

[21] E. E. Liebhafsky, "Migration and Labor Force: Prospects," *Monthly Labor Review,* Vol. 91 (March 1968), p. 7: "Whether the South will continue to lose large numbers of workers depends upon the ability of . . . the South to . . . produce and retain the skilled workers, technicians and able managers essential to the development of a diversified urban-industrial economy in which capital-intensive industries account for an increasing proportion of employment."

A. Economic Opportunity as a Determinant of Destination

It is rare to find an explanation for the destination of migrants which does not have as a crucial factor some measure of economic opportunity, and the importance attached to this is supported by a number of studies. Whether or not this factor maintains its importance when considering poor migrants alone can only be indirectly ascertained. It could be argued that destinations characterized by evident economic opportunity would be a more powerful attraction for the poor than for the nonpoor. Limited evidence supports this argument.[22]

But even if it be granted that, in the majority of cases,[23] migration is motivated by economic reasons, it cannot be inferred that migrants are, therefore, attracted to destinations of the greatest economic opportunity. Individual migrants do not have before them all possible destinations together with reliable information on job opportunities in each. They have limited information about limited alternative destinations, and this is particularly true for less educated, blue-collar migrants.[24]

A second major premise of this analysis is that, although a poor migrant is indeed attracted to destinations of economic opportunity, his actual destination is chosen not to maximize expected returns but to minimize risk. His perceptions of the risk associated with any destination will vary with the information he has about the destination as well as the presence at the destination of risk-bearing institutions—family, friends, etc.—which he can invoke in his behalf. Thus, areas of high economic opportunity will be considered by the migrant only in the case where high risk does not also prevail.

---

[22] "Though the economic factor was the most important reason for moving for all groups studied, persons at the lower socioeconomic levels more often gave reasons for moving that involved economic or job considerations while those at the upper socioeconomic levels more often mentioned noneconomic factors. . . ." Ralph H. Turner, "Migration to a Medium Sized American City," *Journal of Social Psychology,* Vol. 30 (August 1949), p. 235. Turner's findings were contradicted by Lansing and Mueller, ibid., p. 62.

[23] Lansing and Mueller, ibid., pp. 36–38, report that 58 percent of moves were for purely economic reasons and an additional 14 percent were for partly economic reasons. This can be compared to 63 and 49 percent of moves for job-related reasons reported in two previous studies which he cites.

[24] Only one-third of all recent movers in the Lansing and Mueller survey considered any alternatives to their chosen destination. Also, half of the movers used only one source of job information. For recent movers with an eighth grade education or less, only 18 percent considered alternative destinations and 60 percent had only one source of job information. The same figures for blue-collar workers were 22 and 56 percent respectively. In sum, the authors noted: "in most cases a potential mover concerns himself only with a narrow range of alternatives, in terms of timing, destination and job" (ibid., p. 222).

B. Risk and Information

Nelson notes:

> Potentially people are surrounded by a sea of low-quality (general) information. Newspaper stories, popular conceptions of a place, the movies, all provide some information about the character of job opportunities at a distance. However, the very general character of this information produces considerable risk in migrating on this information alone.[25]

Therefore, migrants prefer specific information on job opportunities, which may be provided by an employer, some agent of the employer, or friends and relatives of the receiver. Poor migrants rely, to a considerable extent, upon friends and relatives for specific as well as general information.[26] The employer or his agent will be the sender only in exceptional cases.[27]

Unless migrants can travel themselves to the alternative destinations (on a trip, vacation, etc.) and obtain their own specific information,[28] they must rely on friends and relatives to supply information on job possibilities as well as other conditions at the destination. The willing migrant's sources of information then become very important, for where the individual decides to migrate will be determined by the location of senders of information. The migrant's destination would have to be some location in the set of all locations from which he received information. Therefore, if senders are located only at great distances, his alternative destinations will be at great distances and there is no possibility that he will migrate only a short distance.[29]

---

[25] Nelson, *supra* n. 2, p. 2.

[26] See C. Wright Mills, C. Senior, and R. K. Goldsen, *Puerto Rican Journey* (New York: Harper, 1950), pp. 53–55, for discussion of migrants' reliance upon extended family communications before migrating. Interestingly, and related to the lack of alternatives considered by the migrants, Lansing and Mueller find that "people who moved to a place where they had relatives or friends . . . were considerably less likely to consider alternative locations" (ibid., p. 216).

[27] Blue-collar workers and heads of household with high school education or less rely heavily upon friends or relatives for job information (60 percent reported this as their single source of job information). Other information sources (employers, unions, employment agencies, etc.) were considered much less helpful. See Lansing and Mueller, ibid., p. 227.

[28] Gathering information by taking a trip to the destination under consideration was the second most important source of job information for the less-educated and blue-collar migrants. Lansing and Mueller, ibid., pp. 227–29.

[29] This is not to say that distance is an unimportant constraint upon migration of the poor in general. However, for some subgroups (Negroes, for in-

In summary, the information that a willing migrant receives will assist him in reducing the risks associated with movement into an unknown environment. His possible destinations will be abruptly bounded by the location of his sources of information and will not necessarily cluster within some area determined by conventional distance constraints. Specific information will be preferred to general and migration will await the former unless other means of reducing uncertainty are available.

C. Risk-bearing Institutions

In this context, the important risk-bearing institutions are few. The family is obviously one;[30] so, too, are groups of friends, co-workers, and members of a single ethnic group or voluntary associations. Government welfare agencies and churches may be considered in the same light. Though each may perform a risk-bearing function, it is doubtless true that family and friends must serve this need most often.

Family and friends are obviously well suited for this task, and, in some cultures, they are expected to perform this function. Relatives or friends may provide the migrant with housing and meals upon his arrival at the destination or for a period of time while he looked around for himself before deciding whether the area will be his eventual destination. They may be a very good source of information as to possible jobs. They have a great deal of specific knowledge about the city. In short, they form a "bridge" between the environment which the migrant has left and the new environment within which he now finds himself.[31]

---

stance) distance takes a definite place behind other factors. See Arnold M. Rose, "Distance of Migration and Socio-Economic Status of Migrants," *American Sociological Review*, Vol. 23 (August 1958), pp. 420–23, where he finds that nonwhites (mostly Negroes) have migrated considerably greater than expected distance to Minneapolis and that they probably selected Minneapolis because "friends or relatives have already established a community there." See also Elizabeth M. Suval and C. Horace Hamilton, "New Evidence on Educational Selectivity in Migration to and from the South," *Social Forces*, Vol. 43 (May 1965), p. 539, where the authors noted that "nonwhite persons migrating to different states are more likely than white persons to migrate to noncontiguous states for all educational classes except the lowest, no schooling completed."

[30] See, for example, Walter Firey, *Land Use in Central Boston* (Cambridge, Mass.: Harvard University Press, 1947), pp. 184–86, for comment on family aid to newcomers.

[31] For examples of works dealing with the influence of friends or relatives in the migration and urbanization of ethnic and poor groups, see John S. and Leatrice D. MacDonald, "Chain Migration, Ethnic Neighborhood Formation, and Social Networks," *Milbank Memorial Fund Quarterly* (January 1964); Sidney Goldstein, *Patterns of Mobility, 1910–1950* (Philadelphia: University

D. Distance as a Determinant of Destination

Another accepted determinant of migration is distance. Supposedly, the number of migrants moving from some origin to any destination is inversely related to the distance to the traveled.[32]

When gross migration is formulated specifically as a gravity model

$$M_{ij} = k(M_i^{\gamma i} Ma_j^{\gamma i} / D_{ij}^B)$$

the elasticity of migration with respect to distance is estimated in most cases as greater than 1.0.[33] Since Stewart's work,[34] it has become clear that distance elasticity of migration varies with population subgroups. Stewart, himself, could not reject the notion that it varied by size of

---

of Pennsylvania Press, 1958); Clyde V. Kiser, *Sea Island to City* (New York: Columbia University Press, 1932); Melvin Lurie and Elton Rayack, "Racial Differences in Migration and Job Search: A Case Study," *Southern Economic Journal,* Vol. 33 (July 1966); Eugene Litwak, "Geographic Mobility and Extended Family Cohesion," *American Sociological Review,* Vol. 25 (June 1960); Leonard Blumberg and Robert R. Bell, "Urban Migration and Kinship Ties," *Social Problems,* Vol. 6 (1958–59); Eldon P. Smith, "Nonfarm Employment Information for Rural People," *Journal of Farm Economics,* Vol. 38, Part I (1956).

[32] In the Lansing and Mueller survey, 51 percent of all moves were less than 190 miles in airline distance and almost 80 percent were less than 590 miles. The median distance was approximately 200 miles (ibid., p. 28).

[33] See Theodore R. Anderson, "Intermetropolitan Migration: A Comparison of the Hypotheses of Zipf and Stouffer," *American Sociological Review,* Vol. 20 (June 1955), pp. 287–91, for an extensive review of early tests and writings on the noted hypotheses. Based on the survey, he further concludes that the exponent (elasticity) should be greater than 1.0 but less than 2.0. He also maintains it should be variable, noting that migration from large (population) origins is more accurately captured with a distance exponent of 1.0 while for small origins an exponent of Z provides a more accurate prediction. The formula used for this test was:

$$M = aP_j^{.75} WD^{-x}$$

where

$x = 1 + 125,000/P_i$
M = gross migration from area i to area j
a = parameter
P_j = population of area j
P_i = population of area i
W = 1 or 1.5 depending upon whether the surrounding suborigin was in the same state as the source suborigin

Other more recent works include Lowry, *supra* n. 6.

[34] Charles T. Stewart, Jr., "Migration as a Function of Population and Distance," *American Sociological Review,* Vol. 25 (June 1960), pp. 347–56.

origin region—migrants from larger regions of origin were less affected by distance. In Reilly's earlier study, he noted different "psychologies of distance" between Texans and others.[35]

Our interest must be the extent to which distance inhibits migration of the poor and to what may we ascribe any differentials that exist.[36] If distance inhibits migration because cost is related to distance, then the poor might be more inhibited by distance than the nonpoor. It is true, however, that distance can be overcome in a variety of ways, and the modes of travel for persons as well as household possessions are sufficiently diverse that a great variety of moving costs for any given distance prevail, permitting relatively long distance moves at relatively low total expense.[37] Further, a 1964 ARA study estimates that, in a large majority of cases (80 percent) the costs of moving represent less than 10 percent of the mover's annual income.[38] It appears, therefore, that the direct money cost of moving need not necessarily restrict the distances over which the poor will migrate. Perhaps distance has operated as a relatively severe constraint in the past, influencing the location of friends and relatives and therefore the location of those who are attracted to destinations where kin reside. Further, because trips back to the origin for family reunions and visits are relatively frequent for many of the poor, moves over longer distances may be less desirable.

In summary, poor migrants are presumed to make, on the average, shorter moves than the nonpoor but these shorter distances must remain consistent with the location of friends or relatives. If extended family are located only at great distance, moves will be expected over long distances.

In summary, then, the following assumptions are made with respect to the choice of migration destination by the poor:

1. The decision to migrate to any area is burdened by uncertainty.
2. While it is true that uncertainty affects all individuals to some extent, it remains that the poor—with typically limited financial

[35] William J. Reilly, *The Law of Retail Gravitation* (New York: Pilsbury, 1953), p. 16.

[36] Both Hagerstrand and Dahl, for instance, find working class migrants more sensitive to distance than "intellectuals." See Torsten Fagerstrand, "Migration and Area . . . ," and Sven Dahl, "The Contacts of Vasteras with the Rest of Sweden," both in *Lund Studies in Geography* (Lund, Sweden: C. W. K. Gleerup, 1957), Ser. B, No. 13.

[37] Lansing and Mueller, ibid., pp. 233–46. Also, see p. 276, where the authors note: "Low-income Negro movers . . . often reported . . . moving expenses were small (for instance, the price of a bus ticket) and that they had nothing to take along but their clothes."

[38] *The Cost of Geographic Mobility, supra* n. 3, p. 19.

resources, skills, and educational levels—are least able to cope with uncertainty and risks.

3. Uncertainty, therefore, will pose an important obstacle to migration of the poor.

4. A migrant's perceived risk about any destination can be reduced in at least two ways. First, uncertainty varies inversely with information. Second, risk can be reduced to the extent that risk-bearing institutions at the destination can be invoked in the migrant's favor.

5. Both relevant specific information and general information contribute to a migrant's knowledge of any destination.

6. Relatives and friends of the poor migrant are a key to the migrant's behavior. They provide him with the only relevant specific information he receives about the destination. They also provide some of the general information he may have about the destination. Further, they represent the most readily available risk-bearing institution at the destination. If we know the location of a poor migrant's relatives and friends, we will know the locations to which he is powerfully attracted.

7. The distance to any destination will not determine the migrant's location but will act as a condition upon the migrant's decision.

With this summary as a background, some speculations as to the change in choice of destination may be formulated in the event of a national income maintenance program. Guaranteed income, without reference to residence, should encourage migration to areas not populated by friends or relatives to the extent that the grant can substitute for the information and risk-bearing services provided by these extended contacts. Of course, a certain number of the poor are not reliant on family ties at all. For those poor migrants who may reduce their reliance on family ties, it would be expected that their decision process might more closely approximate the "ideal" economic model: expected returns at alternative destinations are compared with each other as well as those at the origin, and a destination is chosen based on this comparison.

At the same time, it must be noted that the differentials in economic opportunity will be reduced in the event of a national income maintenance program. The characteristics of the particular program are, of course, important. The break-even level, the resource base, and the marginal tax rate all combine to affect the earnings differentials between regions—always assuring that the money income differential is less than the earnings differential at earnings less than the break-even level.[39]

---

[39] For example, with a 50 percent marginal tax rate, a $1,600 minimum guarantee, and a $3,200 break-even level, an earnings differential of $1,000—

Thus, while the grant may reduce reliance on family ties, it also reduces the motivation for migration on economic grounds, particularly if the migrant perceives opportunities at a distance with more uncertainty than opportunities at the origin. Thus the outcome of these evaluations by individuals is far from clear. A major complicating factor is that, after all that has been written on the influence of friends and relatives in the migration decisions, the relative importance of family ties and economic opportunity has not been established. Providing some groups with fairly extensive information on job opportunities in locations to which they are not oriented by virtue of family ties might permit assessment of the relative weight of these two factors.

V. CHARACTERISTICS OF AN INCOME MAINTENANCE PROGRAM AND THEIR EFFECT ON MIGRATION BEHAVIOR

The specific characteristics of any income maintenance program will affect the foregoing speculations in important ways. The length of the accounting period is of obvious importance. The foregoing hypotheses have implicitly assumed that grants will follow closely upon income losses. The longer the previous period over which income is computed for grant purposes, the less influence to be expected on migration rates or destinations.

Both the break-even level of income and the marginal tax rate will affect the calculation of money income differentials for those migrants who include differential economic opportunity as a factor in their decision process.

Also the combined effect of program parameters on work effort may reduce regional differentials in wage rates. If the program causes a significant reduction of the labor supply at the origin thus increasing wage rates while destination wage rates fall in response to an oversupply,[40] differential wage rates will, of course, be reduced. Again, these differentials should affect migration to the extent that migrants respond to differentials in economic opportunity.

Coverage of the program should also modify our expectations. If only families are included, as in the Nixon administration's Family As-

---

from $2,000 at origin to $3,000 at destination—is reduced to a $500 money income differential.

[40] Wage rates do not have to fall at the destination. It is enough that they remain constant or, in the case of rising demands at the destination, that wage rates be less elastic with respect to demand changes than at the origin.

sistance Plan (FAP), changes in the propensity to migrate of individuals may not be significant. An important part of this is the manner in which members of the family are treated for grant purposes. If nuclear family membership is required for support, young adult members of the family will receive support only if they remain in the immediate family. However, if this requirement does not hold—if proof of support is all that is needed —movement among extended family or friends should be expected. Young adults would then join relatives with the assurance that the cost of their support would be offset in part by an increase in grant to the receiving family, if it is eligible. Further, if an individual relative were to assume support responsibilities for the young migrant, this would form a new family unit which would presumably be eligible under the program for the basic grant of $1,000. This particular combination is thus characterized by significant incentives.

The family coverage plus the employment requirement of FAP could also foster more movement of young, newly formed families. It must surely occur to teenage individuals who are considering marriage that they may marry, become eligible under the program for grants, and then move to whatever area strikes their fancy under the assurance that employment or training awaits them at that destination. This aspect of the program may diminish the now-felt need for temporary separation of the family in the migration process. The result, again, should be a higher propensity of females to migrate and maybe less attraction of the migrating unit to destinations with family or friends in residence.

VI. CONCLUSIONS

The net result of these expected changes is difficult to anticipate. It is the author's opinion that migration of the poor will become a more dichotomous phenomenon. Among the young adult poor, the propensity to migrate should increase and the flow of migrants should be more responsive to differentials in economic opportunity. Among the remaining poor, the opposite should hold true. On the theory that differentials in economic opportunity are more significant between metropolitan and nonmetropolitan areas than they are between regions, the short-run consequences would appear to be a relative concentration of the young poor (who are potentially more productive, but also more demanding of social services) in metropolitan areas and a corollary concentration of the remaining poor in the nonmetropolitan areas. The long-run consequences of this, if this tendency is simply extrapolated, would be a growing incidence of the poor in the metropolitan areas[41] as future generations of young people migrate. This would be analogous to the shift of the Negro from the South. Even though birth rates have been high among southern Negroes, migration from the South has been substantial enough to reduce the nationwide percentage of Negroes in the South from 91.5 percent in 1870 to 60 percent in 1960.[42] More relevant to our point is the clear trend of Negro concentration in urban areas, though this growth has been largely by migration only in the South. In the northern metropolitan areas most of the recent growth has been through natural increase.

In short, if the objective is to reduce migration between regions or between city size classes, a national income maintenance program would probably be a successful policy only in the short run. Because the major effect of the program will probably be an increasing responsiveness of the labor supply to differential labor demand, the long-run effects cannot be separated from the long-run trends in the distribution of economic activity, and these trends show increasing incidence of activity in the metropolitan areas of the nation.

---

[41] Their distribution within the metropolitan areas would be an important subject for further study.

[42] C. Horace Hamilton, "The Negro Leaves the South," *Demography,* Vol. 1 (1964), p. 275.

THE EFFECTS OF A NATIONAL INCOME MAINTENANCE PROGRAM ON THE LEVEL AND INDUSTRIAL COMPOSITION OF ECONOMIC ACTIVITY IN METROPOLITAN AREAS

Ernest Bonner

I. INTRODUCTION

This paper concerns an effort to measure the influence of an income maintenance program on the local economy—in the case at hand a metropolitan area economy. In the process, information about consumer expenditure patterns will necessarily be required.

II. THE SPATIAL DISTRIBUTION OF CHANGES IN DISPOSABLE INCOME RESULTING FROM A NATIONAL INCOME MAINTENANCE PROGRAM

1. A national IM program will result in changes in the disposable income of participating units.
2. The *amount* of that change in disposable income for any given participating unit will depend upon the characteristics of the participating unit, the characteristics of the program, and the

relationship between the transfer provided under the program and the change in disposable income.

3. The *spatial incidence* of changes in disposable income will then depend upon the spatial distribution of participating units, their characteristics, and the characteristics of the program.

4. Let ΔY_{ijk} = the change in disposable income realized by participating units of type j living in subarea k under program i.

5. $\Delta Y_{ijk} = n_{jk}\Delta y_{ij}$

   where: n_{jk} = number of participating units of type j living in subarea k.

   Δy_{ij} = change in disposable income to a participating unit of type j under program i. This change will bear some functional relationship to the transfer schedule decided upon for participating unit j under program i.

6. The number of participating units, n_{jk}, may be found—for any point in time—in published data compilations or basic tapes of the Bureau of the Census.

7. The change in disposable income, Δy_{ij}, is set by decisions concerning the program and eligible participating units. It is assumed that these decisions will be the point of entry into the analysis for public policy.

8. Thus the spatial distribution of changes in disposable income will be the result of public policy decisions concerning the characteristics of the program and eligible participating units, along with the actual spatial distribution of eligible participating units.

9. The spatial distribution of changes in disposable income as a result of the program can change with:
   a) changes in the public policy decisions concerning the program;
   b) changes in the public policy decisions concerning eligible participants; and
   c) changes in the spatial distribution of eligible participants.

10. Changes in public policy decisions concerning either the program or the definition of eligible participants are considered exogenous.

11. Changes in the spatial distribution of eligible participants can occur through natural increase or migration. Clearly, migration will affect the location of eligible participants. Natural increase will also affect the location of eligible participants to the extent

that eligibility is defined with respect to the number in the participating unit. Let

$\Delta Y_{ijkt} =$ the change in disposable income realized by participating units of type j living in subarea k under program i over some time interval t

and

$$Y_{ijkt} = n_{jkt*}\Delta y_{ij} + \Delta n_{jkt}\Delta y_{ij}$$

where n_{jkt*} is the number of participating units of type j living in subarea k at the beginning of time interval t. Δn_{jkt} is the change in the number of participating units of type j living in subarea k over the time interval t.

12. On the assumption that Δy_{ij} is a truly exogenous variable in the above relationship, and that n_{jkt*} is given to the analysis, the remaining variable to be explained (predicted) is Δn_{jkt}. This variable can change in three basic ways:

a) A participating unit of type j may move from or to subarea k.

b) A participating unit of type j may change to another type, say $j + 1$, through birth or death of members of the unit, or through some other change in its status.

c) Part of the participating unit may migrate from subarea k. This may result in changing the type of participating units which remains, as well as increasing the number of participating units at the destination of the migrant.

The latter two changes will be called participant mobility inasmuch as they are changes in the participant status of the receiving units. This can then be distinguished from that geographic mobility which the unit may exhibit in the first change. Thus changes in the number of participating units will depend upon the participating unit's geographic and participant mobility.

The problem, of course, is that geographic and participant mobility are not parameters but are dependent upon factors not entirely clear either in their specificity or in their influence. Further, the change in income (Δy_{ij}) resulting from a given program i to the particular participant type under consideration probably also influences the two kinds of mobility. The rural experiment now under way, for example, may lead to some insights into the relationship between changes in income under any program and migration.

At the moment, then, I do not see any simple or direct way to forecast the changes expected in the number of participating units in any subarea of analysis. It is clear, however, that the change in number of participants is related to factors not associated with the program as well as characteristics of the program itself. For the moment, then, I will assume that changes in n_{jkt} are zero, recognizing that the analytical scheme pursued may be enlarged later.

III. THE SPATIAL DISTRIBUTION OF CHANGES IN CONSUMPTION RESULTING FROM A NATIONAL INCOME MAINTENANCE PROGRAM

It has been shown how a national income maintenance (IM) program will change the spatial distribution of income. It is presumed that these changes in income will cause changes in consumption. Changes in consumption are changes in demands for goods and services in the local (and national) economy. An estimate of the changes in income through an IM plan can be obtained experimentally. An estimate of the multiplier effects of this increased demand for local goods and services may be obtained from an impact model such as input-output analysis.

Suppose we know that additional income is to be provided to receiving units of certain characteristics under a specific IM program, within some subarea of the space economy. It will also be assumed that the change in consumption of goods and services affected by this change in income can be estimated in the following way:

Let $\Delta C_{ijl} \Delta Y_{ij} = b_{ijl} \Delta Y_{ij}$
where: ΔC_{ijl} = the change in local consumption of good or service l by participating units of type j under program i.
      b_{ijl} = the change in local consumption of good or service l by participating units of type j under program i, per dollar change in income received by the participating unit j under program i.
      ΔY_{ij} = the change in income to participating units of type j under program i. This is estimated from the relationship discussed in the previous section.
(Note: all quantities are for subarea k and time interval t.)

Therefore, *for each IM program selected for study,* the above relationship provides an estimate of changes in consumption in the following matrix format:

$$
\begin{matrix}
\Delta C_{i11} & \Delta C_{i12} & \cdots & \Delta C_{i1l} & \cdots & \Delta C_{i1p} \\
\Delta C_{i21} & \Delta C_{i22} & \cdots & \Delta C_{i2l} & \cdots & \Delta C_{i2p} \\
\cdot & \cdot & & \cdot & & \cdot \\
\cdot & \cdot & & \cdot & & \cdot \\
\cdot & \cdot & & \cdot & & \cdot
\end{matrix}
$$

$$\begin{array}{cccc} \Delta C_{ij1} & \Delta C_{ij2} & \Delta C_{ijl} & \Delta C_{ijp} \\ \bullet & \bullet & \bullet & \bullet \\ \bullet & \bullet & \bullet & \bullet \\ \bullet & \bullet & \bullet & \bullet \\ \Delta C_{in1} & \Delta C_{in2} & \Delta C_{inl} & \Delta C_{inp} \end{array}$$

The sum of the jth column will be the total change in consumption of good or service l by all participating unit types under program i in subarea k over time period t. The row of column sums resulting provides an estimate of final demand increases as a result of program i. Because federal taxes to sustain a national income maintenance program will *reduce* disposable income of some members of the community, a vector of reductions in consumption resulting from reduced disposable income among nonparticipating units of the community would have to be estimated and subtracted from the row vector estimated above.

The estimation of this vector could not rely upon the experimental data. Possibly some insights may be found in studies of the effect of the 1964 tax cut or the more recent tax surcharge. Most probably any estimates made of changes in disposable income gained in this way would not be area specific. Further, the changes in income would depend upon the characteristics of the program and the eligibility requirements for participants insofar as these would in some way determine the revenue needs and consequently the tax rate changes needed to finance the program. In short, the problems associated with estimation of the vector of changes in consumption on the part of nonparticipating members of the community probably cannot practically be resolved without considerable loss of precision.

It is possible, however, to speculate upon the probable effects of an IM program on a local economy drawing upon the foregoing analytical framework and some related research. These speculations follow in the form of hypotheses to be tested:

1. The overall effect of an IM program on the *level* of economic activity will be greater in metropolitan regions than in less urban regions. More specifically, the total direct and indirect change in local production, employment, or income per dollar change in consumption by members of the community (the so-called multiplier), will be greater in the larger, more fully integrated metropolitan areas than in the more "open" and less urban regions.

2. The *net* effects of an IM program on consumption will be positive even though the *net* change in disposable income may be negative.

3. Thus the *net* effects nationwide will be to shift income from rural and less urban to metropolitan areas.

IV. SOME NOTES ON THE CONSTRUCTION
OF A RESEARCH MODEL

Because the total (direct, indirect, and induced) effects of a national income maintenance program on the level and composition of economic activity are in question, the Leontief[1] interindustry model is the obvious choice. In this case, the vector of changes in consumption estimated as above becomes the motivating change in final demand and the model then estimates the "impact" of these changes on the level and composition of economic activity in the region under consideration.

Though the use of the input-output model for this kind of impact study is clearly called for, the development of the transactions table— basic to use of the model—is an admittedly expensive and time-consuming task. It may be possible, however, to use one of several existing tables (with necessary modifications) in this research effort. Completed tables exist for at least two metropolitan areas (St. Louis and Philadelphia), two states (West Virginia and Utah), and several smaller urban areas (Boulder, Colorado; Lansing, Michigan; Erie, Pennsylvania; Sabine-Neches area, Texas; southwestern Wyoming). A judicious design of the experiment along with some relatively inexpensive modifications of existing tables would probably suffice to test the hypotheses presented.

The alternative is development of a new transactions table for a selected area. As is well known, this is an expensive process. But there would be advantages. Most important, the table and resulting impact model could be specifically designed to test the hypotheses presented, clearly lending greater validity to the outcome of the test. However, at least two years would be required to complete a table for a metropolitan area.

---

[1] See William H. Miernyk, *Input-Output Analysis* (New York: Random House, 1965), for an introductory discussion of input-output analysis. Leontief's original exposition of the analysis is included in his work, "Quantitative Input-Output Relations in the Economic System of the United States," *Review of Economics and Statistics,* Vol. 18 (August 1936), pp. 105–25.

THE EFFECT OF A NEGATIVE INCOME TAX ON THE NUMBER OF SUBSTANDARD HOUSING UNITS*

Hugh O. Nourse

In recent years a number of economists and sociologists have proposed that a negative income tax be implemented to help alleviate poverty. Support for some form of income supplement has come from a wide

Reprinted from *Land Economics* (November 1970), © Regents of the University of Wisconsin, with permission.

* The author wishes to acknowledge an embarrassing amount of assistance. This study has been financed in part by the Institute for Research on Poverty, the University of Wisconsin, for a summer research appointment and computer time. Partial funding was also received through the summer studies program of the Center for Urban Studies at the University of Illinois, Chicago Circle Campus financed by the Department of Housing and Urban Development. Certain data used in this report were derived by the author from a computer tape furnished under a joint project sponsored by the U.S. Bureau of the Census and the Population Council and containing selected 1960 Census information for a 0.1 percent sample of the population of the United States. Neither the Census Bureau nor the Population Council assumes any responsibility for the validity of any of the figures or interpretations of the figures herein based on this material. Harold Watts, Burt Weisbrod, Larry Orr, Eugene Smolensky, other members of the staff of the Institute for Research on Poverty, and Richard F. Muth have made many useful comments. In addition I have benefited from discussions with Jane Leuthold, Ralph Husby, Harold F. Williamson, Jr., and Julian Simon, all members of the Department of Economics, the University of Illinois. Between the preliminary version of this study and its final draft William G. Grigsby allowed me to have a copy of a preliminary paper of his on this same

spectrum of political positions.[1] Milton Friedman in particular has suggested a 50 percent negative income tax as a substitute for current welfare programs.[2] His argument is that the poor would be better off with a lump sum of money than with particular benefits, such as public housing, because they could choose to spend the funds in any way that they wished.

Although there have been many studies on the impact of a negative income tax on work incentives and the federal treasury, no one has attempted to determine if such a policy would substitute for current housing policies which attempt to improve housing to some standard level.[3] It would be useful to know what impact a negative income tax would have on the quality of housing, the better to plan other housing legislation.

An immediate difficulty in such a study is the definition of standard housing. On the one hand, a criterion based on market efficiency would be that standard housing is that quality that would cause the marginal social benefit (reduction of neighborhood cost of fire insurance, police protection, and welfare) to just equal the marginal cost of improving quality an additional degree, whatever that might be. On the other hand, a criterion might be that standard housing is that quality of housing that society believes to be minimal for decent living. Either criterion is nearly impossible to implement empirically. We will use the definition used by many housing analysts and which relies mostly on the latter criterion. It is in negative form, defining substandard instead of standard housing. Substandard housing will be defined as a unit that lacks some or all plumbing facilities, or is dilapidated. Dilapidation is the presence of defects making a structure unsafe.

This study is an attempt to estimate the effect of one specific

---

subject. I have benefited from his careful analysis of the complexities of the relation between a guaranteed income plan and the housing market. Needless to say, I alone am responsible for remaining errors of commission and omission.

[1] For a general survey of these proposals and the reasons for their support see Clair Wilcox, *Toward Social Welfare* (Homewood, Ill.: Irwin, 1969), pp. 248–69.

[2] Milton Friedman, *Capitalism and Freedom* (Chicago: University of Chicago Press, 1962), especially pp. 190–95.

[3] For a recent bibliography see Gail Schlachter, "Guaranteed Annual Income: A Selected Bibliography of Current Materials," unpublished paper, University of Wisconsin, Institute for Research on Poverty, 1967. Since beginning my own research, I have learned of another similar study on the impact of guaranteed annual income on housing markets: William G. Grigsby, "Possible Impacts of the Guaranteed Annual Income on Housing Markets," unpublished paper, March 1969. I have benefited from his study.

negative income tax plan on the number of substandard housing units, as defined above, in the United States. An operational model showing how a change in income distribution might affect the quality of housing is presented first. It is followed by empirical estimation of the impact of a 50 percent negative income tax on the housing market of 1960. Specifically, we will use the 50 percent Friedman plan. That is, when a family's income falls below its tax deductions and exemptions, it will receive a benefit equal to 50 percent of the difference between its allowable deductions and exemptions and its income. Under the current tax law the allowable deductions and exemptions are as follows: A basic $200 deduction for each family plus $100 for each person in the family and the standard $600 exemption for each member of the family. Thus the allowable deductions and exemptions for a single person would be $900 and for a family of four, $3,000.

I. THE MODEL

In this study we want to determine whether a given improvement in housing units will occur. In the real estate market, investors often make this kind of decision. They have to estimate whether to build a particular kind of property in one place or another, or whether to improve a property and, if so, by how much. Their investment decision depends on whether the present value of incomes from the property will support the costs of construction. The problem is identical to the one undertaken in this study, so that we shall also use this approach.[4]

The present value of annual net income from real property can be expressed in the following way:

$$V = \sum_{n=1}^{N} \frac{a}{(1+r)^n} = \left[\frac{(1+r)^n - 1}{r(1+r)^n} \right] a = Ba \qquad (1)$$

Where V = present value of income from property[5]
a = expected gross annual income and is also equal to the rent expenditure of the tenant

---

[4] Ralph Turvey, *Economics of Real Property* (London: Allen & Unwin, 1957), pp. 8–24.
[5] Actually there should be no depreciation of land, so that the present value of land (V_1) would be calculated as follows:

$$V_1 = \frac{a}{r}$$

where

N = the economic life of the structure, or the period of time during which the investor wants to recapture his investment
r = the sum of the tax rate, rate for maintenance and repair, a vacancy rate, and the opportunity cost of capital
n = years 1 through N

$$B = \frac{(1+r)^n - 1}{r(1+r)^n} = \text{gross rent multiplier}^6$$

At any time an investor will convert, merge, or improve real property, if the cost is equal to or less than the increase in value caused by the change. An improvement will occur if

$$C \leq V' - V \tag{2}$$

where V' = the present value after change
V = the present value if there should be no change
C = the cost of conversion, merger, or improvement

The rule applies to conversion of land from agricultural to urban use, as well as the conversion of single-family houses to rooming houses, the demolition of old houses to construct an office building, or the improvement in quality of a residential building. In each circumstance the investor must estimate the expected annual income from the property before and after change, the expected life of the investment before and after change, and the opportunity cost of his capital.

An alternative way to represent the decision equation can be constructed as follows:

$$C = B'c' - Ba \tag{3}$$

where B' = the gross rent multiplier after change
c' = the gross annual rent after change necessary to make $V' - V$ equal cost
B = the gross rent multiplier before change
a = the gross annual rent expected before change

---

a = annual net income to land
r = the opportunity cost of capital

Appraisers of a real property investment would calculate the land value separate from building value, compute the return necessary for land, and deduct this from the net annual income of the property. Equation (1) would then be used to calculate the present value of the building. Nevertheless, any separation of land and building value is arbitrary and fictitious (ibid., pp. 21–24).

[6] For a proof that this is the multiplier necessary to make a constant annual sum equal to its present value see John G. Kemeny et al., *Finite Mathematics with Business Applications* (Englewood Cliffs, N.J.: Prentice-Hall, 1962), pp. 312–20.

If the gross rent multiplier (B') after change is equal to the multiplier (B), then equation (3) becomes

$$C = B(c' - a) \tag{4}$$

and the expected change in value would be

$$V' - V = B(a' - a) \tag{5}$$

where a' equals the expected gross annual rent after change. Thus an improvement, conversion, or other change would be undertaken as long as

$$C \leq V' - V \tag{2}$$

Substituting equations (4) and (5) into (2),

$$B(c' - a) \leq B(a' - a)$$

Dividing through by B, we obtain

$$c' - a \leq a' - a$$

or

$$\frac{c' - a}{a} \leq \frac{a' - a}{a} \tag{6}$$

This inequality shows that under the above assumption that $B' = B$, an investor will undertake a given change as long as the percentage increase in rent required to make the change in value equal to cost is equal to or less than the expected percentage increase in rents. The assumption that gross rent multipliers are equal before and after a change in use would be inappropriate for most types of changes in real property because the multiplier is a function of the economic life of the structure, the tax rate, rate for maintenance and repair, vacancy rate, and the opportunity cost of capital. Nevertheless, the equality of the multipliers may be a reasonable approximation for the rehabilitation of substandard housing.

We now need to determine how the gross annual rent, a, of any property is established. The gross annual rents, hereafter called the rents, are established in local housing markets. The operation of these local housing markets can be shown to be similar to an assignment problem.[7] Consider a given community with a finite number of housing

---

[7] Martin Beckmann, *Location Theory* (New York: Random House, 1968), pp. 94–96; and Wallace F. Smith, "The Housing Stock as a Resource," *Papers and Proceedings of the First Far East Conference of the Regional Science Association* (1965), pp. 77–92.

units of varying quality. There are as many families seeking housing as there are units. Each family is willing to bid a particular rent for each of the available housing units. The rent bid depends upon family preferences, incomes, the quality of housing, and the location of the units. In particular, location includes the distance of the dwelling from jobs and shopping, its access to recreational facilities and distance from nuisance effects such as air pollution and who is living in adjacent sites. If the families were already housed, these bids would represent bids on other houses and reservation bids on the one that they occupied. The latter, of course, must take account of the cost of moving to a new dwelling.

Koopmans and Beckmann have shown that if each household rent bid is dependent upon who occupies the adjacent site, there is no set of rents that will cause an equilibrium.[8] There will always be at least one household that will find itself better off by moving to a new location. Such a result makes it awkward to apply comparative statics analysis because there is no settled equilibrium in the competitive housing market from which to analyze the impact of change. Therefore, in the analysis that follows we shall assume that each family's rent bid is independent of those families on adjacent sites.

If there is competition in the property market, assignments of families to housing units will be such that rents will be maximized. Each family will occupy that house that it prefers the most and for which it can offer more rent than others. The rents established in this way are *short-run* equilibrium rents.

We shall try to adapt the short-run model to long-run equilibrium by introducing rehabilitation and repair into the analysis. Perhaps some families after their assignments would be willing to pay increases in rents in order to improve the quality of the units that they occupy. Whether such quality improvements occur depends upon costs and the families' willingness and ability to pay, as indicated by inequality (6). If the percentage increase in rent families would pay is greater than the percentage increase in rent necessary to pay off the cost, then the improvements would occur. If the improvements would be sufficient to make the housing unit competitive with previously better housing, the supply of such housing would increase, and the rents on that quality would have a tendency to fall. These rents would continue to fall until they were equal to the rent necessary to pay off the cost of improvements. After all such improvements have been completed the long-run equilibrium for a stable population would be achieved.

---

[8] Tjalling Koopmans and Martin Beckmann, "Assignment Problems and the Location of Economic Activities," *Econometrica* (1957), pp. 53–76; and Beckmann, loc. cit.

Consider a change in the distribution of income among the families, such as would occur with a negative income tax. The above long-run equilibrium would be disturbed. Some families would find their incomes reduced by the increased taxes necessary to finance the negative income tax. Other families would find their incomes increased because their earnings were below their allowable deductions and exemptions. Since rent bids are a function of income, some rent bids will rise and others will fall. Furthermore, since there are many more families who will be taxed than there are families for whom benefits will be allowed, individual decreases in incomes and rents will be much smaller than increases. We shall consider these decreases to be negligible and we shall therefore ignore them.

Because of the redistribution of income there would be a new array of rent bids for each of the existing housing units. At the upper end of the distribution there would be no change in rank order of bids, although each bid might be somewhat less. At the lower end, however, there would be a new income floor below which families do not fall. The income floor is different for different-sized families, being higher for families with more persons. Since the benefits vary by family size and income, some families might be able to move up in the rank order by income. Therefore, there might be some initial shifting of families into different quality units. In particular families with more persons may be able to shift up at the expense of smaller families. Since the average income of families receiving benefits has risen, all bids of these families would tend to rise. Nevertheless, with higher incomes, higher bids can also be made for improvements in quality. Thus, after the initial rise in bids there would be the secondary effect of families that would pay more to have their assigned unit improved. In some cases their bid would be sufficient to improve quality. Improvements would continue to occur until the increase in rents was forced down to equality with the cost of improving houses to better quality.

To work out the empirical problem we need to make several assumptions with respect to the above model. They will cause our results to be only approximations, and to the extent that these assumptions are unacceptable to others, the results will be questioned. Since there is no possibility at this time of estimating the accuracy of the predictions, we must look to the reasonableness of the assumptions.

As noted above, the first assumption that is necessary is that a family's demand for housing is independent of the decisions of other families. Obviously this assumption is not true. Indeed, the interdependence of consumer preferences for housing has been considered as one of the factors preventing rehabilitation of neighborhoods, when such rehabilitation would otherwise be profitable.[9] If one house in a blighted neighborhood were to be improved, its rent would not rise much and might not rise sufficiently to pay the cost of the improvement. The rent is held down by the general quality of property in the neighborhood. In such a situation the private market may be unable to improve blighted neighborhoods, even if it should be profitable to do so. It is important to recognize, however, that such neighborhoods may not generate sufficiently high rents for improvement, even if the interdependency of consumer demand were not present. There are at least three reasons for accepting the reasonableness of the assumption that consumer demands are independent for our analysis. First, a negative income tax plan would cause a general shift in demand in the same neighborhood, so there might be pressure for a general improvement of a neighborhood. Second, there is an allowable amount of variation among rents in the same neighborhood even when preferences are interdependent. Third, as long as there are vacancies in the stock of housing, competition to hold families with negative income tax benefits would result in improved housing. Families with income supplements might be able to pay the higher rents for vacant standard housing. If substandard housing vacancies rose as a result, their owners would be forced to improve them or lose all revenue.

The second assumption is that the income elasticity of demand for housing is unity. The percentage increase in rent that families would be willing and able to pay would be equal to the percentage increase in their income. Recent studies of the income elasticity of demand for housing in the United States and other countries show a range between .3 and 2 or 3.[10] Most estimates are in the range of .6 to 1.

The third assumption is that there will be no change in the costs of home repairs and improvements because of any increase in construction activity caused by the negative income tax benefits. I have been able to find no studies of the supply elasticity of the residential construction industry. There are, however, several facts indicating that the industry is a constant cost industry. One study found that the expansion and contraction of the industry was swift during periods of change and showed

---

[9] Otto A. Davis and Andrew B. Whinston, "The Economics of Urban Renewal," *Law and Contemporary Problems* (Winter 1961), pp. 100–110.

[10] Margaret Reid, *Housing and Income* (Chicago: University of Chicago Press, 1962); Tong Hun Lee, "Housing and Permanent Income: Tests Based on a Three Year Reinterview Survey," *Review of Economics and Statistics* (November 1968), pp. 480–90; and Hendrik S. Houthakker, "An International Comparison of Household Expenditure Patterns, Commemorating the Centenary of Engel's Law," *Econometrica* (October 1957), pp. 532–51.

little change in costs per dwelling unit.[11] Although a massive increase in home improvements could cause increases in such costs in order to bid resources away from alternative employments, the shift may cause the industry to reorganize and find more efficient ways of doing operations currently performed on a custom basis. Greater efficiency might result in home improvement costs decreasing in the long run. Since there seems to be no clear-cut evidence for either decreasing or increasing costs, the assumption that no change in costs will occur is made.

The investment model together with the last three assumptions allows estimation of the effect of the negative income tax on the number of substandard housing units improved to standard quality. For each substandard housing unit, one needs to estimate the percentage increase in rent necessary to support the rehabilitation of that house to standard quality, $(c' - a)/a;$ and the percentage increase in rent that families would pay out of increases in income from negative income tax benefits, $(a' - a)/a$. Applying inequality (6), the total number of housing units for which the latter exceeds the former is a measure of the impact of a negative income tax.

Such a census would be exceedingly costly. An alternative is to randomly select a number of families, pay them the benefits that they would receive from a negative income tax plan, see how they spend their increase on rent, and count how many of their housing units are improved to standard quality. An experimental study along these lines on many aspects of a negative income tax is being tried for a three-year period.[12] The main difficulty in using this study for an analysis of housing is its short time horizon. Many home improvements will require longer than three years to be paid off through increased rents.

In this study, probability distributions of the percentage increase in rent families would pay for improved housing with income supplements and of the percentage increase in rents required to improve substandard housing units to standard quality will be estimated from two separate data sources. On the basis that they are independent events, these two distributions will be combined into a joint probability distribution from which one can estimate the proportion of substandard units that will be upgraded to standard quality.

---

[11] Sherman J. Maisel, *Housebuilding in Transition* (Berkeley: University of California, 1953).

[12] Harold W. Watts, "Graduated Work Incentives: An Experiment in Negative Taxation," *American Economic Review* (May 1969), pp. 463–72.

II. EMPIRICAL ANALYSIS

The probability distribution of the percentage increase in rent that families would pay for improved housing was estimated by applying a 50 percent negative income tax to a selected group of families in the 0.1 percent sample of the 1960 Census. Because of the limitations of the data, the analysis was restricted to primary families or individuals who occupied substandard nonfarm housing units by paying rent for a unit in any structure, or by right of ownership of a single-family unit detached from other housing units or from a business establishment. The study group was further restricted to the above families and individuals whose head earned income solely from wages and salaries or self-employment.[13]

The study group was restricted to nonfarm housing because the cost data were generated from an urban blighted area. Costs in that area may not be representative of rural farm rehabilitation costs. Of course, the same logic may apply to the use of the cost information for rural nonfarm housing, but we will take the chance.

Total family income reported by the Census includes a third category besides wages and salaries and self-employment income. This third category includes welfare payments, pensions, social security payments, patent payments, and royalties and rents. We would have liked to exclude only families currently receiving welfare payments, but that was impossible with the data. Instead we excluded all families whose head earned any income from the third category mentioned above. Because families may include several subfamilies and other earners, members other than the head may be on welfare, but it seems unlikely since receipt of welfare payments depends on evidence of need. To the extent that poor families in substandard housing earn income wholly or partly from some source other than wages and salaries or self-employment the study group will yield an underestimate of the number of families receiving benefits.

There were three reasons for the basic selection of the study group. The first was that if families receiving welfare payments had not been excluded, the study would add negative income tax benefits to current welfare benefits. This would surely inflate the benefits that would be received under any negative income tax program. The second was that

---

[13] There were 3,282 families in the study group as defined in the text. 1,136 were in owner-occupied units and 2,146 were in tenant-occupied units. Multiplication by 1,000 yields the size of the universe in 1960 from which the families were sampled.

occupants of substandard housing now receiving welfare have not moved from substandard to standard housing. The supplements proposed in the income guarantee plans fall below the assistance payments now made to families with dependent children in two-fifths to two-thirds of the states.[14] Thus, if these families received a negative income tax benefit instead of their current benefits they would certainly not move into standard quality housing. The third follows from the second. If current welfare payments are higher than a negative income tax benefit, they could be meeting needs that a negative income tax plan would not, so that any negative income tax plan that is implemented will probably assist families not covered by the current welfare programs, rather than substitute for them.[15]

There is one final problem that needs to be covered before presenting the data. The families and individuals defined by the Census may not be the same group as the unit filing an income tax return. For example, married children may live with one set of parents and file separate income tax returns, so that they would be separate families for income tax purposes. In the Census, however, they would be counted as one family living in the same housing unit. Total income reported is that for both families and not just for the head of the household. Therefore, this study will probably underestimate the benefits received. Some families living with relatives might find it possible to set up separate housekeeping if a negative income tax program were instituted. This reinforces the underestimation caused by excluding families whose income is low, and is earned from sources other than wages and salaries, or self-employment.

Estimates of the benefits to the study group from a 50 percent negative income tax can be expressed as a relative frequency distribution of the percentage increase in income. These estimates were calculated from data grouped by income class and family size. For the most part the families were grouped by $250 income classes and exact family size so that the estimates are fairly refined. Because of our assumption that the income elasticity of demand for housing is equal to unity, this relative frequency distribution also shows the distribution of families by the percentage increase in rent that they would pay should they receive benefits under a 50 percent negative income tax plan. The distributions for owner- and tenant-occupied units are shown in the last row of Tables 1 and 2.

An estimate of the probability distribution of the percentage increase in rent that would be required to cover the cost of rehabilitating housing to standard quality was taken directly from a study by Schaaf in which

---

[14] Wilcox, op. cit., p. 258.
[15] Ibid., pp. 257–59.

Table 1. Tenant-occupied Units in Study, Relative Frequency Distribution

Percentage increase in rents required to improve housing[b]	Percentage increase in rents families would pay[a]											
	0	1–10	11–20	21–30	31–40	41–60	61–80	81–100	101–120	121–140	141–160	Over 160	Total
0	0	0	0	0	0	0	0	0	0	0	0	0	0
1–10	.085	.011	.004	.007	.003	.006	.004	.003	.002	.001	0	.015	.142
11–20	.057	.007	.003	.005	.002	.004	.003	.002	.001	.001	0	.010	.095
21–30	.043	.005	.002	.004	.002	.003	.002	.001	.001	.001	0	.008	.072
31–40	.043	.005	.002	.004	.001	.003	.002	.001	.001	.001	0	.008	.071
41–60	.077	.010	.004	.007	.003	.005	.004	.002	.002	.001	0	.014	.129
61–80	.065	.008	.003	.006	.002	.005	.003	.002	.002	.001	0	.012	.109
81–100	.060	.007	.003	.005	.002	.004	.003	.002	.001	.001	0	.011	.101
101–120	.047	.006	.002	.004	.002	.003	.002	.001	.001	.001	0	.008	.079
121–140	.059	.007	.003	.005	.002	.004	.003	.002	.001	.001	0	.011	.099
141–160	.031	.004	.002	.003	.001	.002	.002	.001	.001	.001	0	.006	.052
over 160	.030	.004	.002	.003	.001	.002	.001	.001	.001	.001	0	.005	.050
Total	.599	.074	.031	.051	.021	.042	.029	.018	.014	.010	.003	.107	1.00

[a] Equals percent increase in income resulting from 50% negative income tax as a result of assuming income elasticity is one. Calculated from 0.1 % sample from 1960 Census.

[b] Recalculated from A. H. Schaaf, "Economic Aspects of Urban Renewal: Theory, Policy and Area Analysis, Research Report No. 14, Real Estate Research Program, Institute of Business and Economic Research, University of California (Berkeley), 1960, pp. 34, 37, by dropping units requiring no rehabilitation costs.

Table 2. Owner-occupied Single-family Units in Study, Relative Frequency Distribution

Percentage increase in rents required to improve housing[b]	Percentage increase in rents families would pay[a]								
	0	1–10	11–20	21–30	31–40	41–50	51–100	Over 100	Total
0	0	0	0	0	0	0	0	0	0
1–10	.106	.017	.007	.013	.005	.005	.013	.033	.200
11–20	.106	.017	.007	.013	.005	.005	.013	.033	.200
21–30	.076	.012	.005	.010	.004	.004	.010	.024	.143
31–40	.076	.012	.005	.010	.004	.004	.010	.024	.143
41–50	.046	.007	.003	.006	.002	.002	.006	.014	.086
51–100	.091	.014	.006	.011	.004	.004	.011	.029	.171
over 100	.030	.005	.002	.004	.001	.001	.004	.010	.057
Total	.530	.085	.033	.067	.026	.026	.067	.167	1.00

[a] See Table 1.
[b] See Table 1.

these calculations were made for a slum area in Oakland, California.[16]
A 25 percent simple random sample of residential properties in Census
Tract 17 in Oakland were appraised for quality using the American Public
Health Association (APHA) point system. A subsample of 56 properties
were inspected by an experienced architect and a contractor. They made
an estimate of the cost of upgrading each property to a specified standard,
a standard similar to that used in this study. The standard was defined
as follows:

> In effect the standard requires the provision of private bath,
> toilet and kitchen facilities for each dwelling unit plus remedying
> of any imminently dangerous conditions for which the code (Oak-
> land) reference is clear and unambiguous. It is assumed that the
> work would represent the absolute minimum needed and would
> generally be done in a spirit of unwilling compliance. The em-
> phasis would be upon the avoidance of prosecution rather than
> upon the possibility that the work done might increase the value
> of the property.[17]

These code compliance cost estimates for the subsample were projected
by Schaaf to the whole sample by means of regression equations estimated
from the subsample relating the code compliance cost per room to APHA
points. From market data on interest rates, economic life, taxes, and
maintenance expenditures, gross rent multipliers were estimated. Then,
using equation (3) above, estimates of the increase in rent necessary to
pay off the code compliance cost were made. Converting these estimates
to percentages of current rent, Schaaf obtained the distribution of percentage increases in rent required to pay off rehabilitation costs shown in
the last column of Tables 1 and 2.[18]

Since the distribution of rents families would pay has come from a
different study than that of rents required to pay off rehabilitation, and
since the Schaaf study did not indicate the association between family
income, family size, and cost of code compliance, there is no direct
evidence about the association between the percentage increase in rents
families would pay and the percentage increase in rents necessary to pay
off the rehabilitation cost. In the absence of such evidence we shall

---

[16] A. H. Schaaf, "Economic Analysis of Urban Renewal: Theory, Policy
and Area Analysis," Research Report No. 14, Real Estate Research Program,
Institute of Business and Economic Research, University of California (Berkeley), 1960.

[17] Ibid., p. 20.

[18] There were 655 renter units and 41 owner units for which cost estimates
were made. Some did not require any rehabilitation. These were dropped so
the distributions in Tables 1 and 2 are based on 634 renter units and 35 owner
units.

assume that these two events are independent random events. The relative
frequency distribution for each event represents its probability distribution.
By making this assumption the joint probability of any pair of possible
increases in rents families would pay and required rent increases can
be calculated. It is simply the product of (1) the probability that any
family in substandard housing without welfare payments will receive a
given percentage increase in income from negative income tax benefits
(which means they will be willing and able to increase rent a given
percentage) and (2) the probability of a substandard housing unit requiring a given percentage increase in rent to pay off the rehabilitation
cost. These probabilities are shown in Tables 1 and 2.

All those families for whom the percentage increase in rent they
would pay is greater than the percentage increase in rent that would be
required to pay off rehabilitation costs would be able to improve their
substandard housing unit to standard quality. The step lines through
Tables 1 and 2 divide the cells into those groups that can improve their
housing to standard quality and those that cannot. All of those cells above
the line are groups for whom the rent increase they could pay is greater
than that required to rehabilitate. For those cells below the line the rent
increase required for rehabilitation is greater. Summing over all the cells
above the line, the probability that a tenant living in substandard housing
who receives income only from wages and salaries or self-employment
will rehabilitate his house to standard quality is .24—that is, 24 percent
of such families will be likely to rehabilitate their housing to standard
quality. In the same way, 43 percent of those families living in their own
substandard detached housing unit and receiving income only from wages
and salaries or self-employment would rehabilitate their house to standard
quality.

Applying these percentages to the appropriate estimates of the total
number of families in owner- and tenant-occupied substandard nonfarm
housing units and earning wage and salary income or self-employed income, we find that the total number of units that would have been improved to standard quality in 1960 would have been about 857,000 units.
If the income elasticity of demand for housing should be only .5 rather
than the 1 that was assumed, this estimate of the reduction of substandard housing would be reduced to about 465,000 units. As a point
of comparison, 850,228 public housing units have been constructed in
almost thirty years.[19] Nevertheless, there were about 11 million substandard housing units in the United States in 1960.[20]

---

[19] U.S. Bureau of the Census, *Statistical Abstract of the United States: 1968*
(89th edition) (Washington, D.C.: U.S. GPO, 1968), p. 706.
   [20] Ibid.

III. CONCLUSION

The magnitude of our estimate of the number of housing units that would be improved to standard quality because of benefits received from a 50 percent negative income tax suggests that a guaranteed income policy could be as important an influence on the quality of housing as current public housing policy. Its impact is great enough that it is worth further study.

The model described in the first part of the paper outlines the considerations necessary for analyzing the problem of the impact of a change in income distribution on the quality of housing. In empirically implementing the model, however, several assumptions were required. In particular it was assumed that the income elasticity of demand for housing is unity, and that the home repair and improvement industry is a constant cost industry. The first assumption can be defended by a number of statistical studies. The second assumption cannot be defended by reference to statistical tests. The tests do not exist.

The estimates of the percentage increases in rent required to rehabilitate substandard housing are weak. Further study is required into the supply side of the housing market. We know very little about the nature of rehabilitation costs. Although there have been many demonstration projects, the data from these studies have not been analyzed in such a way as to be useful for understanding the supply of improvements. There is also a noticeable lack of information on the housing of welfare recipients. For the purposes of this study it would be useful to know how the quality of their housing changed, or if it did at all, as a result of welfare benefits received.

The model presented was not constructed for the sake of building a model, but to help understand the impact of a negative income tax on the number of substandard housing units. The model itself is useful because it outlines the major facts needed in any such analysis. The empirical implementation has shown that such a policy may have as important an impact as current housing policy. But more importantly, the attempt at implementation has indicated the kind of further research required to do a better analysis.

ALTERNATIVE CONCEPTIONS OF POVERTY AND THEIR IMPLICATIONS FOR INCOME MAINTENANCE*

Seymour Spilerman and David Elesh

I. INTRODUCTION

In the narrowest use of the term, living in poverty means having low income. As a concern of social agencies and social scientists, however, poverty is associated with a range of disabilities, some spawned by low income, others producing this condition. Psychologically, poor persons are likely to feel powerless, have low self-esteem, have short temporal horizons, and be weakly motivated in their occupational roles. At the level of individual behavior, low income is associated with inadequate nutrition, poor health care, living in dilapidated housing, unemployment, economic dependency, illegitimacy, and crime, to cite but a few concomitants. Poverty-ridden communities have some characteristics which are aggregates of these individual level disabilities—high rates of unemployment, crime, economic dependency—but also others which emerge only in a context of dense concentrations of poor persons, such as gang delinquency and a paucity of formal organizations to advocate interests which are shared by residents of a neighborhood.

* We would like to thank Harold Watts and Jerald Hage for their criticisms on an earlier draft of this paper.

Income definitions of poverty are attractive for a number of purposes. Income definitions provide explicit criteria for measuring the prevalence of poverty, for charting over-time changes in the size of the poverty population, and for estimating the financial cost of eliminating this condition, at least in the sense of raising low-income families to the subsistence level. Income definitions are also useful to researchers who are principally concerned with the social disabilities which often accompany low income since they provide a convenient summary indicator of the magnitude of these problems.

At least in part, the motivation behind eliminating poverty stems from a concern with alleviating some of the correlative disabilities of low income. The presence of poor persons in a society creates substantial costs for the more affluent who not only must sustain the impoverished but suffer their asocial behavior as well. Many programs in the panoply of social welfare have therefore been designed to combat disvalued behavior of one sort or another which accompanies low income (delinquency, illegitimacy) rather than alter the income level itself.

However, the fact that a syndrome of conditions carries a name which designates an income state—poverty—signifies the prevailing assumption as to the interrelations among the specific variables, namely that low income somehow plays a central role in the perpetuation of these conditions. Consistent with this perspective, a range of social welfare programs have been directed at altering factors which impinge upon income: job training, anti-discrimination laws in hiring, and job creation (for a review of these programs see Elesh, Ladinsky, Lefcowitz, and Spilerman, 1971). In recent years, however, attention has focused more upon the advisability of manipulating the income variable directly, rather than factors related to it, however closely. Reflecting this interest, income maintenance programs are currently undergoing field experimentation in New Jersey, Pennsylvania, Washington, Iowa, and North Carolina.

Income maintenance programs, indeed all plans which propose to eliminate a syndrome of conditions by manipulating one or a few variables, embody specific assumptions about the interrelations among the variables. Implicit in an income maintenance policy is the belief that many correlative characteristics of low income can be altered by an exogenous intervention which raises family income; in short, that income level is an antecedent variable in a causal relationship between low income and other poverty characteristics. If this assumption is correct, income maintenance could provide an efficient strategy for treating a range of social problems since only a single variable would need to be manipulated. On the other hand, if this assumption as to the variable linkages is wrong and the correlative characteristics of low income prove intractable to income adjustments, we will find ourselves contending with these same problems under a new label such as "disabilities of the near-poor."

Unfortunately, we have only limited experience with income support programs that are not restricted to narrow categories of the destitute who are incapable of significantly altering their work behavior (e.g., the incapacitated, the aged, and female heads of families). When applied more broadly, it is likely that some correlates of poverty—hunger, insufficient clothing, poor health care—could be quickly eliminated, but what about factors which are only indirectly related to family income such as educational aspirations of the young, one's sense of personal efficacy, family stability, and delinquency? Can we expect fewer family breakups or a decrease in illegitimacy under income maintenance? Also, how long will it take for these responses to develop if, indeed, it is reasonable to expect such changes?

Analogous questions can be raised concerning the variation across individuals in response to an income maintenance program. Economists have been primarily interested in the *average* individual adjustment. However, it is conceivable that different persons in the poverty population will adapt to income support in very different ways. If the variation is indeed large then the simplification of the welfare structure which would be achieved by adopting a uniform national program of income maintenance would be attained at the cost of not meeting the needs of a great many poor persons.

The intent of this paper is to discuss some of the dimensions along which individual variation in response to an income maintenance program is likely to occur, and to indicate the relevance of different explanations of poverty to experimentation in income maintenance. Our perspective here is that (a) the different poverty theories predict divergent adaptations by recipients of income maintenance, (b) a given explanation of poverty is likely to be valid for some individuals but not for others, and only for particular correlates of low income, and (c) much of the inter-individual variation can be attributed to differences in response among *social* groups. Consequently, we propose that future research should be directed at identifying the characteristic types of adaptations which are likely to occur, and associating particular groups in poverty with each adaptation.

II. ALTERNATIVE THEORIES OF POVERTY

Theories of poverty are broadly of two types, situational (commonly characterized by simple causality) and cultural (functional). Situational explanations view the behavioral characteristics of low income individuals as an adaptation to environment and circumstance. If a poor person tends not to defer gratification and invest in the future, it is because the future is precarious for him, too unstable for a long-range perspective to be rational. If he robs for a living, it is because the socially acceptable occupations which show similiar financial returns are outside the pale of vocations available to him. Thus the view that the destitute share a deviant culture, with values which are in opposition to those of the dominant society, is not invoked. The fact that in seemingly diverse settings poor persons exhibit similar behavioral characteristics is taken as evidence for their having to contend with analogous problems which permit few alternative adaptations, rather than their holding like deviant values.

By comparison, cultural explanations of poverty argue that the behavior and attitudes of poor persons are components of a coherent life style. These factors are seen as an expression of established rules or norms which prescribe what is desirable or important, rather than as an application of general societal values to the circumstance of the poor. Since cultural theories explain behavior and attitudes in terms of concepts like values, expectations and social pressure, cultural theories of poverty take the guise of "functional explanations."[1] From this perspective, then, the poor in different settings behave in a similar fashion because they share common values.

These two types of explanations have very different underlying logical structures and often imply contradictory adaptations by recipients of income maintenance. Since our interest here is with developing the implications of the different theories by examining their logical structures, the substantive examples that are considered in the following sections will necessarily be elementary and are intended for illustrative purposes.

A. Situational Explanations

In their most elementary form, situational explanations which relate low income to correlative behavioral characteristics may be viewed as causal sequences. For example, low and variable income leads to insufficient nutrition and inadequate housing, which result in poor health, impairing, in turn, the individual's ability to work. Or, low income implies inadequate home study conditions for children, poor nourishment, and a continual state of financial need by the family, which combine to reduce a child's ability to concentrate on school affairs. In each of these chains,

---

[1] Following Stinchcombe (1968: 80–85) we identify a functional explanation with a self-adjusting system which involves negative feedback. This point is elaborated in the following section.

as in causal theory generally, there is an implication that by manipulating a prior factor the variable of primary interest can be altered; an increase in family income would be translated into an improvement in work performance in the first illustration, and into an increase in scholastic attainment in the second example.

In order to obtain the most return from an intervention, it is vital that the variable chosen for manipulation be prior to most of the conditions which one is interested in altering. Thus, in the first example, if one improves the state of health of an individual by bringing exogenous factors to bear which impinge directly on health—providing vitamin pills rather than raising income—only the variables subsequent to state of health (the individual's work performance) will be improved by the manipulation. By intervening earlier in the causal sequence, however (in this illustration by raising family income), a large number of factors can be altered *without particular attention having to be given to these disabilities.* From the perspective of altering the behavioral concomitants of poverty, then, an income maintenance program represents an assumption as to the causal ordering, namely that family income is causally prior to many of the other elements in the constellation of poverty characteristics.[2]

There is another form of causal explanation, often employed in studies of the intergenerational transmission of poverty, in which it is less apparent that the link at which the intervention should occur is material. We refer to the "cycle of poverty" explanations (The Negro Family, 1965: 47; House Committee on Education and Labor, 1964: 49). If a causal sequence can be closed by adding links to connect the final and initial variables (in the first illustration, low capacity to work can be linked to inadequate income in the succeeding time period; in the second, low academic attainment implies poor labor market situation which results in inadequate income) then, theoretically, intervention can be made at any link with a consequent improvement in the levels of all factors. In practice, however, even where a cycle provides a valid representation of reality,[3] the selection of a variable for manipulation remains an important decision because the cost of intervention can differ considerably

---

[2] Likewise, alternative proposals for combating poverty—job training, more effective schooling, maintaining a tight labor market—represent different assumptions as to the causal ordering.

[3] It should be noted that where a cycle of poverty explanation is appropriate, the relationships must necessarily be nonlinear. For example, in the first illustration, after a certain period of time a unit increase in an individual's level of health must have a negligible impact on his work performance. Otherwise, the system of relationships would "explode," resulting in infinite health and commensurate income.

by link, and because societal values are more permissive of some manipulations (e.g., raising educational attainment, income maintenance) than of others (e.g., limiting family size).

More complex situational explanations can be represented as path models. Recent empirical work on the interrelations among poverty associated characteristics have used this methodology (Duncan, 1969; Duncan and Duncan, 1968; and Featherman and Duncan, 1968). It must be recognized that the use of a causal methodology such as a recursive system of equations represents an *assumption* regarding the validity of a situational explanation. A path model enables the variation in the dependent variable to be partitioned among the several paths (causal sequences). Only rarely, however, can the suitability of the underlying causal framework be tested.[4]

There is a considerable literature, both theorizing and research, in support of a situational explanation for the behavioral and attitudinal correlates of poverty. In a now classic essay, Robert Merton (1957) introduced a fivefold typology relating the goals pursued by individuals to the means employed. Merton contends that where the societal goals are accepted but the sanctioned means are unavailable, an innovative response—the use of illicit means—is likely to ensue. Applying this perspective to the poor, it would appear that precisely the individuals who subscribe to the middle-class conception of success—wealth and its appurtenances, to put matters crudely—would be most likely to resort to illegitimate means. Conversely, if well-paid and steady work were available in the "respectable labor market," the muggers and pimps could presumably be enticed away from their current vocations.

Support for a situational perspective is also provided by Miller, Riessman, and Seagull (1968). Miller and his colleagues argue that while impulse following and a preference for immediate gratification are characteristics of lower-class life styles, this behavior derives from the opportunity structure facing the poor, rather than from distinctive cultural values on their part. For a middle-class person the world is orderly and stable, making an investment in the future relatively secure and economically rational. By comparison, the present-time orientation of poor persons is a calculated response to an unstable reward structure, a world

---

[4] Sewell Wright's comment (1960a) on the interpretation of a path coefficient which is greater than one is suggestive of the operation of negative feedback and may provide a test for this condition. Wright (1960a: 194–95) writes, "Such a value shows at a glance that direct action of the factor in question is tending to bring about greater variability than is actually observed. The direct effect must be offset by opposing correlated effects of other factors." Compare this statement with the discussion pertaining to Figure 1 in this paper.

characterized by garnishment and unemployment. In this circumstance, one might well choose to get his kicks while he could rather than plan for extensive gratification in the future. Thus, in this view, it is not so much different orientations to time which account for the differential class tendency to invest in the future as it is the different future of the poor and the affluent.

Elliot Liebow (1967), in a study of Negro men who hang out at a particular street corner, provides compelling descriptive evidence for the impact of the opportunity structure on their behavior, although in values and attitudes toward work the men are essentially middle class. Liebow argues that the lethargy and uninterest these individuals bring to the job is due to their *acceptance* of the dominant societal values toward work. The jobs which they have access to are, typically, "hard, dirty, un-interesting and underpaid" (Liebow, 1967: 58). More importantly, they are dead-end jobs, not stepping-stones to better positions even for those who are willing to do them faithfully. "The busboy or dishwasher in a restaurant is not on a job track which, if negotiated skillfully, leads to chef or manager of the restaurant. The busboy or dishwasher who works hard becomes, simply, a hard-working busboy or dishwasher" (Liebow, 1967: 63). The disdain which these men have toward their work, then, is no different from the view which middle-class individuals accord to these same positions; they are accurately reflecting the values of the society.

These works are illustrative of research supporting a view of poverty which attributes the behavioral characteristics of poor persons to their material situation. The poor are not seen as carriers of an independent culture with values and aspirations that are at variance with those of middle class society. Rather, their behavior deviates from established norms because the application of the societal values to their circumstance leads to different results. One immediate implication of situational theory for income maintenance is that the characteristics of low-income indi-viduals which are causally subsequent to income level will respond to a change in this variable. Indeed, it is expected that the resulting adap-tation would approximate middle class mores since, by assumption in this explanation, the values of the poor are not different from those of more affluent persons.

However, situational theory does not suggest what the waiting time would be for a particular response to income maintenance to develop. It is basically a theory of static relationships and rarely directs attention to the dynamic behavior of the adjustment process. Assuming the ap-propriateness of the situational assumption, other questions which must be addressed, in order to construct a particular situational explanation, concern the location of the income variable in the causal sequence, and the manner in which the linkage among variables differs by individual. These and related matters which impinge upon income maintenance are discussed after the logic of the cultural explantions has been outlined.

B. Cultural Explanations

The main contrary thesis to situational explanations is represented by the cultural theories. In this perspective, individuals living in poverty share distinctive values and aspirations which set them apart from the dominant culture. Some of the values which are characteristic of this subculture are action seeking, impulse following, a strong present-time orientation, belief in luck or fate, and a predisposition toward authoritarianism (Lewis, 1966: xlviii). As derivative attributes, individuals subscribing to these values are generally hostile toward education (which is incompatible with action seeking and an orientation toward present-time gratification) and unable to identify with a job as a career.

Culture of poverty explanations, like much of functional theory, are weak in their ability to account for the emergence of the culture. The commonly presented view is that a poverty culture originates when a population has been economically depressed for a very long period of time (Lewis, 1966: xliv). In this situation, values and aspirations develop which allow the population to achieve some modicum of success or status even in their deprived state. Individuals decide that the really important goals are ones which they can attain, that the standards according to which they should measure themselves are ones which they can reasonably compete for. Albert Cohen (1955: 121) describes the adolescent gang culture in this vein: "Certain children are denied status in the respectable society because they cannot meet the criteria of the respectable status system. The delinquent subculture deals with these problems by providing criteria of status which these children can meet."

One assumption common to cultural explanations is that the values originating in this manner attain an existence which is relatively independent of the situational considerations which gave them birth. Daniel Moynihan suggests such a development in his controversial work on the Negro family. Moynihan is concerned with "whether the impact of economic disadvantage on the Negro community has gone on for so long that genuine structural change has occurred, so that a reversal in the course of economic events will no longer produce the expected response in social areas" (Moynihan, 1966: 155). He suggests that "three centuries of injustice have brought about deep-seated structural distortions in the life of the Negro American. At this point, the present tangle of pathology is capable of perpetuating itself without assistance from the white world" (The Negro Family, 1965: 47). It is not our intention here to enter into a discussion concerning the substantive merit of his argument,[5] only to illustrate a typical presentation of the origin of a culture of poverty.[6]

The essential feature of a culture of poverty argument is that the value structure forms a self-maintaining system which perpetuates itself from generation to generation. By a self-maintaining value system we mean one in which the dominant norms and aspirations are accepted by members of the group, are interrelated in such a way as to sustain one another in an individual's internal organization of values, and are reinforced through social pressure upon deviants in the value setting institutions of the group (e.g., family, street-corner gang). The most explicit formal representation of a self-maintaining system, or functional relationship, is given by Stinchcombe (1968). (See also Coleman [1968: 439] on a methodology for analyzing functional relationships.) In this conceptualization, a particular variable (the homeostatic variable) is maintained at a constant level due to the activity of a negative feedback structure despite the action of forces attempting to alter it (exogenously induced change).

We can illustrate this arrangement by considering how an income support program might fail to produce a particular consequence such as raising the scholastic performance of children. Normally, an increase in disposable income would be expected to promote higher academic attainment by children in the household (presumably through the intervening variables discussed earlier in the illustrative causal chain). However, if an adolescent belongs to a peer group which rewards manliness, emphasizes immediate gratification, and scorns scholastic interests, then we might expect the exertion of peer group pressure to offset the increased opportunity to concentrate on academic concerns. Figure 1 illustrates this situation. The improvement in scholastic performance which is expected from income maintenance (positive effect) induces peer-group pressure in opposition to this activity (positive effect) which, in turn, compels the child to reduce his involvement with education (negative effect), main-

---

[5] For extensive commentaries on Moynihan's analysis, see Rainwater and Yancy (1967) or Valentine (1968).

[6] To our knowledge, Moynihan never explicitly claims that a coherent culture with institutionalized values has come into existence as a result of the many years of deprivation and neglect. He speaks of *structural changes* which are capable of *perpetuating themselves*, terms which are suggestive of a cultural explanation. They are also consistent, however, with a "psychological maiming" argument (see following section) which does not assume the presence of autonomous cultural standards.

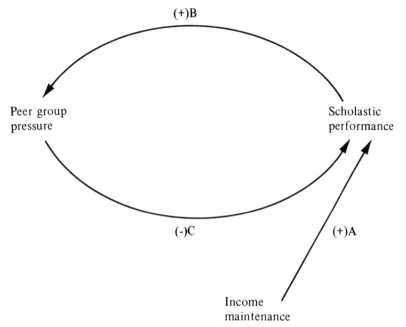

Figure 1. Illustration of a functional explanation

taining scholastic performance at near its original level. Assuming magnitudes of the individual effects equalling A, B, and C as indicated in Figure 1, it can be shown (Stinchcombe, 1968: 136–38) that the net contribution from an income change of magnitude A upon scholastic performance will equal $A(1 - BC)$. Since C is negative, the denominator of the fraction is greater than 1 and $A(1 - BC) < A$, the effect which is expected from income maintenance in a simple causal relation.[7]

In this manner, the interrelations within the value system and the presence of cultural institutions which support the traditional values can offset exogenously induced change and inhibit the effect one would expect from a causal relationship. This is one essential notion of the culture of poverty concept. A second relates to the process by which poverty is perpetuated. The preceding discussion of situational explanations suggested that the intergenerational inheritance of poverty could result from children having to adapt to the same environment as their

---

[7] As Figure 1 suggests, nonrecursive path models would probably provide an appropriate methodology for studying the effects of cultural factors on the perpetuation of poverty. No empirical work of this nature is known to the authors. For a discussion of the relevant methods consult Wright (1960b).

parents before them, and making similar adjustments. In a culture of poverty explanation, by comparison, the transmission is through socialization of the young into the value system of their parents. Oscar Lewis writes, "By the time slum children are age six or seven, they have usually absorbed the basic values and attitudes of their subculture and are not psychologically geared to take full advantage of changing conditions or increased opportunities which may occur in their lifetime" (Lewis, 1966: xiv).

According to a culture of poverty argument, then, a set of values has come into existence (perhaps as an adaptation to having lived in poverty for a long period) which discourages certain behavior such as investing time in education or developing a career orientation toward work. Were social agencies to intervene and increase the payoff or the probability of a return from these actions (by providing income maintenance to make the future more determinate and deferral of gratification more rational) the cultural values which support the status quo would be stressed by the traditional institutions of the group. Supplementing the effects from socialization to these values, individuals would be reminded of their obligations to kin, friends, and tradition, and thereby socially pressured to refrain from adopting life styles which are disvalued in the culture.[8] As a consequence, one implication of a cultural explanation of poverty for income maintenance programs is that the behavioral correlates of low income may prove intractable to these manipulations and have to be treated directly. This, incidentally, is the type of policy recommendation which Daniel Moynihan makes in his assessment of the Negro family structure (The Negro Family, 1965) and, in the context of a cultural explanation, it is an appropriate conclusion.

C. Conceptual Distinctions Between These Explanations

In practice, circumstances in which a situational explanation provides an appropriate assessment for why individuals remain in poverty can be difficult to distinguish from ones in which a cultural explanation is valid. One reason is that "psychological maiming" may have occurred, and this would prevent individuals from responding to a change in conditions (such as might be provided by income maintenance) although one would predict such response from the values which they hold.

---

[8] These mechanisms of social control are common to religious sects which try to maintain unambiguous boundaries between themselves and the secular society. Neither the Amish nor many Hasidic groups (Poll 1962: 147) would be likely to encourage university education for their youth even if it were offered free.

Psychological maiming refers to the complete demoralization of an individual as a result of repeated failure in the main institutions of society. For example, Liebow reports that the experience of being a drop-out from school, continually having difficulty in finding satisfying work, and failing to adequately support one's family often generates low self-esteem and a fear of being tested. "Convinced of their own inadequacies, not only do they not seek out those few better paying jobs which test their resources, but they actively avoid them, gravitating in a mass to the menial, routine jobs which offer no challenge—and therefore pose no threat—to the already diminished images they have of themselves" (Liebow, 1967: 54).

In this circumstance, the values to which the individual is socialized are those of the dominant culture, yet his ability to respond to an altered situation is drastically impaired. In Merton's paradigm, the condition is one of withdrawal or retreatism (Merton, 1957: 153), and is exemplified by the "disreputable poor," the dregs, drifters, and hoboes. According to Gans (1969: 224–34), persons in this circumstance must be aided in reestablishing a link between values and behavior. "How much security, economic and other, must be provided for how long before people can take the risk of grasping at new opportunities and be able to give up present behavioral norms and associations?" Thus the failure of an ex-pected response to result from a change in environment can result either when a causal explanation is correct but the linkage between the variables has been attenuated (psychological maiming), or when a functional (cultural) explanation is appropriate and the variable of interest is maintained at an approximately constant level through negative feedback.

Second, in circumstances for which a situational explanation is appropriate, the time to adjustment following the introduction of income maintenance may be considerable, incorrectly suggesting the operation of cultural values and aspirations which counter the requisite behavior for exploiting new conditions. However, the essence of a situational ex-planation is not that adjustments to an exogenous change are immediate, but that there are no negative feedback structures which impede the adjustment. Thus, some behavioral correlates of low income, such as an inability to defer gratification, may be slow to disappear because poor persons may require several years of evidence that the income support payments are not a transitory phenomenon. Other possible adjustments, such as an increase in educational attainment by the family head, are unlikely to ever develop, even in the absence of cultural interference. The location of these individuals in the life cycle no longer permits a major response on this dimension. Unfortunately, existing analyses of adjust-ments to exogenously induced change rarely consider the dynamic aspects of the response (see Lieberson and Fuguitt [1967] for a contrary instance). These studies are largely cross-sectional and focus on changes in the equilibrium relationships.

Third, even where a cultural explanation is appropriate, by drastically altering the environment a *causal* response to the manipulated variable can often be effected. A self-regulating system such as a culture can maintain behavioral patterns homeostatically only for limited ranges of exogenously induced change. Therefore, concerning culturally supported behavior, the appropriate question is not whether it can be altered by exogenous manipulations but how extensive an input would be necessary. What is required is either a disintegration of the cultural values which normally prevent the response, which will occur if the traditional patterns are no longer viable in the altered context, or a readjustment of the culture to a new equilibrium in which the intended behavior is sanctioned (redefinition of the values). If alternative adaptations to a new situation are few, it is likely that the equilibrium would be in the direction of the dominant societal values since these represent one adaptation with which all individuals have some familiarity. To illustrate, it may not be necessary to treat the instability of the Negro family directly, as Moynihan (1966) contends. Even accepting his evidence concerning the lack of responsiveness of the Negro family's stability to economic conditions, an *extensive* alteration of employment opportunities and the welfare structure may accomplish this purpose if it makes the matrifocal family less viable.

III. ELABORATIONS AND IMPLICATIONS FOR RESEARCH ON INCOME MAINTENANCE

In the preceding sections we have reviewed the logic of the main types of poverty theories and have indicated some immediate inferences to be drawn for an income maintenance program. However, the discussion has been superficial in two ways. First, we have not differentiated among the various groups of persons in poverty to allow for the possibility that while a situational explanation may be appropriate to the circumstance of some, a cultural explanation may provide more accurate predictions of the response by others. Second, explanations should probably be behavior specific as well as population specific. As Gans (1969: 209) has pointed out, it is a mistake to view culture as a holistic system. In any culture some areas of behavior will tap few values or mores and therefore will respond situationally to exogenous interventions, while in other areas the culture will rigidly prescribe what is appropriate behavior.

Some early researchers into the relation between culture and poverty conceived of a universal poverty culture. Oscar Lewis, who has presented the most elaborate version of this type of explanation to account for the behavioral characteristics of low income individuals, argued that a poverty culture exists which "transcends regional, urban-rural, and national differences" (O. Lewis. 1966: xlviii). While this contention of universality is probably extravagant[9] (Clark, 1965; Liebow, 1967; H. Lewis, 1968: 441), the reaction to the contrary evidence has been to discount the possibility that culture plays any role in the perpetuation of poverty. However, refuting the universality of this concept does not mean that culture is unimportant in every instance of poverty. What has been neglected is precisely the research which would permit specification of the range of conditions under which a cultural explanation is likely to be appropriate.

It is hardly controversial to claim that a diversity of groups live in poverty, and that much of the interindividual variation in response to an antipoverty program is likely to be explained by the group means. In designing income maintenance programs, for example, allowance is commonly made for different responses (in the size of the work disincentive, in educational investment) according to whether the family head is male or female, able-bodied or incapacitated, young or approaching retirement age. Our contention here is that *social* groupings will also differentiate among persons in their response to income maintenance and, furthermore, that cultural explanations will be appropriate for some of these groups, situational explanations for others. The importance of investigating the variance in the response is that alternate programs may be necessary to meet the needs of individuals who are unresponsive to an income support arrangement. To the extent that different groups can be associated with one or another of these theories (with respect to particular behavioral characteristics) their adjustments to income maintenance should be more predictable.

One factor which is likely to influence an individual's adaptation to income maintenance is ethnicity. Writing about the West Enders, an

---

[9] The lack of precision in Lewis's discussion on the geographic location of poverty cultures makes testing the validity of the universality concept an impossible affair. According to him the poverty culture is (1) universal, yet (2) does not apply to all poor persons (Lewis 1966: xlviii). Logically, a contention of this sort can never be rejected. It would be correct if the poor in only one nation exhibited the characteristics of the poverty culture, and even if the poor in no nation had these traits. Lewis does state conditions under which the poverty culture is likely to develop (Lewis 1966: xlviii), but even in these circumstances it characterizes only a small proportion of the poor (e.g., 20 percent of the poor in America [Lewis 1966: li]). The culture of poverty therefore seems to be universal in the sense that it exists wherever it exists.

Italian community in Boston, Herbert Gans maintains that work, for them, is primarily a means of obtaining income in order to maximize the pleasures of life within the family circle—type of work and considerations of job advancement are of secondary importance. "Achievement and social mobility, for example, are group phenomena. In the current generation, in which the Italian is still effectively limited to blue-collar work, atypical educational and occupational mobility by the individual is frowned upon" (Gans, 1962: 39).

The West Enders provide an example of an ethnic culture which would appear to retard economic mobility since group pressure functions to discourage exceptional attainment. However, an ethnic culture could also support this goal. The dominant Jewish-American and Japanese-American cultures are cases in point. In each, economic achievement and occupational status in the external society are encouraged by the group's values and also rewarded within the ethnic society.[10]

More generally, there is considerable evidence that ethnic affiliation is an important component of social mobility, although there is some doubt as to whether the influence operates primarily through cultural values, or is a residue of the economic opportunities which were available to an immigrant group upon arrival to this country. There are reasons to believe that cultural factors play at least some part. Duncan and Duncan (1968), using data which identify the country of origin for native white males of immigrant fathers, report that after controlling for father's SES (education and occupation), some 2.8 grades of schooling still separate the mean scores of the highest achieving and lowest achieving national-origin groups. "Membership in a particular national-origin group can rather clearly constitute a substantial 'handicap' or 'bonus' in the stratification process" apart from the class of social origin (Duncan and Duncan, 1968: 360). Comparable findings are reported by Katzman (1969) in an analysis of the economic position of fourteen ethnic groups: "The educational attainment of the second generation is only weakly related to metropolitan educational opportunities and the educational level of their parents. Consequently, we interpret intergenerational gains as an expression of subcultural values" (Katzman, 1969: 365).

The intention of the above comments was to indicate that ethnicity

---

[10] An illustration of high occupational attainment in the external society being disvalued within an ethnic group is given by Poll. After indicating that the norms of the Hasidic community in Williamsburg discourage Hasidic youth from law training, he writes: "The lawyer is considered a somewhat despicable person. His services are not sought if it can be at all prevented" (Poll, 1962: 150). For an ethnic group to be socially mobile it would seem necessary that a substantial portion of the occupational statuses which are rewarded in the external culture also be accorded prestige within the ethnic group.

may differentiate among persons in many areas of response to an income maintenance program. Extrapolating from the cited material we would suggest the following propositions:

(1) The *variability* of the response across individuals will be smaller among members of an ethnic group in which the traditional culture remains intact (in the sense of retaining distinctive values and institutions) than among individuals who lack an ethnic identity or for whom ethnicity no longer corresponds to a distinctive subculture in America.

(2) Although the presence of an ethnic culture should reduce the within-group variance, the *direction and magnitude* of departure of the group mean from the average response by all persons in the program will reflect the particular cultural values. Consequently, among ethnic groups for whom cultural values influence the response to income maintenance we can expect characteristic, and different, average group responses. Among individuals for whom the adaptation is situational rather than cultural we can expect only a large variance in individual response.[11]

These propositions must be qualified in two ways. First, as was indicated earlier, it is likely that with any ethnic group some behavioral correlates of poverty will be best approached through one type of theory, other characteristics through the second type of explanation. Second, the category of individuals upon whom the cultural mores tend to fall most heavily will probably differ by ethnic group. The constraints may be most severe on adult behavior, permitting children considerable flexibility in responding to altered conditions, or they may apply most rigidly to females, restricting their behavior, for example, as secondary wage earners. Research should therefore be directed at determining for which categories of persons, among ethnic groups with large numbers in poverty, behavior is likely to be prescribed by cultural mores, and what kinds of behavior are most likely to be so governed.

In the above discussion we have argued that ethnicity is likely to condition an individual's response to income maintenance in many important ways as it relates to whether his adaptation will be culturally specified or a situational adjustment. A second consideration involves the demographic and organizational characteristics of poor neighborhoods since these factors will affect the strength of the cultural norms which can be exerted by an ethnic group.

In order for a culturally distinctive group to effectively control

---

[11] It is not possible to distinguish the "psychological maiming" thesis from a cultural explanation by examining the response pattern in this manner. A small variance with a weak group response would result under "psychological maiming" or where cultural values operate to hinder the situationally expected response. To determine the appropriate explanation in this circumstance one must examine the internal organization of the group.

behavior it is necessary that an unambiguous rule exist for deciding when the norms of the external system are to be followed, and when the norms of the subculture are operative. Were this not the case, individuals would constantly find themselves cross-pressured, faced with contradictory specifications for behavior. Residential segregation provides one common way for avoiding this dilemma since the operation of the ethnic culture can be tied to geographic boundaries. Moreover, the fact that one resides with others of the same culture permits interpersonal pressure in support of the group's values to be exerted upon a deviant individual, especially when population turnover in the neighborhood is low so that social bonds are stable. Extrapolating from these considerations, we can scale the likely ability of an ethnic group to effectively control behavior according to the following structural characteristics of a neighborhood:

High cultural control over behavior (1)	(2)	(3)	Low cultural control over behavior (4)
Single ethnic group in a neighborhood; stable population	Single ethnic group; geographically mobile population	Multi-ethnic neighborhood; stable population for the ethnic group under consideration	Multi-ethnic neighborhood; mobile population for the ethnic group under consideration

Holding neighborhood composition constant, a major determinant of a group's extent of control over its membership lies in its degree of institutional completeness (diversity of formal ethnic organizations). Residential segregation provides a setting which is conducive to the emergence of ethnic institutions—ethnic schools, churches, newspapers, and social clubs. However, the diversity of organizations which actually develops in a neighborhood will differ by ethnic group, reflecting such considerations as the magnitude of differences between the ethnic and native cultures (Breton, 1964). To the extent that these organizations do proliferate, an individual will have more of his social needs satisfied within the neighborhood, be embedded more thoroughly in ethnic networks, and be less likely to violate the expectations of the group. Such an argument suggests, for example, that the response to income maintenance by poor Italians (commonly an institutionally complete ethnic group) would be more closely governed by ethnic values and norms than would be the adjustment by poor Negroes (for whom ethnic institutions are less diverse).

In determining the response to an income maintenance program, these neighborhood characteristics would probably interact with ethnic membership in the following way: where an ethnic group does not place constraints on a behavioral response—deciding whether the wife should seek employment, for instance—the neighborhood social structure would be largely irrelevant to behavior. However, in cases where the ethnic values function either to prevent or encourage a particular adaptation, the organization of the neighborhood should be an important intervening consideration.

In the above discussion we have presented instances in which cultural groups are likely to influence the response to an exogenous intervention such as would be represented by income maintenance. The fact that an ethnic group may impede certain adjustments to income maintenance does not imply that the individuals actually desire to be poor. Rather, it is that the responses which are necessary in order to emerge from poverty are usually individualistic and detrimental to group cohesion, and may conflict with the values and mores which are central in the culture.

IV. CONCLUSIONS

In the economic literature on income maintenance (Green, 1968; Kesselman, 1969), the analysis of work disincentives and other effects from income manipulation proceeds as if, aside from universalistic considerations such as gender and physical condition of the family head, the poverty population can be treated as a homogeneous group. In this paper we have attempted to demonstrate the deficiency of that simplification. It is our contention that the diversity of adaptations to income maintenance which are likely to ensue cannot be adequately understood unless account is taken of the distinct social groups in poverty, and of the different mechanisms which can maintain persons in that state.

Field experimentation with income maintenance is designed to answer a number of questions such as which behavioral correlates of poverty will respond to this intervention, what will be the time rate of response by different characteristics and, more generally, how should limited financial resources be allocated to maximize the rate at which individuals are removed from economic dependency. An appreciation of the different mechanisms through which persons are maintained in poverty is important to this enterprise for two reasons. This would allow for more efficient programming, enabling the range of response by different groups to be predicted beforehand. Also, if antipoverty programs are to actually move persons to self-sufficiency and not merely maintain them above the poverty line, then an understanding of the diverse social contexts in which poor persons are embedded is a necessary preliminary for designing successful interventions.

V. REFERENCES

Breton, Raymond. 1964. "Institutional Completeness of Ethnic Communities and the Personal Relations of Immigrants," *American Journal of Sociology* 70 (September), 193–205.

Clark, Kenneth B. 1965. *Dark Ghetto: Dilemmas of Social Power.* New York: Harper.

Cohen, Albert K. 1955. *Delinquent Boys.* New York: Free Press.

Coleman, James S. 1968. "The Mathematical Study of Change," in H. M. Blalock and A. B. Blalock (eds.), *Methodology in Social Research.* New York: McGraw-Hill.

Duncan, O. D. 1969. "Inheritance of Poverty or Inheritance of Race?" in Daniel Moynihan (ed.), *On Understanding Poverty.* New York: Basic Books.

———, and Beverly Duncan. 1968. "Minorities and the Process of Stratification," *American Sociological Review* 33 (June), 356–64.

———, David L. Featherman, and Beverly Duncan. 1968. *Socioeconomic Background and Occupational Achievement: Extensions of a Basic Model.* Washington, D.C.: U.S. Department of Health, Education, and Welfare, Office of Education.

Elesh, David, Jack Ladinsky, M. J. Lefcowitz, and Seymour Spilerman. 1971. "The New Jersey-Pennsylvania Experiment: A Field Study in Negative Taxation," this volume.

Gans, Herbert. 1962. *The Urban Villagers.* New York: Macmillan.

———. 1969. "Culture and Class in the Study of Poverty: An Approach to Anti-Poverty Research," in Daniel Moynihan (ed.), *On Understanding Poverty.* New York: Basic Books.

Green, Christopher. 1968. "Negative Taxes and Monetary Incentives to Work: The Static Theory," *Journal of Human Resources* 3 (Summer), 280–88.

House Committee on Education and Labor. 1966. "1964: A Report." In Hanna H. Meissner (ed.), *Poverty in the Affluent Society.* New York: Harper & Row, pp. 43–67.

Katzman, Martin T. 1969. "Opportunity, Subculture and the Economic Performance of Urban Ethnic Groups," *American Journal of Economics and Sociology* 28 (October), 351–66.

Kesselman, Jonathon. 1969. "Labor-Supply Effects of Income, Income-Work, and Wage Subsidies," *Journal of Human Resources* 4 (Summer), 275–92.

Lewis, Hylan. 1968. "Child Rearing among Low Income Families," in L. Ferman, J. Kornbluh, and A. Haber (eds.), *Poverty in America.* Ann Arbor: University of Michigan Press.

Lewis, Oscar. 1966. *La Vida.* New York: Vintage Press.

Lieberson, Stanley, and Glen Fuguitt. 1967. "Negro-White Occupational Differences in the Absence of Discrimination," *American Journal of Sociology* 73 (September), 188–200.

Liebow, Elliot. 1967. *Tally's Corner.* Boston: Little, Brown & Co.

Merton, Robert. 1957. "Social Structure and Anomie," in *Social Theory and Social Structure.* New York: Free Press, pp. 131–60.

Miller, S. M., Frank Riessman, and Arthur A. Seagull. 1968. "Poverty and Self-Indulgence: A Critique of the Non-Deferred Gratification Pattern," in Louis A. Ferman, Joyce L. Kornbluh, and Alan Haber (eds.), *Poverty in America.* Ann Arbor: University of Michigan Press, pp. 416–32.

Moynihan, Daniel. 1966. "Employment, Income, and the Ordeal of the Negro Family," in Talcott Parsons and Kenneth B. Clark (eds.), *The Negro American.* Boston: Beacon Press, pp. 134–59.

The Negro Family. 1965. U.S. Department of Labor. Washington, D.C.: U.S. GPO.

Poll, Solomon. 1962. *The Hasidic Community.* New York: Free Press.

Rainwater, Lee and William L. Yancy. 1967. *The Moynihan Report and the Politics of Controversy.* Cambridge: M.I.T. Press.

Stinchcombe, Arthur. 1968. *Constructing Social Theories.* New York: Harcourt, Brace and World.

Valentine, Charles A. 1968. *Culture and Poverty.* Chicago: University of Chicago Press.

Wright, Sewell. 1960a. "Path Coefficients and Path Regression: Alternative or Complementary Concepts?" *Biometrics* 16 (June), 189–202.

————. 1960b. "The Treatment of Reciprocal Interaction, with or without Lag, in Path Analysis," *Biometrics* 16 (September), 423–45.

PROVISION OF SOCIAL SERVICES TO RECIPIENTS OF INCOME MAINTENANCE

Irving Piliavin

I. INTRODUCTION

The association between public assistance and social service for the poor dates back virtually to the inception of public assistance itself. Yet the consequences of this association for those who supply assistance and service, as well as those who receive it, has been given appallingly little attention. Given this historical relationship, the design of an income maintenance program should include specification of the relevance of social services for the poor, the appropriate delivery system for such services, and the proper providers of the services.

This paper focuses on the question of whether or not the provision of social services should remain tied to the public assistance program, as at present. An experimental design for testing various modes of service delivery is proposed.

II. CURRENT STATE OF KNOWLEDGE

Social service workers currently operating in public assistance programs have a variety of responsibilities, among the more important of which have been:

1. The assessment of eligibility and appropriate budget for applicants for public aid and the periodic review and budget determination of current recipients.

2. The provision of direct rehabilitative services (counseling, advice, support, information) to assist recipients in performing their social

214

roles and coping with problems which otherwise they might not be able to handle.

3. The referral of welfare recipients and members of their families to a variety of community agencies (health, child care, etc.), whose rehabilitative services are presumed to help clients perform their social roles.

The degree to which social service workers have been successful in meeting any of the above responsibilities is uncertain. While there is some indication that fraud is not very prevalent among public assistance recipients, data collected to date indicate this is not due to the diligence of social service workers. Hoshino[1] reports, for example, that, under a declaration system where worker surveillance is minimal, there is little apparent increase in fraud among welfare applicants. On the other hand, there are data which indicate that some social service workers in public assistance agencies engage in their own fraud in that they illegally deny, curtail, or discontinue financial aid to recipients.[2]

Studies of the rehabilitative impact of the efforts of social service workers in public agencies have been limited in number and, frequently, quality. Some of these studies have indicated that intensive casework (the primary mode of operation among public assistance workers) increases discontinuance rates and improves family functioning. However, the one well-designed study in this group, investigating the impact of relatively intensive social work services provided by two professionally trained social workers, reveals no significant differences between the results obtained by these workers and those obtained through less intensive efforts by nonprofessionals.[3] While an investigation of two workers is hardly even an exploratory study, the results obtained are generally in line with the few other reasonably well-designed experimental studies of the consequences of professionally provided casework services.[4]

Despite these negative findings, a number of considerations suggest

---

[1] G. Hoshino, "Simplification of the Means Test and Its Consequences," *Social Service Review,* Vol. 41 (September 1967), pp. 237–49.

[2] Greenleigh Associates, *Facts, Fallacies and Future: A Study of the AFDC Program of Cook County, Illinois* (New York: Greenleigh Associates, 1960).

[3] G. Brown, *The Multi-Problem Dilemma* (Metuchen, N.J.: Scarecrow Press, 1968).

[4] J. Meyer, E. F. Borgatta, and W. C. Jones, *Girls at Vocational High* (New York: Russell Sage Foundation, 1965); J. W. Wrightstone et al., *Evaluation of the Higher Horizons Program for Underprivileged Children* (New York: Bureau of Educational Research, Board of Education of the City of New York, 1964); J. Meyer and E. F. Borgatta, *An Experiment in Mental Patient Rehabilitation* (New York: Russell Sage Foundation, 1969); New York City Youth Board, "An Experiment in the Use of the Glueck Social Prediction Table as a Prognosticator of Potential Delinquency" (mimeo., 1961).

that it is still too early to conclude that social work services of the type that are given or could be given to recipients of public assistance are of no value. These considerations include the following:

1. The assessment of impact in the studies cited above are problematic. In some studies they are open to serious question because they have been couched in terms which are vague and involve subjective judgments.[5] In other studies, impact assessment has been based on criteria involving major changes in life style including the move from economic dependency to self-sufficiency, and/or from chronic delinquency to conventional behavior.[6] It may be asking too much of casework counseling to effect such major changes in the absence of a host of economic, vocational, health, and other services. Rather, its impact may be more appropriately assessed in less dramatic but nonetheless significant terms, some of which are discussed below.

2. The services whose impact has been studied have been generally rendered to those who did not request them. It is certainly questionable whether provision on this basis could have much effect since service would not be necessarily related to any experienced desire for help.[7]

3. Some social agencies have enormous control over those who receive their services. Under these circumstances client suspicion and fear may counteract whatever benefits could result from service.

4. At least two studies indicate that the orientation of social workers, professional and nonprofessional, is adversely affected by the policing emphasis found in public welfare and correctional agencies.[8] Thus the failure to find that clients of these agencies benefit from casework service may reflect the debilitating influence of the organization rather than the inadequacies of the service.

5. Casework services as provided by professionals in private practice as well as in family service agencies and psychiatric clinics are in strong demand by the middle-class families served by these workers and agencies. Similar services provided to poor families by nonprofessionals in neighborhood service centers and welfare rights organizations also are in some demand.[9] This suggests casework services are relevant in the

---

[5] *Supra* n. 3.

[6] Meyer et al., *supra* n. 4.

[7] I. Piliavin, "Restructuring the Provision of Social Services," *Social Work,* Vol. 13 (January 1968), pp. 34–41.

[8] H. Piven, "Professionalism and Organizational Structure," D.S.W. Thesis, Columbia University School of Social Work, 1961; P. Blau, "Structural Effects," *American Sociological Review,* Vol. 25 (1960), pp. 178–93.

[9] The fact that poor families have received relatively little service from voluntary agencies reflects the traditional belief that they would be more properly served by public welfare agencies.

sense that they tap problems of personal significance and, at least from the consumer's (client) perspective, accomplish something.

In summary, then, one can say very little about social work counseling services other than that a rather substantial number of (primarily middle-class) families and individuals desire them. While such a conclusion may furnish solace to some social work advocates, to many it has been a cause for deep concern. The impact of few enterprises of comparable scope and cost is so little known.

III. IMPACT OF VARIOUS MODES OF PROVIDING CASEWORK SERVICES

The delivery of social services has become an increasing concern of social workers in recent years. Inequalities in the availability of services and conflicting demands on those supplying services are but two of the problems which have led to consideration of new modes of service delivery.

In a fairly recent article, Piliavin[10] has argued that only a total reorganization of the provision of social services could mitigate the vitiating effects of current agency sponsorship of service. The reorganization which was suggested was that social workers withdraw from social agencies and establish private practices. The service reorganization advocated was general. It included services now intended for inmates of prisons and hospitals, middle-class families experiencing marital problems, and, among others, welfare recipients. The system advocated by Piliavin was based on the assumption that such services should be available to all but imposed on no one. That is, the use of social services by anyone, including welfare recipients, criminals, and the mentally ill, should be voluntary. In order that these services be available to all, their costs would have to be borne in large part by government. There are a variety of ways in which this could be done including an insurance system similar in form to the health insurance system in England or to Medicare. The central feature of these services would be that the dominant economic and political interests in the community would have less control over workers' activities. On the one hand this means that nonservice-oriented, punitive, and demeaning activities would no longer be part of workers' jobs and they would be freer to serve the interests of their clients.[11] On the other hand, the lack of community con-

---

[10] *Supra* n. 7.

[11] It has been pointed out that government financing will bring about government control. While this may be true, there is a difference between the kind

trol raises the possibility that private practitioners will overcharge, operate without responsibility to their clients, etc. Presumably these possibilities can be controlled for by quality control procedures, licensing, and, according to Pascal, the competition among practitioners for clients.[12] Additional problems, not insurmountable, would have to be worked out if a private practitioner, government-insured system of providing social services became public policy. These would include the setting of appropriate fees, establishing training facilities, providing for professional standards, etc.

At about the same time that the Piliavin article was published, a number of social workers were beginning to attend to the somewhat narrower concern of social services in public assistance agencies. These workers suggested that social services which are now provided to recipients of public assistance be provided by public welfare workers who have no responsibility in the area of income maintenance. While not all these commentators thought that these services should be supplied only at recipients' requests, those who took this view were expressing a position close to that voiced by Piliavin. A possibly significant difference is that the private delivery system advocated by Piliavin may provide greater autonomy of workers from interest groups and policies which would compromise service features of public welfare. Whether this would in fact be the case can be tested.

Another recent and important change in the provision of social services in poverty areas has been the creation of agencies whose policymakers consist largely of representatives of service recipients. While the programs of these agencies vary, they generally cover a substantial segment of that which is considered social work. Thus these agencies suggest another alternative to the public welfare agency-based social worker, namely the neighborhood agency-based worker.

IV. INDEPENDENT VARIABLES

The alternative modes of service delivery outlined above can be ordered by the degree of workers' freedom to act in behalf of the client. On the

---

of close administrative control operative in welfare agencies and that which would exist over workers in private practice. At the very least, private practitioners would not experience conflict between service and control aspects of their relationship to clients, nor would there be conflict between practitioners and supervisors.

[12] A. Pascal, *New Departures in Social Services* (Santa Monica, Calif.: RAND Corporation, 1969).

basis of our prior discussion, social service workers having income maintenance responsibilities have the least freedom to serve their clients' interests and public welfare social service workers without income maintenance responsibilities have somewhat more freedom. At the other end of the scale, private practitioners are assumed to have the greatest freedom to act in clients' behalf[13] and workers in neighborhood-controlled service centers somewhat less.[14]

If the preceding assumptions are valid, the four modes of service delivery that are described above should have different degrees of benefit for those who receive them. In particular, the ordering of these workers in terms of the service and benefits they provide should be as follows:

1. Public welfare worker with income maintenance responsibilities
2. Public welfare workers without income maintenance responsibilities
3. Neighborhood-controlled agency service worker
4. Private practitioners

Before discussing a possible design and some procedural elements of a study intended to test the above predictions, let us turn briefly to another question. This question is the effect of workers' education on the provision of effective services. The study reported by Brown[15] suggested that professionally trained workers vary little from nontrained workers in the impact their services have on clients. As noted above, the Brown report notwithstanding, the data are still far too meager to allow conclusions on this question. Examination of the relevance of workers' attributes for service impact is easily incorporated in the design of an investigation of service delivery.[16]

Figure 1 portrays the essential design of such a study. The control cell is intended to test the hypothesis that no worker background effects will be observed. It should be noted that, while the worker background variable is specified in Figure 1 in terms of training, it could be specified on other dimensions (e.g., indigenous to community vs. nonindigenous to community). For ease of discussion we will confine ourselves to the dimensions specified in Figure 1.

---

[13] *Supra* nn. 7, 12.

[14] It is probably true that workers' self-interests operate in whatever setting they are located. However, for reasons elaborated in Pascal, it is assumed these interests will tend to work toward the clients' behalf as agency-client interests cease to be in conflict.

[15] *Supra* n. 3.

[16] Some procedural difficulties are encountered. However these do not completely vitiate opportunity to examine the question. These problems will be discussed shortly.

Workers' freedom to serve clients' interests

Worker educational background	None	Little	Moderate	Large
	Worker in income maintenance program	Public welfare worker: no income maintenance responsibilities	Working in neighborhood-controlled service agency	Private practitioners
Professional training	C_{11}	C_{12}	C_{13}	C_{14}
College graduate, no professional training	C_{21}	C_{22}	C_{23}	C_{24}

Control cell: income maintenance and no service

Figure 1. Study of service impact of variations in service delivery and workers' training

V. DEPENDENT VARIABLES: IMPACT MEASURES

It is possible and important to measure two types of impact of the various service provision arrangements depicted in Figure 1. One is the *service impact* of workers' efforts. The other is the client demand impact of workers' efforts.

As indicated earlier in this paper, past efforts to measure service impact are subject to serious criticism in that they either (1) have been based on subjective judgments of questionable validity or (2) have utilized relatively objective criteria of change which reflect major life style changes (e.g., absence of arrests) and may demand too much of social work counseling service. Since these criteria can be used with relatively little expense, they might be used in the proposed study in the hope that some variations of service delivery and worker training will produce major life-style changes. However, they will have to be supplemented by other criteria, some of which will have little if any significance for long-term change. Perhaps an analogy with the service supplied by the physician is appropriate. In the typical case, the patient of the general practitioner seeks help for a temporary problem whose major symptom may be subjectively experienced distress or pain. In the vast majority of such cases the problem will ease even without the aid of the physician and comparison of examination findings some weeks prior to treatment with those some weeks after will reveal little change in the patient's physical condition. Yet an important service is typically rendered in such cases. The period of distress may have been lessened. In consequence, work effort may not have been adversely affected or, perhaps, the patient simply "felt better." Casework services may achieve such "lower-order" consequences even if they do not attain, as does medicine at times, more momentous and striking consequences.

Another consideration in developing service impact criteria follows from the argument of a number of writers that services must deal with problems that clients articulate if they are to be effective.[17] This viewpoint suggests that an important source of information about the consequences of service is the point of view of the client himself in contrast to the "social service expert."

A full specification of criteria relevant to service impact which takes into account "lower-level" achievements and the client's perspective is not yet possible, simply because so little attention has been given them. However, a partial listing for income maintenance recipients might well include: (1) the degree to which these recipients receive the income maintenance benefits to which they are entitled; (2) the number and comparative success of appeals made by recipients relating to welfare agency decisions; (3) the frequency of, and comparative success in, referring recipients to health and community service agencies; (4) the speed with which these agencies provide recipients with requested service; and (5) the recipients' own assessment of the degree to which their problems have been dealt with.[18] Additional criteria for assessing service impact can be obtained by means of a pilot project examining the

---

[17] *Supra* nn. 7, 12.

[18] While it is true that this assessment involved subjective judgment, it is no less valid than the complex judgments made by professional clinicians. On the other hand it has relevance for assessing potential demand for service.

problems presented by clients in social agencies. (Although studies of "presenting problems" may already exist, their appropriateness is questionable because of the tendency for clinicians to conceptualize problems in "deeper," as opposed to client, terms.)

The measurement of *client demand* has yet to be undertaken in relation to social services. In the present context, its significance stems from the aforementioned argument[19] that services should be rendered only to recipients who request them.[20] Supposedly some political jurisdictions are moving in this direction. However the services so supplied will probably be only those of the types indicated in cells C_{21} and C_{22} of Figure 1. According to the Piliavin and Pascal arguments concerning service impact, any demand developing for these services will be demand for the potentially least client oriented and effective social services. Also, the manner in which these services will probably be provided is such as to raise doubt that a valid measure of demand for them is possible.[21] Thus the fact is that, although the idea has developed in many quarters that service should be provided in response to demand, the demand level is not known for any mode of service delivery, level of worker performance, or any other significant characteristic of social service.

Some inroads on this problem could come from the present study. These are a variety of criteria by which demand could be measured. One possibility is simply to count the number of times workers are asked to provide a service by income maintenance recipients. (It will be necessary of course to control for the distance and inconvenience encountered by recipients in obtaining service.) Another is to determine how much service people are willing to buy when service is priced at different levels. Either of these measures could be utilized in the present study.

A. Procedures

One approach for implementing the design in Figure 1 is to assign workers fitting any one cell description to the same geographic area. This homogeneity of service within neighborhoods would help avoid

---

[19] *Supra* nn. 7, 12.

[20] For similar arguments by public policy markers see Assembly Office of Research and Staff of the Assembly Committee on Social Welfare, *California Welfare: A Legislative Program for Reform* (Sacramento: California Legislature, 1969).

[21] Thus in many if not all public welfare agencies some arbitrary limit on the number of workers will be set. Insofar as this limit may lead to high case loads and decreased quality of performance, demand for service will probably decrease from or fail to attain that based on "optimal" service.

comparisons among income maintenance recipients about the quality of service they receive and confusion among them concerning the possibilities of changing of service arrangements. This approach would also control for the inconvenience entailed in obtaining service (e.g., the mean distance traveled across neighborhoods for service would be roughly the same) among neighborhoods; service-area workers could engage in whatever efforts are required to make people conscious of the availability of service and improve the quality of service rendered. It should be noted that, insofar as demand is to be assessed by a count of various kinds of service, the design in Figure 1 can be applied in a straightforward manner. If, however, we wanted to determine demand for various forms of service at different price levels, we would have to replicate each cell of Figure 1 for each of the price levels.[22]

The assignment of personnel to some cells of Figure 1 may offer some problems. For example:

C_{11}—professionals are rarely found in income maintenance programs, particularly in practitioner positions. Special efforts to obtain these workers may fail.

C_{14}—professionals in private practice will be difficult to obtain in small communities, although relatively easy in large urban areas.

C_{24}—nonprofessionals in private practice are rarer than professionals who provide direct services in public assistance agencies (C_{11}).

The research should probably be confined to urban areas, since obtaining personnel for certain cells will be easier because there are already professionally trained social workers in private practice and public agencies within these communities. There is indication that purchase of time from privately practicing workers for service to income recipients should offer no problems.[23] There is an additional advantage of locating the study in urban areas. It has been suggested above that certain advantages will accrue if only one service arrangement is rendered in a given neighborhood. A problem with such a setup is that measurement of impact may be contaminated if variations exist among the neighborhoods within which different service arrangements are provided. There is a good possibility, however, that proper sampling of neighborhoods in a few large urban communities will ease this problem considerably.

---

[22] The suggested experimental assessment of demand in terms of the prices individuals are willing to pay for service is not intended to imply that costs would necessarily be associated with service in a national welfare program.
[23] Communication from the board of directors of the Social Work Treatment Service, Los Angeles.

B. Anticipated Additional Findings

Although the major trend of the proposed research has been described there are two other important questions which it can address.

First the research can provide information about the relationship between individuals' characteristics and their demands for service. At the present time we know little about those who request social service and the institutions which lead them to make their requests. This information would be of considerable value in that it could help determine: (1) how potential demand for social services varies among different ethnic and racial groups in the United States; (2) whether there is any relationship between demand for social services and the experiencing of personal and/or interpersonal problems; and (3) how demand is related to prior experience with social services, etc. Second, the research will be able to reveal whether and why services offered under different delivery systems develop different emphases. The development of different emphases has been predicted elsewhere[24] but for social policy purposes it would be important to know just what form these variations would take. Later studies might seek to test means for enhancing or mitigating certain service trends found in the study discussed here.

C. Costs

A specification of the costs of the study proposed here will not be attempted. However it is important to note that some of the service costs may be absorbed by existing programs. Thus, staff fitting the descriptions of cells C_{11}, C_{12}, C_{21}, and C_{22} could consist of personnel now employed in public welfare agencies. While more careful consideration must be given this possibility, if feasible it would dramatically cut the costs of the proposed study.

---

[24] *Supra* n. 7.

PART FOUR

INTRODUCTION: RESPONSES TO NONFINANCIAL PARAMETERS OF INCOME MAINTENANCE PROGRAMS—AN OVERVIEW

Larry L. Orr

In the previous sections primary attention has been devoted to only two of the many parameters which characterize any given income maintenance program: the income guarantee and the implicit tax rate. This narrow focus is, incidentally, typical of much of the literature in this field. However, a number of other program characteristics may be expected to exert some influence on the behavior of program beneficiaries. Such features as the definitions of income and the family unit, the accounting period, associated work tests, and administrative arrangements may have a crucial bearing upon the response of recipients to the program. A number of these aspects are discussed in the papers included in this section. Others will be briefly noted here, with some indication of their potential significance for public policy. In what follows, I have grouped these issues according to the listing of program parameters which serve as column headings in the behavioral response matrix described in the Introduction to Part One.

Many of the issues discussed below, especially those relating to equity, are not basically research questions in the usual sense, but rather are questions of public policy. Still, an understanding of the policy implications of these features of program structure is essential to competent research in this area. Many of the features of income maintenance raise conflicts between equity and efficiency. These conflicts must be explicitly recognized if they are to be effectively resolved. It is for these reasons that equity issues are included in the present discussion.

I. THE DEFINITION OF INCOME

As in the positive tax system, the concept of "taxable income" can be a potent vehicle for altering the economic behavior of covered individuals, either deliberately or inadvertently. Just as the determination of the tax base constrains the revenue-generating capacity of the system under the positive tax, the income concept selected for an income maintenance program crucially influences the transfer cost of that program. Moreover, in both cases, the definition of income embodies the concept of horizontal equity upon which the program is based; in the former case it is the measure of "ability to pay," and in the latter it is the standard of need.

A strict economic definition of income or need would rest upon the family's command over goods and services during a specified period. For a variety of reasons, however, program definitions tend to be based upon some variant of money income. The disparities between these two concepts are likely to give rise to a number of horizontal inequities in practice. The principal source of such inequities is the large number of individuals who consume goods and services not purchased directly in any market. Examples of such "in-kind" income include the housing services consumed by farmers, and the implicit subsidy enjoyed by beneficiaries of government programs which provide goods and services at no charge or at prices below their market value. The latter include such programs as Medicaid, food stamps, public housing, Head Start, and a variety of others. To provide an accurate measure of economic need, income should be defined to include the market value of in-kind consumption and the implicit subsidy value of in-kind transfers. Such a definition would, of course, raise serious administrative problems, and has been steadfastly rejected by policymakers on those grounds.

The costs of excluding these types of income, in terms of equity and efficiency, ought to be explicitly recognized, however. Their exclusion will result in a disproportionate share of benefits going to less needy families, will increase program costs for a given benefit structure, and will distort economic choices, as, for example, between homeownership and renting, or between farming and other occupations.

Even within the broad concept of money income, there are a number of definitional decisions which may affect equity, cost, and behavior. The problem of allowable deductions from income is an important one.

At the one extreme are obvious costs of earning a living, such as the expenses of a self-employed businessman, which should be deductible. At low incomes, however, work-related expenses tend to merge imperceptibly with consumption. The cost of clothing, transportation, and meals away from home are examples. The approach taken in the proposed Family Assistance Plan is to allow a flat $60 per month exemption against earnings for these expenses. In terms of equity, this is probably an adequate, if crude, adjustment. In terms of program cost, however, it is estimated that this exemption would increase the cost of the program in 1971 by about $650 million. Moreover, the cost of such an earnings exemption tends to rise rapidly as the income guarantee is increased, since it raises the break-even income level by an equivalent amount and greatly expands the coverage of the program. With a $2400 guarantee, for example, a $60 monthly exemption would increase the cost of the program by $2.9 billion.

A unique feature of the Family Assistance Plan is its discrimination between "earned" and "unearned" incomes. While the former would be taxed at 50 percent under the federal program, the latter would be taxed at 100 percent. Adopted as a device for reducing program cost, this provision opens the door for a number of alterations in individual and institutional behavior. For FAP beneficiaries, it would reduce to zero the income value of Social Security, unemployment and workmen's compensation, veterans' benefits, private pensions and savings, rental income, strike benefits, and private charity, to the extent that such income is less than the family's benefit would otherwise have been.

This program feature thus creates a severe disincentive for low-income families to save or invest. It may also have a substantial effect on the policies of private institutions which provide cash benefits for low-income families. Private charities may find that the bulk of their outlays simply displace federal dollars. Pension funds may be induced to adjust their benefit schedules in an attempt to avoid subsidizing low-income families. At present, we have no way of predicting the strength or ultimate consequences of these disincentives.

While there is no apparent justification for discriminating among private sources of income on equity grounds, a case can be made for the 100 percent taxation of other government transfers. If one views existing transfers as income maintenance, then the relevant need standard would be total *private* income, and income maintenance benefits should be defined broadly to include all government transfers. In this view of the world, benefits under any existing program should be fully offset against benefits under a new program. If, on the other hand, one views existing transfers as benefits to which the recipient has earned a right quite apart from his income status (e.g., through past payroll contributions, or military or civilian government services), then these benefits ought to be treated just like any other income in determining need. The ambiguous goals of most existing programs make clear delineation between income maintenance payments and "entitled" benefits exceedingly difficult.

II. THE INCOME ACCOUNTING PERIOD

The period over which income is measured may be as important as the definition of income itself in arriving at an equitable need standard and in conditioning the response of recipients.

The specification of the income accounting period has important implications for horizontal equity among households receiving the same average income over long time periods; payment levels under any particular accounting scheme could vary greatly among such families, depending upon the time-form of their income streams. In addition, the speed of response of payments to changes in family income, and therefore to emergency needs, depends critically upon the accounting period; if benefits are based on a lagged average of past income, as is usually proposed, they will adjust more or less slowly, depending on the length of the lag.

From the viewpoint of behavioral response, the length of the accounting period may affect the recipient's perception of the marginal tax rate and, thus, his work effort. If the worker bases his work effort upon the returns to labor over a fairly short time period, then a short accounting period, with rapid adjustment of payments to changes in earned income, may be perceived as involving a higher tax rate than a longer accounting period with slower adjustment, even when the statutory tax rate on earnings is the same. If this is the case, there is a conflict between the goal of making payments respond rapidly to need and the goal of minimizing the work effort disincentive.

In addition, the definition of the accounting period may create important incentives for recipients to manipulate the timing of their income stream in order to maximize payments. A short accounting period, for example, may induce greater seasonality in work effort.

The often conflicting goals which must be served by an income-accounting system, and ways of mediating these conflicts, are the subject of the paper by Bawden and Kershaw presented in this section. They propose that a basic accounting period of three months be supplemented with a twelve-month "carry-forward" of income above the break-even point, to ensure that equity is preserved on an annual basis. This system allows relatively rapid response to need without sacrifice of horizontal equity. Whether such an accounting period is sufficiently long to minimize the work disincentive of adjustments in benefits to earnings is an empirical question which can only be resolved through further research.

III. DEFINITION OF THE FAMILY UNIT

It has long been recognized that the eligibility criteria for transfer payments in terms of family structure can create strong incentives for change in family structure, e.g., the alleged incentives for family breakup under AFDC, which provides aid only for female-headed families. In general, when eligibility is defined categorically, people will attempt to alter their behavior in order to become categorically eligible.

For example, while the Family Assistance Plan would greatly expand welfare coverage and reduce some of the discriminatory family structure requirements of the old system, it would perpetuate many of the old categorical distinctions. Benefits would still be restricted to families with children. This provides some incentive (up to $1300 per year) for young couples to have their first child earlier than they might otherwise have, and for parents of illegitimate children to marry and keep the child, rather than give it up for adoption. In the light of the conjecture of some demographers that a prime cause of poverty is early marriage and childbearing, these may be very significant adverse effects. Given the loosely structured living arrangements of the poor, the restriction of benefits to families with children may also induce some shifting of children from their natural homes to the homes of childless couples, in order to create new "families" eligible for benefits. The Family Assistance Plan would also continue the long-standing AFDC incentive for marital breakup (albeit in reduced form), since only female-headed families would be eligible for state supplementary payments, which in many cases would be larger than the FAP benefit itself.

Many of the incentives discussed above would be eliminated, or substantially reduced, under a universal income maintenance system covering unrelated individuals and childless couples. Unfortunately, a universal program would introduce other incentives, and some adverse incentives are virtually unavoidable, regardless of the coverage of the program. Indeed, it seems safe to say that there is no such things as "neutrality" with respect to family composition.

For example, a universal program would provide incentives for youths and members of extended families to set up independent households and qualify for benefits. Such incentives could have a very substantial effect on program costs, since these split-offs could occur in families throughout the income spectrum. A particularly dramatic example is the possibility of large numbers of young "hippies" from affluent families living on government support. (While this possibility can be easily exaggerated, it is not the kind of prospect political decisionmakers like to contemplate.) At the opposite end of the age spectrum, there may be a large number of aged individuals for whom the prospect of independence from their families, even at a reduced living standard, would be attractive. While, theoretically, any support these new households receive from their families would be treated as income and partially offset against their benefits, such transactions would be very difficult to monitor.

Quite aside from the question of categorical requirements for eligibility, any income-conditioned transfer system inevitably contains some incentives for alteration of family structure. Any individual whose earnings reduce the family's transfers by more than his marginal income guarantee can increase the total income of the unit as a whole by leaving the family. Under FAP, with marginal guarantees of $300 and a 50 percent tax rate, this would include any secondary earner earning more than $600 per year, as well as family heads. Thus, even if male- and female-headed families were treated identically, there would be financial incentive for desertion among single-earner families above the break-even point. The only way to avoid this incentive would be to define the family unit to include estranged spouses and youths, regardless of whether they contribute to the family's support.

Similarly, there is the question of whether the income of a stepfather should be applied against benefits to his stepchildren. To do so would reduce the (re)marriage prospects of female heads of family (possibly their most promising route out of poverty!), but to do otherwise would raise problems of horizontal equity vis-à-vis intact families.

Another troublesome area in the definition of family is the status of college-age students. The paper by Ribich in this section deals with the interrelated problems concerning students and education. It is often proposed (as in FAP) that youths aged 18–21 attending school away from home be treated as children and part of the family. This is clearly an incentive to continued education, but it may also be deemed inequitable treatment vis-à-vis the poor youth who choose to leave home and work at low wages, if benefits are limited to families with children. Under a universal program, this incentive might actually cut the other way for students who are truly independent of their affluent families; they would be denied benefit on the grounds that their family income was too high.

In nearly all of the cases discussed here, the direction of the response to particular incentives is fairly clear on the basis of a priori theorizing. The quantitative importance of these responses, however, is uncertain in the extreme. Very little research has been undertaken on the influence of financial incentives upon family structure. Even the long-standing allegations of the incentives for marital instability under AFDC have never been adequately tested empirically. While one tends to feel that many of these incentives will have only a negligible impact under the type and level of transfer programs currently being considered, their significance will surely increase as coverage is expanded and benefit levels rise in the future. The area of effects on family structure, therefore, presents a number of opportunities for empirical research.

IV. ADMINISTRATIVE FEATURES
OF THE PROGRAM

The ultimate outcome of any income maintenance system, in terms of behavioral response, equity, cost, and coverage, will be strongly conditioned by the administrative features of the program. Indeed, some of the strongest objections to the current welfare system are directed not as much at its benefit structure as at the arbitrary, inefficient, and demeaning way in which it is administered. It is widely agreed that one of the primary goals of welfare reform should be to move to a more depersonalized system, with less discretionary intervention in the lives of the recipients at the local level.

An important result of a more automatic, depersonalized system, in terms of behavioral response, might be a reduction in the unwillingness of recipients to work their way off the welfare rolls. Because enrollment is presently such a trying, demeaning process in many localities, it is quite probable that, once on the rolls, recipients are loath to relinquish their welfare status lest at some future time they might have to go through the enrollment process again. This reluctance may constitute a serious work disincentive. By simplifying eligibility requirements and procedures, families working their way off the rolls could be assured prompt reinstatement in the event of future financial setbacks.

The most desirable system on these grounds would, of course, be a self-administered system similar to the positive income tax, with enforcement through auditing and spot-checks. Such a system presents serious administrative problems, however. It is an open question whether many low-income families possess the required literacy and sophistication for self-administration, although there is some indication that they do if care is taken to keep forms and requirements straightforward. Auditing also poses problems. Low-income families receive a significant proportion of their income from sporadic activities under relatively informal arrangements, which would be difficult to monitor even on a spot-check basis. While on grounds of cost one might be willing to ignore these sources of income, that would create an incentive (and a strong one, under high tax rates) for recipients to prefer irregular, possibly illicit, activities to regular employment.

There will also be a number of special groups who pose significant administrative problems. Two obvious examples are migrants, whose mobility and low level of literacy will make administration difficult, and persons who speak primarily a foreign language and may therefore require special forms and counseling.

The traditional techniques of social science research are not well-suited to resolving such administrative problems, yet it would be vastly preferable to attempt some resolution in advance of any major reform or extension of the existing income maintenance system, since some of these arrangements must be specified legislatively, while others will be made willy-nilly (and perhaps almost irrevocably) by local authorities unless firm guidelines are imposed from the outset. The most promising approach to these problems is probably the experimental, or "pilot project" route of "learning by doing." Kershaw discusses some of the administrative lessons learned in the New Jersey income maintenance experiment, as well as giving some general methodological guidelines for administering this type of experimental program.

The administrative complexities of income maintenance do not end with program-recipient relationships, however. Any income maintenance program will have a number of administrative interfaces with other programs. The administrative structure designed to handle these interrelations will be important to the resulting interactions among programs. An important issue here is the locus of certification of eligibility and determination of benefits under related programs, e.g., Medicaid, food stamps, General Assistance, Emergency Assistance, and public housing. Centralized certification procedures might facilitate application of uniform standards, as well as auditing and enforcement; centralization would probably increase the power, and opportunity for abuse, of local discretionary authority, however. On the other hand, decentralization of certification may lead to wasteful duplication of effort and needless intervention in the lives of recipients. At a minimum, it would seem that administrative arrangements should be made for an efficient system of referrals and information exchange among programs.

One effect of close coordination of the various existing programs designed to aid the poor with a broad-coverage income maintenance program may be to substantially increase the number of applicants and beneficiaries under other programs. For example, it is estimated that integration of food stamp administration with the proposed Family Assistance Plan will add some $400 million to the federal cost of food stamps. If our goal is to achieve maximum coverage of the target population of each program, this "case-finding" effect is wholly beneficial, and administrative procedures ought to be designed to facilitate it.

Unfortunately, experimentation with alternative administrative arrangements between programs is probably beyond the scope of a relatively small-scale self-contained income maintenance project like the New Jersey experiment. Pilot projects in this area require extensive interrelationships with existing program structures on a formal, legal basis. Perhaps the most promising strategy would be to "try out" new programs in one or more states, with a number of experimental variations within the state, in advance of setting up the national program.

Particularly difficult problems of administration arise when, as in the Family Assistance Plan, income maintenance eligibility is made conditional upon employment status or willingness to work or undertake job training. "Work tests" of this sort are analyzed by Munts in his contribution to this section. Munts discusses the rationale for a work test, then analyzes the various components that may make up such a screening device and the experience with such requirements under existing programs, notably unemployment compensation.

As he points out, work tests have both positive and negative aspects: they exclude the "undeserving," but they also serve to select those individuals who need employment counseling or lack employable skills, so that efforts can be made to help them. As administered under the unemployment compensation program, "the" work test is really a series of screening devices: What is the applicants' past employment experience and, therefore, for what type of work is he suited? Is his present unemployment voluntary or involuntary (and, if the latter, was his discharge for misconduct)? Is he really available for work for which he is suited? And so on. Each separate test serves a specific function, not all of which are necessarily appropriate to the program goals and clientele of income maintenance. Some (e.g., determination of skill levels) may be very difficult to apply to this population because of its unique characteristics (intermittent work history, or in some cases, no work experience at all). All involve a good deal of discretionary judgment, and are therefore subject to abuse at the lowest administrative levels.

While the analogy is by no means exact, a good deal can be learned from the long experience with work tests under existing pro-

grams. Inferences can be drawn about the way in which local administrators will interpret specific requirements, and the effect of a given provision on eligibility rates can be analyzed. Judgmental predictions as to
the differential impact of such requirements on a lower-income population can then be made.

While Munts makes no attempt at quantitative predictions, his
qualitative assessment of various work tests throws a good deal of light
on their workings. It enables identification of those tests which can be
uniformly and efficiently applied, and those which further the goals of
income maintenance. It emphasizes the need for central administrative
controls over the application of work tests, and identifies the distinctions
which can and cannot be made through work tests, and those which
should be made under a work test related to income maintenance.

V. INTERACTIONS WITH OTHER PROGRAMS

The behavioral response to income maintenance cannot be discussed
in isolation from the context of other influences and incentive structures
impinging on the lives of recipients. An important set of incentive structures which has received little attention in existing income maintenance
literature is the large number of governmental tax and transfer programs,
both cash and in-kind, which affect the low-income population.

Several programmatic interactions have been briefly discussed earlier
in this volume. The (hopefully beneficial) interactions between income maintenance and manpower service programs—employment counseling, job training, day care, etc.—were proposed in Part Two as an appropriate area for experimental research. In his discussion of income
maintenance and the aged in that section, Hollister explored in some
detail the relationship between the existing Social Security system and
any future extension of income maintenance for the aged. Finally, in
considering the definition of income earlier in this paper, the treatment of
benefits from other transfer programs in defining income for transfer
purposes was discussed.

There remain, however, a number of other programs which will
involve significant interactions with any income conditioned transfer program. Indeed, virtually every feature of income maintenance raises issues
of potential interactions with other programs.

Perhaps the most substantial potential source of adverse interactions is the compounding of tax rates when low-income families are
faced with a variety of income-conditioned tax and transfer programs.
This problem is considered at some length in Hausman's contribution to

this section. As he points out, there are implicit taxes on earnings under Medicaid, food stamps, public housing, rent supplements, and day care for welfare mothers. In addition, earnings are subject to Social Security taxation and, above a minimum level, the positive income tax. In some programs, the marginal tax rate can, at certain income levels, become infinite, as when the recipient passes a cut-off or "notch" and loses all benefits from the program. Even when benefits are reduced smoothly to zero, so that there are no notches, the compounding of these separate tax rates with whatever tax rate is implicit in the income maintenance program can present severe work disincentives. It has been estimated that the combined marginal tax rate under only three or four of the programs, when taken in conjunction with a 50 percent income mainte-nance tax, would be as high as 75–80 percent over substantial portions of the low-income range.[1] When these taxes are superimposed on a 67 percent income maintenance tax, the combined rate runs as high as 88 percent.[2]

These disincentives are, of course, the cumulative result of a number of independent legislative decisions made with little consideration of their effect in the context of other programs, coupled with the perennial insistence upon providing earmarked assistance for the poor. If income maintenance is not to prove self-defeating, careful thought must be given to its coordination with other income conditioned benefits and, equally importantly, to the rationalization of implicit tax structures in earmarked programs.

The introduction of high marginal tax rates on the earnings of the poor may also have other, less direct, behavioral consequences, aside from their effect on work effort.[3] Suppose, for example, that state and local taxes may be deducted from income in determining income maintenance benefits. This amounts to a federal assumption of a speci-fied share (equal to the marginal tax rate) of the state and local tax bill of low-income households. As a consequence, the "price" of public services provided at these governmental levels would decline substan-tially for those low-income households that pay state and local taxes. Standard economic theory suggests that the demand for public services on the part of these households should rise significantly as a result. This

---

[1] D. Lee Bawden, Glen Cain, and Leonard Hausman, "The Family Assist-ance Plan: An Analysis and Evaluation," University of Wisconsin, Institute for Research on Poverty, Discussion Paper 73 (1970), p. 23.

[2] Ibid., p. 21.

[3] The following discussion draws heavily on A. J. Heins, "Income Main-tenance and the State and Local Tax-Expenditure Package" (unpublished paper, 1969).

price effect would also be reinforced by a positive income effect upon adoption of the program. The significance of both effects, of course, depends on the level and coverage of the income maintenance program, and upon the ability of the poor to translate their preferences into political action.

At the same time, the state and local tax structure may be altered in the direction of greater regressivity, since the net burden of a given level of state and local taxes on low-income households would be substantially lessened by high federal tax rates (assuming deductibility). Thus the poor might be willing to trade off higher nominal local tax liabilities for increased public services, while high-income taxpayers might demand a shift of tax burdens toward the poor—who, in turn, can pass on the bulk of the tax increase to the federal government.

All of this is, of course, highly theoretical, and relies heavily on the rationality of taxpayer attitudes and the responsiveness of political processes to taxpayer preferences. Still, if the coverage and benefit levels of the income maintenance program are substantial, some response may be expected to occur. At the present time we have virtually no means of making quantitative predictions of such responses; it would seem worthwhile, therefore, to develop predictive models of the impact of income maintenance in this area.

VI. CONCLUSION

The scope for variations in the structure of income maintenance goes far beyond the twin parameters of income guarantees and tax rates, upon which the preponderance of academic research effort has been focused to date. Decisions with respect to definitions, eligibility criteria, administrative arrangements, and interactions with other programs will all have an important bearing on the response of recipients and institutions, horizontal equity, and program costs. Yet there is little in the way of existing research or experience to provide reliable guides in many of these areas. The need for careful, quantitative research, utilizing the skills and insights of a variety of disciplines, is compelling. It is hoped that the papers of this section will constitute a meaningful first step in filling this void.

WORK TESTS: A REVIEW OF ISSUES

Raymond Munts

I. INTRODUCTION

As used in Social Security programs, "work tests" are measures of the applicant's relationship to remunerative employment. Both his expressed opinions and behavior in holding or seeking a job are evaluated by these tests. A complex work test may be thought of as a series of screens that sift both the statements of intent and any evidence of past and current work-related behavior to answer the question, "Is this person in the labor force?" Underlying the question is a judgment whether the applicant should or should not be working as a condition for income support.

Commitment to work establishes eligibility for support in some plans; inability to work establishes eligibility in others. In public assistance, it is the categories that serve as proof of eligibility. They are the acceptable reasons for being dependent, whether because of advanced age, disability, a broken family, or unemployability. The categories constitute a work test because they exclude certain persons. This is particularly the case where AFDC-UP is not one of the categories. In unemployment insurance, the work test measures availability and attachment to the labor market, including the reasons for past work separation. Benefits are accordingly granted or withheld for varying periods of time. In both public assistance and jobless pay, the work test screens out the undeserving who shall not receive aid.

Although the nature and use of work tests vary, in every case a judgment is made that entails some reward or penalty, and the consequence is immediate and specific. Since society holds to a work ethic, it requires that a moral decision be made and also establishes a bureaucracy to make these judgments operational for millions of people.

It has become increasingly difficult to make such judgments in a society where there is much part-time and intermittent work, and where the work roles of family members are much less clear cut than a generation or two ago. In the sixties there was a mounting dissatisfaction particularly with public assistance. Much of this criticism was directed at the categorical features, particularly at the unpredictability of its administration. The wide variation among states, and even within the same counties, seemed to be a function of the broad discretion exercised by those who processed applications for assistance. These criticisms found official expression in the report of the Advisory Council on Public Assistance that recommended the categories be abandoned and be replaced by a test of need only. The negative income tax proponents have also been moved by concerns of horizontal equity among recipients; their proposals also dispensed with the work test. Nevertheless, when the welfare reform debate reached its culmination in the Nixon administration, it was the work test proponents who won the day.

Why? From the debates one can cull two underlying purposes or roles for a work test that were deemed appropriate for the new family assistance benefits. First, the work test can be the contact point for initiating manpower services. After ten years of experimenting with stepped up counseling, training, and placement services, there is in the federal government a strong predisposition to see this as a meaningful form of economic rehabilitation. It was felt that the work test would aid in identifying those who needed job placement services and in selecting for training those who are lacking in job-related skills. The second underlying argument for the work test was an economic one; that it served to limit the cost of the program. The argument was not cast so much in the moral terms of keeping out the "undeserving," but rather of holding total expenditures within acceptable budget limitations. These are the same thing in fact, and there appears now to be little question that the estimate was a shrewd one from a political point of view. The vigorous rejection by the House of standards and qualifications added to the work test by the Ways and Means Committee suggests that the work test, as a simple moral judgment, is still an important force in public thinking. By following the politicians rather than the professors on this issue, it would appear that the administration gave its family assistance benefits a much better chance in the Congress.

In the drafting stages of the family assistance benefits plan, as in the Congressional deliberations, it has been clear that some vestige of the idealism in the guaranteed income movement continues. That movement has been motivated not only by a desire to end poverty but also by hopes for a system of rules and governance by law rather than the whim of lower level bureaucrats. There is still some optimism that a new income maintenance program can adopt more explicit and rational work-test rules. For this purpose, the legislative drafters turned to concepts in unemployment insurance. The ideas of "availability" and "suitable work" as used in unemployment insurance have been applied and interpreted in great detail, through thirty years of experience in more than fifty jurisdictions. There appears to be widespread belief that the notion of "availability for suitable work" is a satisfactory working criterion for a good welfare work test. So far as the author knows, this proposition has not been subject to investigation.

The purpose here is to sketch the outlines of the unemployment insurance experience. Variation between states is limited by federal surveillance and by court review, but there is still a considerable range of experience on a number of questions: (1) There are questions about how to make the work test consistent with the goals of the program it serves. (2) There are questions about economics and costs, such as what proportion of claimants are disqualified under different tests and the effects of alternative kinds of penalties or benefit denials. (3) There are important issues of administrative feasibility, such as how much discretion is required at each level, or whether a test is sufficiently objective that its administration can be consistent and fair.

The central lesson from unemployment insurance is that statutory provisions are of crucial importance but, at the same time, the eventual impact will be enormously affected by the regulations and operating rules for its administration.

II. CRITERIA OF THE WORK TEST

A. Previous Work

Throughout their three decades of history, all unemployment insurance laws have required a record of work during the year or eighteen months prior to the filing of a claim for benefits. But it has never been clear whether this is part of a work test or whether it is necessary to fulfill the "insurance" character of the system; that is, to demonstrate a record of recent work for which contributions have been made thereby giving the insured a right to his benefit. This latter is probably the best explanation. No state has even experimented with giving benefits to new entrants to the labor force on the grounds that their benefits have not been funded. (The cost of benefits for discharged veterans is paid for by the federal government.) It is frequently argued, however, that the previous earnings requirements do at least create a presumption that the claimant has had enough recent work experience to constitute "labor force attachment" and serve as one part of the work test.

In a welfare program, such a work test would be wholly inappropriate, simply because the support functions of a welfare plan are directed to both working and nonworking poor. A record of recent work experience could, however, be used to exempt the applicant from such other work tests as registration for work or training on the grounds that he is a worker already, even if an intermittent one.

The extent of intermittent work is not fully appreciated. State studies of the effects of previous work requirements in unemployment insurance laws show that large proportions of persons can be disqualified by what appear to be modest work requirements. In general, the data seem to indicate that, among otherwise qualified persons, as many as one-fourth are eliminated from unemployment insurance by a requirement of twenty weeks of work in the base year.[1]

It would be a mistake to assume, in a welfare plan work test, that people who work intermittently are not in the labor force. People work intermittently for many reasons, only some of which are personal preference. It is true that a considerable number of people leave the labor force or enter it each year as shown by the much larger number of total persons who work at some time compared with the average size of the labor force over the year. People quit to look for other jobs; they may be discharged after brief periods. But these personal factors do not explain the wide variation among industries. A substantial part of the explanation lies in industries' demand for labor, which fluctuates narrowly in some industries and widely in others.

The work test in a welfare program can help persons make the transition to more stable forms of employment, but in no case should it be constructed on the premise that intermittent employment is of itself an indicator that the individual is not work committed.

How can labor force attachment be measured? Special care should be taken not to blanket out the intermittently employed as unattached to the labor force. Using a specified number of work weeks a year fails to distinguish intermittent employment from cases where the individual has worked steadily for a short period of time and then withdrawn from the labor force. A more sensitive measure would consider the distribu-

---

[1] William Haber and Merrill G. Murray, *Unemployment Insurance in the American Economy* (Homewood, Ill.: Richard D. Irwin, Inc., 1966), p. 263.

tion of work over the year. In unemployment insurance it is not uncommon to require some work in at least two quarters, or to require earnings throughout the year of 1¼ or 1½ times high quarter earnings. Whatever test is used will necessarily be arbitrary and wrong in some cases. The more simple and straightforward it is, the more arbitrary and unjust it can be in application.

The value of having specific tests, even if arbitrary, is that they limit the area of discretion for those administering the work test. The dangers of arbitrary measures can be minimized by using several of them, and then stringing them together as alternatives.[2] In no case should arbitrary measures be multiplied or compounded since this magnifies the effect of their artificiality. The individual should not have to meet a series of arbitrary tests; he should have to meet only one of various alternative tests.

A properly functioning work test in a welfare system would require some measure of who have been workers, because it would be necessary to make decisions about who needed manpower services. It may be decided that only nonworkers should register for work or manpower services; it may be decided that everybody should register. In either case it would be necessary to decide when a benefit recipient was demonstrating sufficient work on his own that he could refuse training or referral to a job without losing his cash payment.

If we exclude "previous work," the essentials of the work test in unemployment insurance consist of four parts: (1) an inquiry into the reasons for termination of the applicant's last employment, particularly whether it was a voluntary quit or discharge for misconduct, since these circumstances create a presumption that unemployment is voluntary; (2) whether the applicant is "able and available for work"; (3) whether he is registered for work with the employment service and, in some states, actively seeking work in addition to being registered; and (4) whether he has refused suitable work.

B. "Voluntary Quit" and "Discharge for Misconduct"

While "voluntary quit" and "discharge for misconduct" criteria can contribute to a finding of whether a claimant is involuntarily employed, there have been serious difficulties about applying them in unemployment insurance.

They open a vast area of complex equity questions. It is not al-

---

[2] Only the New York unemployment insurance law has applied this principle.

ways possible to determine what is a voluntary and what is a compelled decision, or who really initiated a work termination. There are circumstances under which there may be "good personal cause" for quitting, although more and more states have limited this to "good cause attributable to the employer." Some states allow voluntary quitting where the work is "unsuitable" and some allow voluntary quitting where the quit is in order to fulfill marital obligations (such as staying with a husband who has been transferred).

The law on discharge for misconduct attempts to distinguish such shadings as "willful misconduct," "wrongful intent or evil design," and "deliberate violations." Such actions are treated differently than inefficiency," "failure because of inability or incapacity," or "ordinary neglect." Motivations of the individual are weighed as is the seriousness of the consequences of the negligence.

While these criteria began as mere operating rules to test work attachment, they have expanded into a rich jungle of issues that can delight the legal scholar and the moral philosopher. Part of the reason for this lies in the employer financing and in experience rating which tend to fasten attention on "employer fault" rather than on "general welfare" as an underlying consideration.[3] Even without this influence, a general revenue supported welfare program using these criteria in the work test would develop a substantial body of equity law. Also, procedures would have to be established for getting the employer's side of the story as well as the worker's, because the subtleties of many questions cannot be decided on the basis of one view alone. The conclusion is that "voluntary quit" and "discharge for misconduct" should not be part of any statutory language in a welfare plan work test. This judgment is not intended to preclude an inquiry into the individual's own version for past terminations in the course of a counseling interview for purposes of estimating his retraining needs or capacities.

C. Relationship of "Availability" and "Suitable Work"

Availability for work is the keystone of the work test and the most frequent reason for disqualification. In unemployment insurance it is usually considered along with "ability to work," but "ability to work" would serve a different purpose in a welfare system. "Inability to work" is a reason for disqualification in a program such as unemployment in-

---

[3] The "employer fault" notion has resulted in a number of states restricting good cause for leaving to causes attributable to the employer or connected with the work. This effect is to make the "voluntary quit" disqualification much more severe. This appears clearly in higher disqualification rates for those states restricting "good cause."

surance that is only for unemployed members of the work force. It is not a reason for disqualification in a welfare program. Ability to work is appropriately rewarded in unemployment insurance; inability to work is appropriately rewarded in a welfare system.

The harshness of the ability to work test has been questioned in unemployment insurance. An otherwise qualified applicant who slips on the stairs of the employment office and breaks a leg will be disqualified because he could not accept a job if one were offered. Several states have mitigated the severity of this ability to work disqualification. Nine states provide that if, during a period of temporary disability, the claimant is registered for work and no suitable work is offered the benefits will be continued nevertheless.

We cannot distinguish the relative frequencies of disqualification for inability to work from those for unavailability because they are lumped together in statistical reporting, but informed persons estimate that the former are relatively infrequent. The discussion that follows will be limited to the questions of availability since this serves similar purposes in unemployment insurance and in a welfare test.

Ralph Altman has made the most thorough study of availability for work in unemployment insurance.[4] In the following paragraphs he describes the primary role of the availability criterion and the relationship with the test of "refusing suitable work":

> The role of the availability requirement (and the other eligibility conditions) in the unemployment compensation structure may be best conceived as a broad, rough test that the claimant must meet. It is a gross sieve designed to block the clearly unfit from entering or remaining in the benefit system. So operated, it becomes a routine check of the claimant's work history, the circumstances of his work separation, his more prominent physical and other personal circumstances, and his expressed work restrictions. Some claimants will get past such a preliminary examination despite their actual unwillingness and inability to work. They will not be numerous. For them there is a secondary line of defense to prevent them from penetrating too deeply, a finer sieve. That is the test of offered suitable work. It is recognized that a work offer is not always possible and that the job of the employment office is placement and not policing. If that office is, however, doing its job well and the employment level is fairly high there will be work opportunities offered to most claimants.

> The offer of suitable work, if rejected by the claimant, may reveal previously undisclosed aspects of his availability. The reason for

---

[4] Ralph Altman, *Availability for Work: A Study in Unemployment Compensation* (Cambridge, Mass.: Harvard University Press, 1950).

the refusal may indicate that the claimant is not, in reality, sufficiently attached to the labor force. The unemployment compensation agency then discovers the error of paying him benefits and
holds him ineligible. On the other hand, the claimant's reason for
refusal may be entirely consistent with availability for work. In
that case if the reason is not strong enough to be "good cause,"
the claimant is disqualified.

Altman is distinguishing between a preliminary estimate of availability and subsequent behavior when confronted with specific job offers.
What the claimant professes in a general way may or may not be confirmed by how he actually behaves when a job offer is tendered.

1. *"Availability."* We will first suggest policy questions on "availability" and then look at those relating to the meaning of "suitable
work." Does a claimant have to want full-time work to be considered
available? Two states require full-time work in their statutes, most
others do so by rules and administrative practice. Can a claimant's
availability be limited to his own occupation? In several states this is
permitted by statute. Practice in other states has never been thoroughly
studied, though it is known that the duration of one's unemployment is
considered. For example, limitation to one's occupation may be permitted
for the first six weeks but thereafter a broader range of jobs must be
considered. Practice also varies in cases where one's occupation is rare or
nonexistent in the community, most states holding that such a limitation
does not constitute availability.

Can a claimant limit his hours of availability because of marital
obligations or for other reasons? Two states specify by law that women
are not required to be available between 1 and 6 A.M., but in general,
and particularly for men, availability cannot be limited to specific hours
of the day.

Does registration for work at a local public employment office satisfy
the availability requirement? This was the original intention, and it was
part of the plan that the local employment office would test availability
for work by the offer of suitable jobs. But since the "penetration rate"
of the employment service in the total picture of job placements is
something less than 15 percent, a number of states have gone further
and require more initiative by the claimant. Thirty states by statute require that, in addition to being registered, the claimant must "actively
seek work." A degree of flexibility may be allowed, however, as some
of these states do not require active search for work during temporary
lay-offs or when the job market is loose. There are also significant
differences in the administrative application of "actively seeking work"

provisions, and a thorough study of their administration would shed a guiding light for policy development. The best judgment to date is that an inflexible application of "active search for work" is pointless, leading to fictitious visits and complaints by employers who are unnecessarily bothered by claimants. Certainly the policy should be eased in loose labor markets and during short lay-offs. Haber and Murray agree with Altman that in other cases there should be a "guided but active search for work," meaning that the employment office should give the claimant labor market information to help him look for work, should counsel him as to jobs for which he is fitted, and should help him make a plan for his job search.[5]

When should a student or trainee be considered as not available for work? Some states appear to rely on a test of the availability of a student for full-time work. However, eight states automatically disqualify students who have voluntarily left work to attend school; another nine disqualify claimants during school attendance even if a voluntary quit was not involved. As for those engaged in vocational training, thirty-one states now consider an otherwise eligible claimant to be available for work (and therefore eligible for benefits) if he is attending a training or retraining course approved or recommended by the employment security agency. This trend is consistent with the relatively new appreciation of unemployment insurance as part of a comprehensive labor market program. To avoid charging benefits during approved training to particular employers, the cost may be allotted to noncharged accounts (or pooled funds).

Should there be special tests on the availability of women, or workers who are not the heads of households, or persons who have no dependents? A majority of states have special disqualification provisions with respect to voluntary quitting because of marital obligations and pregnancy. Twenty-three states disqualify persons who quit to attend a sick child or to move with a husband who has been transferred to another state; most of these states require re-employment to again establish availability. Thirty-eight states have special provisions disqualifying women for stated periods before and after childbirth, and several of these will not pay benefits again until after the woman has proven her continuing attachment by working again after the birth of the child.

In a welfare-oriented program the key questions are somewhat different. The issues in a welfare program are whether all women should have to register for work or training, or whether some can be exempted such as women with children (or preschool children), or women with

---

[5] Haber and Murray, *supra* n. 1, p. 269.

working husbands, or women with such home obligations as caring for other family members. Doubts about the availability for work of some female unemployment insurance beneficiaries arise because of the variation in our society of the values and norms concerning remunerative work as against home and family-directed work for women. This widespread uncertainty about what is good or desirable for the family woman should lead to considerable caution in how a work test is applied to such women, even with the obviously greater income imperative facing poor families.

2. *"Suitable Work."* The questions involving suitable work are restricted somewhat because there are some federal standards to which state laws must comply. Compensation cannot be denied, according to federal law,[6] (a) if the position offered is vacant due directly to a strike, lockout, or other labor dispute; (b) if the wages, hours, or other conditions of the work offered are substantially less favorable to the individual than those prevailing for similar work in the locality; or (c) if, as a condition of being employed, the individual would be required to join a company union or to resign from or refrain from joining any bona fide labor organization.

In addition, the typical state law follows the Social Security Board's original draft bill which reads, "In determining whether or not any work is suitable for an individual, the commission shall consider the degree of risk involved to his health, safety, and morals, his physical fitness and prior training and experience, his length of unemployment and prospects for securing local work in his customary occupation, and the distance of the available work from his residence."

Despite this uniformity in statutory language, differences have developed as a result of court interpretation and administrative application. For example, in most states as unemployment lengthens the worker is expected to take a job at lower skills or earnings. It is suspected that there is considerable diversity among the states in this practice, but the subject has never been thoroughly studied or documented. It is clear that practice varies considerably on the question of how much lower a wage the claimant can be expected to accept with the passage of time. Similarly, there are wide differences of opinion as to the distance a job can be from the worker's home and still be "suitable."

When has a worker been offered suitable work? This is usually taken to mean that it must be clear the claimant has been asked to take the job, that the job conditions are specified, and that there has been

---

[6] Internal Revenue Code of 1954, Section 3304 (a) (5).

definite acceptance or rejection. But what if the job is referred through the employment service and the claimant indicates he is not interested? According to Haber and Murray, "The decision often turns on the conclusion reached by the employment office interviewer as to whether the worker would have refused the job if he had definitely been referred to it."[7] Here, as in so many other instances, we see the operation of judgment and discretion at the lowest administrative level.

When a job offer is made by mail but the claimant does not receive the notice, can he be disqualified? State courts have held differently on this issue.

When has a worker refused suitable work? Most states will disqualify where the worker has failed, without good cause, either to apply or to accept when suitable work is offered. But the difficulties of administering this have again been suggested by Haber and Murray:

> If he deliberately seeks to avoid being hired by acting in a way which causes the employer to withdraw the offer, he will be disqualified in most cases. Delicate questions arise, however. For example, if a claimant tells the prospective employer that he expects a recall to his former job in a few weeks and will only work until he is recalled, should he be disqualified if the prospective employer does not hire him under such conditions? The decision may turn on whether the claimant made the statement in order to avoid being hired or because he felt he should be honest in advising the prospective employer of his intentions.[8]

In his 1953 study of abuse in unemployment insurance,[9] Joseph Becker estimated that as many as 15 or 20 percent of referrals could be manipulated by the worker in such a way as to discourage a job offer being tendered. No study has ever attempted to corroborate this estimate. In any case, there are very difficult problems of judgment involved. There are no simple rules for judging the variety of human behavior involved in accepting or refusing suitable work. It is almost inevitable that considerable discretion shall rest at the lowest administrative level. As we shall see in the next section, the total disqualifications involved here are small; perhaps, as Becker suggests, they should be larger. It would appear, however, that they are more important for the reputation of the program than for its cost.

---

[7] Haber and Murray, *supra* n. 1, p. 267.

[8] Ibid.

[9] Joseph M. Becker, *The Problem of Abuse in Unemployment Benefits* (New York: Columbia University Press, 1953).

III. DISQUALIFICATION FREQUENCIES

The operating data from the unemployment insurance system provide a rough picture of how the work tests operate in terms of their effects on claimants and costs.

In 1969 there were 9,726,000 new spells of insured unemployment. For the same year there were 1,696,000 disqualifications. This ratio of about 17 per 100 holds fairly constant in the last three or four years.

The most frequent reasons for disqualification are the "able and available" category (32 percent of total disqualifications), followed closely by "voluntary quits" (30 percent). In a weak third and fourth place are "discharge for misconduct" (9 percent) and "refusal of suitable work" (3 percent). The remainder consists of miscellaneous disqualifications which do not apply in all states. These proportions also held fairly steady in recent years.

For looking at changes over time it is appropriate to use the number of "claimant contacts" as the base of disqualification ratios. "Claimant contacts" is a better base because it takes into account the duration of the claimants' unemployment, and the longer exposure in which he must maintain his eligibility. It is a base that will rise more than "new spells" of insured unemployment in those high unemployment years when both the number of individuals and the number of unemployed weeks are increasing. The ratio of total disqualifications to claimant contacts declines in high unemployment years, such as 1961. In such years, the objective labor market conditions rise in importance by comparison with individual motivational concerns. Over the entire period from 1951 to 1969, the ratio of disqualifications per 1,000 claimant contacts has risen, suggesting that the work test has become more severe and is being more vigorously applied than at the earlier date. This corroborates the impression of informed persons that equity considerations have loomed larger as the program gets older, casting a longer shadow over income maintenance purposes of the system. This might be considered an ominous warning for the work test of a welfare program.

However, we should note that the major source of this increase appears to be in the "voluntary quits" and "discharge for misconduct" categories. For reasons given in the preceding section, these tests may be only minimally useful in a welfare work test, such as in counseling interviews for evaluating what assistance to prescribe. Disqualifications under "able and available" have been remarkably steady over the last twenty years, and "refusal of suitable work" may have declined somewhat in importance.

The variation in disqualification rates among the states is considerable. For example, in 1969 the rate for "able and available" disqualifications ranged from 1.4 persons per 1,000 claimant contacts in Tennessee to 26.5 in Virginia. The rate for the country as a whole was 8.5 and the mean of the states was 6.4. There appears to be some consistency year after year on which states are likely to be toward the high end and which toward the low end. No study has yet attempted to explain precisely the inter-state variation in disqualification rates.

One problem with state disqualification rates lies in uncertainties about the denominator of these rates, the "number of claimant contacts." It is probable that a good deal of "filtering out" of possible claimants occurs before one ever gets on the statistics as a "claimant contact." The public image of the program may effectively keep some potential claimants away. Preliminary screening and interviews after one enters the local claims office may also result in varying number of persons deciding there is no reason to go further. Not until a record of his base year earnings has been prepared, showing that he meets the "previous work" requirement, does the individual become a "claimant contact" for statistical purposes.

This suggests the need to develop accurate measures for evaluating the administration of work tests. It is important that the responsible authority in an income maintenance program have some indicators that the work test is being uniformly administered. Since it is inevitable that discretion and judgment rest at the lowest operating levels, it is altogether too easy for prevailing attitudes and personal prejudices to enter into administrative decisions.

Some hint as to the magnitude of the problem created by discretion is shown in a recent study.[10] Although prepared to develop guidelines for budgeting administrative activities, this study showed that as many as one-fifth or more of nonmonetary determinations—i.e., those involving the work test criteria—are being incorrectly tallied as such.

The persistence of significantly different rates of benefit denial per 1,000 claimant contacts, even in states with similar work tests, also suggests that administrative influences are significant. There is no evidence to support the hopes of those who believe that the use of unemployment insurance concepts in the family assistance program will of itself assure an equitable application of the work test.

---

[10] U.S. Department of Labor, Manpower Administration, *Work Measurement of the Nonmonetary Determination Function* (Washington, D.C.: U.S. GPO, December 1969).

Table 1. Total Number of Disqualifications and Ratio to Claimant Contacts and New Spells of Insured Unemployment by Issue, Selected Years
(absolute figures in thousands)

	1951	1957	1961	1964	1967	1968	1969
New spells of insured unemployment	10,046	13,726	16,685	12,910	11,013	9,801	9,726
Number of claimant contacts	54,835	84,534	128,899	90,971	69,721	64,176	63,522
Total disqualifications[a]	1,097	1,562	2,261	2,139	1,840	1,708	1,696
Per 1,000 claimant contacts	19.3	18.5	17.5	23.5	26.4	26.6	26.7
Not able or available for work	488	674	970	921	590	548	545
Per 1,000 claimant contacts	8.6	8.0	9.5	10.1	8.5	8.5	8.6
Refusal of suitable work	91	68	90	78	66	58	55
Per 1,000 claimant contacts	1.6	0.8	0.7	0.9	1.0	0.9	0.9
Voluntary quits	313	464	649	625	558	517	514
Per 1,000 spells of insured unemployment	31.1	35.0	38.5	48.5	50.7	52.8	52.9
Discharge for misconduct	91	164	235	214	170	157	153
Per 1,000 spells of insured unemployment	9.0	12.3	13.9	16.5	15.4	16.0	15.7

[a] In addition to the four issues shown, also included are miscellaneous disqualifications which do not apply in all states. Labor dispute disqualifications are excluded.

Source: U.S. Department of Labor, Manpower Administration.

IV. THE WORK TEST AS ENTRY POINT FOR MANPOWER SERVICES

We noted in the introduction that work tests are usually regarded as means for denying community financial supports to those uninspired by the prospect of work. The emotional connotations here have been reinforced over the ages. Society will be a provider only to those who have proven their inability to work. But the development of manpower planning in the United States during the last decade has opened new possibilities in the meaning and use of work tests.

There has been increasing interest during the last decade in making manpower services available in a meaningful way to unemployment insurance beneficiaries. Similarly, the Nixon welfare bill requires the beneficiary of the family assistance benefit to be registered "for manpower services, training, and employment with the local public employment office of the States as provided by regulations of the Secretary of Labor." The Secretary is obliged to provide these persons with such services as counseling, testing, institutional and on-the-job training, work experience, upgrading, program orientation, relocation assistance, incentives to private and public employers to train or hire these persons, special work projects, job development, coaching, job placement, and follow-up services "required to assist in securing and retaining employment and opportunities for advancement." A training incentive allowance is established. Provisions are also made for day-care services.

This innovation, if passed, would provide an opportunity to drain the work test of its emotional connotation and to objectify its function as the juncture between income maintenance and manpower programming.

The word "test" has two different meanings. In one sense it means trial or proof or ordeal, and connotes guilt or innocence. But "test" also means measurement or appraisal, as of one's qualifications or potential. In this latter meaning it has a scientific and constructive rather than a judgmental implication.

Work tests can range over a wide area. At one limit they serve only as a condition or qualification for receipt of a benefit, but, at the other limit, they can encompass the existence of an opportunity available entirely at the discretion of the beneficiary. Such an opportunity to adapt to the world of work does represent a new juncture between income maintenance and the use of manpower. Northern and western European countries have gone well beyond the United States in their programming in this sense. It appears to be more appropriate for the work test in a welfare program to emphasize the opportunity rather than the penalty component.

Several factors will influence where the decisions will fall along this penalty-opportunity axis, including the following:

1. The amount of out-reach practiced in administration, and the frequency with which the transfer beneficiary is actually exposed to the manpower facilities.

2. The quality and "climate" of those exposures, including the amount of salesmanship or personal pressure brought to bear in the counseling and the extent to which the beneficiary comes to feel that the program is being run in his interest.

3. The latitude permitted one to define his availability and to define the nature of a job that is "suitable."

4. The amount of reduction in transfer payments or the duration of their discontinuance when the beneficiary decides against the manpower services available.

5. The incentives existing in terms of training payments, the assistance available in finding a job and overcoming the obstacles of relocation, and the likelihood of a good job at the end of the training period.

Negative and positive incentives operate in any plan designed to shape behavior or provide support, but publicly administered plans always seem to end up emphasizing negative incentives. The reasons for this probably lie in the defensive posture of the administering agency vis-à-vis the public and anxiety over guarding the "public image" of the system. Also related are the difficulties of securing professional personnel at the level of contact with the beneficiary for salaries prevailing in public service. But it is imperative that considerable discretion be lodged at the claimant contact level and that quality personnel, backed up by the bureaucracy, be available to administer the work test. With qualified personnel, a work test can be applied so as to underscore the positive inducements. Emphasizing opportunities rather than penalties reinforces the claimant's self-esteem and commitment to personal growth, an orientation that is appropriate for a program designed to diminish poverty.

There are undoubtedly serious limitations in the capacity of an "old line" agency such as the employment service to realize these principles, but there have been a number of important policy decisions in recent years designed to improve the effectiveness of the employment service. The "one-stop service" idea in which unemployment insurance claims and placement functions were administered in the same place has been criticized as inefficient, and there is some evidence showing that separation of claims and placement functions has produced a better placement record. Computerization and rapid data processing have progressed in some parts of the country, making it possible to dredge files quickly and make responses to job applicants and job seekers within twenty-four hours. Where there is no substantial mechanical assistance, the placements achieved may be in part a function of the size and experience level of the staff in the local employment office. There are other important variables having to do with the image of the employment service and its role as fostered through explanation and experience among employers and employees. Among these is the specialization of employment office staff by sectors, such as the separation of white-collar placement services from others.

The limitations of the employment service are well known and one of the most important is its limited capacity to place people in jobs for which they have been trained. The placement activities of the employment service, as measured by the "penetration rate" (i.e., number of nonagricultural placements per 100 workers hired in nonagricultural employment) is still only a small fraction of total job placements, and about one-third of nonagricultural placements by the employment service are temporary. It has been shown that the success of a training program is closely related to the assurance of a job at the end of the training period, and without this the other manpower services lose the sharp focus that comes with directed purpose.

The performance level required for effective delivery of manpower services in a nationwide welfare work test will be expensive indeed unless there is a sophisticated system for distinguishing among persons by what their needs really are. In its early days, unemployment insurance programming was built on a bland assumption that the work test requirement would be met if everybody registered for work with the employment service. However, it soon became clear that it was not equally compelling to provide placement services for every such person. Some claimants were known to be only very temporarily unemployed and would soon be called back, probably by the same employer. In recent years, there has developed more interest in further differentiating among unemployment insurance beneficiaries in terms of their service needs. A similar development has taken place within the employment service.

A limited demonstration project was undertaken in New York City in 1967–68, known as the Claimant Advisory Service Project.[11] This

---

[11] New York State Division of Employment Research and Statistics Office, "CLASP: Experience of 1967 Claimants," Working Paper, Memorandum No. 6, November 1968 (mimeo.).

study attempted to analyze the nature of the claimant's job separation in order to distinguish between those on temporary layoff but still job attached and those permanently separated from their jobs. The results of the study indicated that, by identifying those who seemed to require attention and assuring the delivery of the services needed, the duration of unemployment could be substantially reduced for such persons.

This experience suggests the utility of a work test that distinguishes between registration for the purpose of diagnosis and registration for the purpose of applying needed services.

A "five cities project" has been initiated by the U.I. Service to apply more broadly the principles in the New York City plan. Considerable emphasis was devoted to perfecting interviewing techniques designed to assess the true nature of the unemployment insurance claimants re-employment problems. One of the tasks of the interviewer is to classify each case by difficulty: (1) those who are temporarily or seasonally unemployed; (2) those who are occupationally set and have employable skills; and (3) the hard-core unemployed. This latter group may include those whose skills are becoming obsolete, those who are unskilled or underutilized, and those who desire retraining or a change of occupation. It can also include claimants who have personal impediments to prompt or stable employment. This group of hard-core unemployed has been shown to have much higher disqualification rates in unemployment insurance; that is, they are less likely to meet the tests that measure involuntary unemployment and availability.

Some test efforts have been directed to ascertaining whether specially trained interviewers can identify the severity of the re-employment problem of claimants, and to what extent concentration of services on those identified as having the most severe problems actually serves to reduce the duration of their unemployment. Tentatively, the findings are that a staff specially trained for the purpose of making the distinction between types of claimants according to the severity of their re-employment problems does show an ability to identify the nature of the claimant's problem.[12] Further testing will show whether the effect of concentrating services on these more difficult placement cases will be to reduce the duration of unemployment.

These investigations have proceeded largely with unemployment insurance claimants. Meantime the employment service is developing a

---

[12] Employment Security Commission of Arizona, Unemployment Compensation Division, "First Interim Report, Evaluation of the Effectiveness of Trained U.I. Interviewers Using the Extended Interview with New Claims Applicants."

new approach called a "Comprehensive Manpower Agency," in major labor market areas that also makes distinctions among job applicants in terms of their job readiness or job search assistance needs. This program has operated in Pittsburgh and Phoenix and will be extended during the coming months to some fourteen cities in all.

Such interrelated developments should become reinforcing. They hold some promise for greater efficiency and greater effectiveness in the administration of manpower services, without which the work test remains primarily a penal rather than an opportunity mechanism.

PROBLEMS IN INCOME REPORTING AND ACCOUNTING

D. Lee Bawden and
David Kershaw

I. INTRODUCTION

The implementation of any national program of income-conditioned transfers requires the resolution of a number of important issues related to the reporting and accounting of income. The effectiveness of such a program, in terms of equity among recipients, responsiveness to need, and accuracy of reporting will depend significantly on the manner in which these issues are resolved. In this chapter we examine the issues surrounding the choice of the accounting period, the frequency of reporting income, and the frequency of payments to families. We then propose a general income accounting and reporting system which, we believe, is the best available resolution of the conflicts which inevitably arise among the goals of any comprehensive income maintenance program.

II. GOALS

We assume that it is desirable to design an income maintenance program such that:
1. Administrative costs are held to a reasonable level
2. Most families will be able to report income and comply with regulations without assistance (i.e., the self-administrative features of the program are maximized)
3. Disincentive to work is minimized

4. There is reasonable responsiveness to the needs of recipients

5. There is a close relationship between the operations of the national program and state or local public assistance programs

6. Equity among all recipients is maintained

Developing a system which serves all of these goals equally well is not possible, since some of them are contradictory. In addition, a national program will have to address the needs of families with substantially varying income circumstances. Some examples are:

1. Families with unemployed heads whose incomes are essentially zero

2. Families with constant, but low, incomes

3. Families whose incomes fluctuate substantially over a year period (both under and over their breakeven points)

4. Farm and other families who receive all of their incomes in a lump sum at one time in a year

5. Families with incomes which steadily rise or which steadily fall over a year period

6. Families whose incomes fluctuate between years

The challenge is to serve as many of the goals stated above for as many income types as possible. The discussion which follows sets forth what we consider to be the best way of doing this. We will discuss each of the four basic components of an accounting system: (1) the *accountable period* (the ex post period over which equity is maintained among families), (2) the *frequency of payments* to families, (3) the *accounting period* (the length of time over which ex post income is averaged for calculating payments), and (4) the *frequency of filing* income statements.

III. ACCOUNTABLE PERIOD

The length of the accountable period depends in large part on the assumed cycles of income fluctuation of those with variable earnings. To insure equity among those with stable incomes, those with monthly or quarterly fluctuating incomes (seasonal workers), and those with incomes fluctuating annually (farmers and businessmen), it is necessary to compute the total payments to recipients on at least an annual basis. An annual accountable period meets this criterion for all but those with year-to-year income variations.

An annual accountable period can be implemented either by a reconciliation at the end of the year (like the federal income tax) or by using a twelve-month "carryforward" procedure. The year-end reconciliation provides equity on an annual basis by rectifying any under-

or overpayments (based on a shorter income averaging period) at the end of the year through an additional payment or a recoupment. While this system is equitable, the New Jersey experience revealed some difficulties with it. In particular, it is administratively cumbersome, it creates very real problems for families who owe substantial amounts of payments at the end of the year, and it is difficult to explain to recipients.

Given these problems, an alternative—the carryforward procedure —was developed.[1] This procedure averts the above problems while still maintaining annual equity. Earned income in any given month in excess of the break-even level (the guaranteed minimum divided by the tax rate) is accumulated in a carryforward sum. If earned income in any successive month falls below the break-even level, the carryforward sum is added to the family income for that month. If the carryforward sum is used up (because the amount by which the family income fell below the break-even level was greater than the accumulated carryforward sum), then the family would receive payments. If the carryforward sum is not used up, the amount in excess of the break-even point remains in the carryforward sum for use in future months. Income above the break-even point earned in any given month remains in the carry-forward sum for up to twelve months, after which it expires.

The carryforward procedure eliminates over- and underpayments and thus eliminates the necessity for an annual reconciliation to maintain equity among families. It is also appropriate for the self-employed who, in some periods, may have cash expenses but no cash receipts. In such a case income would be assumed to be zero for the purpose of calculating payments, but a negative carryover sum representing cash expenses can be carried forward and offset against cash receipts in a later period. Deductions (e.g., for day care and work expenses) could be treated in this way as well.

This system is now in use in New Jersey and in the Rural Negative Income Experiments. Experience to date suggests that it would be an extremely effective way to proceed in a national program.

IV. FREQUENCY OF PAYMENTS

Regardless of how frequently payment levels are recalculated for families, a decision must be made regarding the frequency with which the checks are mailed. The New Jersey experience with biweekly checks

---

[1] This procedure was developed by William Klein and Lee Bawden, staff members of the Institute for Research on Poverty, University of Wisconsin, in the design of the Rural Negative Income Tax Experiment.

seems to us to be an appropriate model. The realistic choices with regard to frequency include monthly, semimonthly, biweekly, and weekly checks. The general goal should be to balance two considerations: (1) to make payments often enough so that families are not required to engage in unreasonable amounts of planning and budgeting, and (2) to minimize administrative costs. A good balance is probably struck at twice each month, although this may prove to be too expensive. The choice between semimonthly and biweekly is, of course, hardly a crucial one. Since most low-income earners are paid by the week, we lean toward biweekly payments because this replicates more closely the family's current experience. Dealing with the New Jersey families has shown that conforming to existing patterns of wage payment is a great help in promoting correct and prompt compliance with regulations and in enabling families to plan more effectively.

V. ACCOUNTING PERIOD AND FREQUENCY OF FILING INCOME REPORTS

The impact of the payment system is determined in large measure by the length of the accounting period, i.e., the period over which income is averaged for calculating payments. The accounting period, in turn, is partly dependent on how often income report forms are filed by families. Within the context of the carryforward system, we will describe what we consider to be the three leading alternative accounting and reporting methods.

A. Reporting Income Monthly with a One-Month Accounting Period[2]

The major advantage of a system which has a short accounting period is its responsiveness to changing income needs of the recipients— its ability to replace income soon after it is lost. Unless a national income maintenance program is fairly responsive to need, there will be a necessity to retain a sizable local welfare program to handle constantly recurring "emergency need." There will always be emergency needs, of course, but a short accounting period would drastically reduce such needs

---

[2] A month rather than four weeks will be used for convenience; the discussion is appropriate for either period. As stated earlier, the choice between a month and four weeks depends on the frequency with which wages are paid for most of the families involved, i.e., weekly or biweekly versus monthly or semimonthly.

and cut the size of the mechanism needed to serve them. The second advantage in a one-month accounting period is its close relationship to the accounting periods now in use in state and local public assistance programs (including AFDC). Such a close relationship would promote a smooth transition from existing programs to a new, nationwide program.

As we indicated above, the carryforward method would eliminate the most serious problem with a short accounting period, namely horizontal inequity. However, while this short accounting period is responsive and equitable, it has the potential disadvantage of inducing a greater work disincentive (rises in income would be associated with rapidly corresponding reductions in payments). Monthly versus less frequent income reporting will also raise administrative costs.

While we think there may be something to the disincentive problem, we feel that the overriding consideration is the administrative one. The ability of both the families and the agency to handle frequent reporting will be discussed below.

B. Reporting Income Monthly with a Three-Month Accounting Period

This method is similar to the one just discussed, except that it "dilutes" the disincentive effects by smoothing income over the previous three-month period. A family's payments would be recalculated each month, but earned income upon which payments are based would be a moving three-month average. Administrative costs would be identical to the previous method, but the disincentive problem would be diminished by lessening the responsiveness of the payments to changes in income. For example, only one-third of the effect on payments of a change in income would be felt in the next month.

C. Reporting Income Quarterly with a Quarterly Accounting Period

Quarterly reporting would presumably reduce the administrative burden for both the families and the agency. While the disincentive problem associated with rapid responsiveness to income changes is minimized, the possibility of unpredictable income declines during a given quarter creates a real problem in coping with emergency needs. If reporting is to be quarterly, one must accept a large local (and possibly highly discretionary) emergency assistance program, given the fluctuating nature of incomes among low-income families.

Presumably, one would choose a quarterly accounting period only if the administrative cost of frequent reporting is so high, or the disincentive effect of rapid response is so severe, as to make a shorter accounting period and more frequent reporting unacceptable.

VI. ADMINISTRATIVE CONSIDERATIONS IN FREQUENT REPORTING

The frequency of filing income reports is crucial to the selection of the accounting period, for obviously the latter must be based on the former. At issue is (1) whether low-income families, many of whom are poorly educated, can handle the paper work required of them to file monthly, and (2) whether processing costs of the administrative agency can be held to a reasonable level.

We have had over a year's experience with monthly income reports in the New Jersey experiment. There are strong indications that rapid reporting is not only possible but desirable in and of itself. Under the assumption that a simple form is used for reporting, frequent contact (by mail) seems to promote greater accuracy and dependability in the reports. Second, frequent reporting enables the agency to adjust quickly (and therefore equitably) to changes in address and family composition.

Quite obviously the kind of form which is used will have a great deal to do with the family's ability to report and the agency's ability to process.[3] We believe monthly reporting is desirable if a "short form" is used—one designed to pick up only those items of income which are most common and which tend to vary the most. For example, this form could include wages and salaries, Social Security payments, pensions, and income from self-employment (including farm income). These sources account for most of the total income of the poor and virtually all of the variable income. When a family initially signs up for the program, and at the beginning of each year thereafter, a long form would be used to report other income earned over the past year, and to estimate other income for the coming year. Other income would include bonuses, trust funds, inheritances, cash gifts, etc. The value of assets could also be declared on this longer form.

The use of such a short form (a single side of an IBM card) would enable recipients to report income easily and frequently and would enable the agency to process forms efficiently.

---

[3] We have discovered that most illiterate recipients can work with numbers and do simple addition. They have generally been able to submit the relatively short New Jersey form promptly and without serious errors.

VII. IMPLICATIONS OF VARIOUS ACCOUNTING PERIOD OPTIONS

While considerable attention has been paid to the importance of the accounting period by researchers, it has been difficult to convince policy-makers that the accounting period issue is more than a technicality of interest to social scientists.

In order to illustrate that the accounting, and accountable, periods which are chosen will have a *major* impact on the coverage, cost, and average payments of an income maintenance system, it is instructive to look at current accounting period thinking by policymakers in Washington and some analysis we recently conducted in Seattle.

It appears that the general thrust of HEW thinking on accounting rules for the proposed national application of the Family Assistance Plan is that families will become eligible for benefits *at any time* that their monthly income falls below the monthly break-even level regardless of previous income level. Thus a family with income of $1000 the previous month (plus all months before that) but with no prospective income this month could get a full FAP payment immediately. To do otherwise, it is argued, will drastically increase the caseload of the general assistance agency, and thus the state welfare budget, under the "no federal match" provisions for GA. A yearly accountable period has been ruled out, at least at this stage, and HEW seems to be leaning toward the proposition that a very short period is the best approach.

HEW is also considering seriously the possibility that families would not file regularly, but only when incomes change (i.e., adapting the Social Security model to FAP families). At the end of a year (either twelve months after an applicant's initial check or at a regular time as under IRS rules), there would be a "roundup," where actual payments made would be compared to annual entitlement. While overpayments are antici-pated, it is generally assumed that very little can be recovered, particularly when incomes are low. To attempt anything approaching full recovery of overpayments could throw recipients onto general assistance; this would effectively mean that FAP was being repaid out of nonmatched state funds, a particularly untenable possibility.

The effect of these procedures would be not only to produce gross inequities, wreak havoc with effective marginal tax rates, and generate an annual administrative hassle of gargantuan proportions, but to vastly increase both costs and caseloads.

In a national program with universal coverage of the working poor, the accounting period will have a tremendous impact on the cost. For a given budget, the accounting period selected will in fact determine the basic parameters which are permitted, i.e., the tax rate and the guarantee level which we can afford. If we assume the costs of the national income maintenance program as currently projected by HEW, we can afford a program with a $1,600 guarantee, a 50 percent tax rate and a work set-aside of $720. This system was costed out assuming that families would receive an entitlement based on their annual incomes.

To estimate the change in program cost caused by shifting from the annual income system to the proposed FAP system, we used a sample of 100 families from an income maintenance experiment currently in progress in Seattle. Under the reasonable assumption that year-end recovery of overpayments is usually impossible, with the proposed FAP system we may be making payments to many families which are equivalent to those we would make under a program with a guarantee level of $3,080 and our total program costs may be increased by 250 percent.[4] The problem is that those who need it most will not be the beneficiaries of this increased budget. In fact, 55 percent of the families who would be recipients under the proposed FAP accounting system will have annual incomes above the annual break-even point.

The purely annual or the purely prospective approaches are both extremes: one sacrifices responsiveness completely to cost considerations and the other does the reverse. What is important to establish is that the selection of an accounting period has a drastic effect on the program— something many have been unwilling to recognize. In addition, it has to be stressed that tightening up the accounting scheme is not for the purpose of insuring that families do not get a little something extra. The currently proposed system is so inefficient that we buy very little additional coverage for people who are poor for the tremendous increase in cost involved.

In order to make a first attempt at determining the outside impact of various accounting period techniques, we pulled a random sample of 100 Seattle families who had a male head and at least one child. These families had been included in the interviewing process because their gross family incomes were below $15,000 annually on a first round of interviews.

Each family had been asked to reconstruct its income over the

---

[4] This level is based upon the most extreme condition that families apply when their incomes are the lowest for the year and maintain payments at that level for the next twelve months. A more realistic set of assumptions based on probabilities of reporting income changes and recapture of overpayments will be included in a paper by Harold Watts prepared for the State of Vermont's Family Assistance Pre-Test Study. Watts' preliminary data indicate a range of total budget increase of from 130 to 180 percent.

preceding year (1969) month by month. We thus had both an annual figure and twelve monthly figures. We calculated eligibility for benefits on two bases: (1) Families were eligible if their incomes fell below their break-even point for the year:

$$.5 (Y_a - 720) \leq 1000 + 300 (n - 2)$$
where Y_a is annual earned income and n is family size

(2) Families were eligible if any one monthly income fell below the monthly break-even point:

$$.5 (Y_m - 60) \leq 83 + 25 (n - 2)$$
where Y_m is monthly earned income

Of the 100 families, 19 percent were eligible for payments under the first procedure, while a total of 42 percent were eligible under the second. The average annual income of the first group was $1,746 and the average for the additional 23 percent was $5,665. Making the admittedly extreme assumption that those whose monthly incomes fell below the breakeven continued to get payments at that level for the next twelves months, the average payment to the first group (average family size 4.8) was $1,327; the average payment to the 42 percent group (average family size 4.4) was $1,494. Looking at the 42 percent group after a year of payments, we would have had to recapture an average of $1,733 from each family at the "annual roundup" to insure annual equity, or an amount equal to over 40 percent of the average annual income of those families! Because the HEW national cost and caseload estimates used annual data from the Survey of Economic Opportunity, the extreme case described above under the monthly accounting system would raise the caseload nationally by a factor of 2.2 over current estimates and the costs by a factor of 2.5.

To illustrate how this is derived, consider the monthly accounting case as it would operate with the sample of Seattle families. If we are unable to recapture any payments, the average payment per family would be $1,494 for the year. Using the average Seattle income of $3,892 for eligible families under the monthly scheme, we will be paying at the equivalent of a program with a $3,080 guarantee level under an annual scheme. This can be seen by using the formula for annual entitlement:

$$\text{Ent} = G - .5 (Y_a - 720)$$
where G is the annual guarantee level

Substituting the Seattle average income and the average payment, we get

$$1,494 = G - .5 (3,892 - 720), \text{ or}$$
$$G = 3,080$$

We will thus have increased the FAP caseload by a factor of 2.2 and the average cost per case by 1.1 for a combined increase in program cost of 250 percent.

Even if we assume that we can reduce this by recapture, the *caseload* will still be as high, since all of these people will be recipients for some part of the year. Any modifications we made in the accounting period would, of course, reduce both costs and the caseload: for example, better methods for getting families to report changes in income quickly, using a quarterly rather than a monthly accountable period at enrollment, at least partial recapture of overpayments, and so forth. It does not seem to me, however, that we could bring it down to within reasonable bounds.

VIII. CONCLUSION

The goals of a nationwide income maintenance program would be best served through the following accounting and reporting system:

1. *A three-month or a one-month accounting period* in which payments would be based on an average of family income for the preceding three-month period, or on income in the previous month
2. *A carryforward method of reconciliation* to promote horizontal equity—income in excess of the break-even level for any accounting period would be counted as income in the next period
3. *A 12-month accountable period* to encompass cyclical changes in income—the carryforward sum would be used under the first-in–first-out principle, and the contribution to the sum from any given month would be the amount by which monthly income exceeds the break-even point
4. *Income reporting monthly on a short form* to insure responsiveness to need—most income (wages and salaries, Social Security, income from self-employment, etc.) would be reported by families every month using a short form
5. *A yearly report of other income on a long form* which would be filed by each family initially and each year thereafter to report income not shown on the short form for the preceding year and to estimate this other income for the coming year
6. *Frequent payment* to avoid burdening recipients with lengthy planning and budgeting problems—checks would be sent to recipients at least once each month and preferably biweekly

ADMINISTRATIVE ISSUES IN INCOME MAINTENANCE EXPERIMENTATION: ADMINISTERING EXPERIMENTS

David Kershaw

I. INTRODUCTION.

From recent discussions in Washington, it has become increasingly clear that one of the major contributions which current and future income maintenance experiments can make to the development of effective national programs is in the administrative sphere: What is the cost per recipient for processing forms and providing services; what sorts of personnel are required; can the system be truly self-administered; what is the impact of the accounting period; how is income to be defined; what constitutes a family unit; what kind of audit is efficient and appropriate, and so forth. It seems to us that one of the dangers inherent in current discussions of the Family Assistance Plan is the very real possibility that the framers will develop a system which does not permit self-administration by recipients because it is too cumbersome, too complicated, and makes demands which exceed the capacities of those the system is designed to serve. This would be tragic, because no other single element distinguishes the FAP from the current welfare system more than the hope held out that we can divorce services from grants and intrude in the lives of recipients only on request.

A second important consideration is that there will be a number of income maintenance experiments in the next few years. The extent to which these experiments together provide a coherent set of findings for policymakers will, in large measure, determine the value of their analytical contribution. In order for such coherence to be maximized, these experiments should be administered in such a way that (1) some recipient responses can be pooled, (2) analysis in one experiment can be compared to that in another, and (3) the entire combination of findings can be replicated in a future national program.

For all of this to happen, some measure of standardization and consistency, particularly in the highly volatile and unpredictable sphere of administration, must be introduced. This paper is an attempt both to provide some basis for a consistent set of administrative approaches to income maintenance experiments and to raise some of the most important administrative issues which lend themselves to experimentation.

The paper has two major sections. The first is a reasonably systematic description of the New Jersey experience, as applied to other experiments which are now being proposed. It is essentially a manual for the operation of other experiments, intended to provide a specific set of administrative guidelines. Many of the subsections indicate areas where major problems still exist; in other areas we are surer of how to do certain things. Within some of these sections we will also make suggestions for ways to experiment with different administrative techniques which can be applied to future experiments. At this stage, it is probably almost as important to learn how to administer experiments in income maintenance as it is to operate a national guaranteed income program.

The second section suggests some of the areas where future experiments can test various administrative techniques which might be used in a national program. We have come to grips with some problem areas and now think we know how they should be handled nationally. On others we have simply done some thinking and will suggest that other experiments include further work and testing. Where we can be constructive about the direction such tests should take, we will suggest some approaches.

II. ADMINISTERING EXPERIMENTS: THE NEW JERSEY TYPE

From the standpoint of administration, the kinds of experiments which are currently being discussed can be grouped into four major categories:

1. New Jersey type: experiments of reasonably limited duration (three to five years) limited in geographical location to a small number of sites, with a sample which is partially dispersed (i.e., a "test boring")

2. Experiments of long duration: experiments which must last a long time because they are testing questions like the impact of income maintenance on fertility, retirement decisions, educational achievement, and so forth

3. Saturation experiments: tests designed to discover "community effects" and other impacts associated with making income maintenance available to all persons within a specified area

4. Widely dispersed sample: generally this means a national probability sample, drawing recipients from widely scattered sites.

This paper will deal primarily with experiments similar to the New Jersey one, since that is where experience currently exists and most experiments will be of this type. This "test boring" kind of experiment is applicable where experimenters are attempting to measure the impact of income maintenance on work incentives among male- and female-headed families, the aged, single individuals, and others; the relationship between income maintenance and child care services, job training, counseling, and other services; the relationship between the accounting period, the frequency of payment, and the accountable period and the incentive issue; the impact of income maintenance on family stability, mobility, migration, the formation of new households, and various political and sociological issues. This section will treat the problem of administering such a test boring experiment in some detail; additional issues which apply to the three other kinds of experiments will be mentioned as they arise.

A. Predicting Costs

The issue of administrative cost is a particularly sensitive one. It is often possible to get support for a large transfer payment program provided the administrative costs are kept to a minimum. In this section we would like to break the issue of cost down into its most common components and discuss some average costs for various activities.

The operation of an income maintenance experiment can be divided into the following steps, each of which has its own special cost considerations: (1) sample selection and initial interviewing; (2) administration of the payments; (3) administration of a panel survey, including counter-attrition programs for the control groups; and (4) administration of the analysis. Within each of these categories, costs in various experiments will differ as a function of the eligibility criteria, where the site is located, how large the sample is, the ratio of experimental to control treatments, the number of different treatments, the duration of the experiment, the frequency of contact with the families, the changes instituted once the experiment is under way, the nature of the interviewing, and the kind of analysis which is performed. Each of these aspects of the experiment should be carefully considered in estimating costs before the experiment begins. As a guideline, the cost of analysis is, of course, least sensitive to changes in the number of families in the sample. With a relatively large experiment (sample size greater than 1,000 units), costs for research staff, report writing, computing, special projects, and so forth, will be at least $200,000 annually. This cost can be regarded as fixed relative to sample size, although it may change significantly as a function of the number and length of interviews administered.

The per unit cost of the other operations, depending again on the factors outlined above, should average as follows:

Operation	Annual cost/family
Sample selection and baseline interviews	$100–$150
Administration of interviews (including counter-attrition programs)	$ 75–$100
Administration of payments (general administration)	$125–$150

As in all activities of this kind, there are substantial diminishing marginal costs. For example, because screening interviews may be administered to a random number of households within a designated area, perhaps ten times the number of eligible persons are interviewed initially. In the New Jersey experiment, the eligibility rate was approximately 4 percent since we were looking for a male-headed, nonaged family with an employable member who was not a full-time student. Given the nature of the interview, however, we have also located single individuals, female-headed families, families with an aged head, and so forth. Other experiments will also develop a rather lengthy file of randomly selected individuals who are not eligible for the experiment at hand. Consequently, one important consideration in the development of new experiments is the fact that some of the existing ones can add families or individuals at virtually zero selection cost (a random run through the files of screening interviews) and at substantially diminished administrative and research costs.

B. The Political Context

We can say very little at this point about operating in a rural area, although the Iowa and North Carolina experiments should yield substantial information on that before long. This section deals with the urban political context which we feel is substantially more difficult than the rural in any case.[1]

By its nature, an income maintenance experiment in an urban area is exposed to the community at its most sensitive experimental stage—while the families are being selected. The potential for bias or fraud or both at this stage is great and care must be taken to insure that the integrity of the sample is maintained. There are several operating rules which we have developed in New Jersey which we feel are important.

First, decisions must be made with respect to who to inform before the selection process begins. It is of great advantage here if the sites selected for the experiment are not known outside of the research staff and if, additionally, there are some alternative sites. The experimenters are in a far stronger position if they have some options which they can exercise at some point during the initial experimental phases. There are two kinds of contacts which are important at this stage: those people who can help the experiment get under way and those people who can do it harm if they so choose. In the first category are individuals with either technical expertise and knowledge of the city (planning departments, Model Cities, local universities, certain individuals) or an official role in the community (the mayor and the chief of police). These people should be told that there is some thought about conducting an income maintenance experiment in the city and that an investigation is currently under way to determine whether the city is a suitable site. The general outlines of the experiment can be spelled out, particularly with respect to an estimate of how much money would be coming into the community if it is selected. It does not seem to be necessary to get very specific with respect to eligibility criteria at this point, and it is usually a good idea to refrain from doing so. If supplied with a few general descriptions of the experiment and a personal visit, these few officials are usually extremely cooperative.[2]

The more difficult liaison problem is with "community leaders." These can be loosely defined as unofficial or official representatives of various segments of the community, where community means community of dwellings, views, ethnic backgrounds, incomes, and so forth. Locating

---

[1] The New Jersey experiment faced some very difficult hurdles in several of the New Jersey cities. In particular, the larger the city, the more difficult were the political problems with the community. In Scranton, which approaches a rural location in some respects, few such problems were encountered.

[2] The chief of police should be informed because most cities require either a special permit for large scale interviewing or a letter of introduction from the police carried by each interviewer. To avoid interviewer arrests (some of which are inevitable in any case), close cooperation with the police is usually a necessity.

some of these people is easy; insuring that everyone who should be contacted has been contacted is more difficult. The approach should be similar to that with the officials of the community: a general description of the experiment (omitting any detailed discussion of eligibility criteria) and what it can do for the community (short term—community people will be hired to interview and supervise, and will be the recipients of the income transfers; long term—we're going to help get rid of the current welfare system which we all agree is terrible). The important thing about informing these leaders is to reinforce their leadership positions in the community; they do not like being neglected by any organization that is working in their territory. Serious trouble may arise if several people who have been interviewed approach one of these leaders to ask him what is going on and he does not know. Two things may happen, both of which we have experienced in New Jersey. First, he may instruct as many people as he leads not to submit to the interview. (In Passaic virtually an entire public housing project refused until we discovered who the leader was and spoke with him.) Second, he may decide that the operation represents a threat to his position and attempt to take more drastic action. (In Paterson members of several community groups infiltrated the interviewing staff with a view toward destroying the organization; in the end they realized that the experimenters had no designs on community control and, more important, that the interviewer salaries were supporting a number of their members.)

The process of identifying contacts should continue through the initial selection process, in order to make sure that no difficulties arise during the process of sample selection. It was our experience that very general pamphlets stressing the help being given to the community and the long-range goal of income maintenance worked very well and that most individuals who were originally either very interested or suspicious of the operation lost interest. Getting as many local people as possible to lose interest in the operation is, of course, the primary goal.

Following the sample selection phase, these same contacts can then be used during enrollment to legitimize the experiment for the recipients. When enrolling families initially, interviewers generally carry the names of three or four such persons who would be known and respected by each selected family. If the family is suspicious or hesitant, they can telephone or write to one of these people for assurance.

As the experiment continues, these people, in addition to the official contacts, should be kept informed of its progress; some of them may also be called upon to provide inside information about the city, help families cash their checks, and so forth.

The key aspect of the urban political context is the existence of violently competing power centers. It is not enough, for example, to locate a Puerto Rican leader and consider the Puerto Rican community fully informed. It is often the case that intense rivalries exist within the Puerto Rican community (e.g., Trenton), within the black community (e.g., Paterson), and between the community leaders and their previous peers who are now in local government positions (e.g., Passaic). The important lesson here is that, while the organization operating the experiment should attempt to contact various groups and individuals within the local area, it should also be extremely careful not to be identified with any one of them.

C. Organizational Considerations

The nature of the organization is important at three levels: (1) what kind of group should operate the experiment in the field; (2) what kind of organization should be responsible for the research, analysis, and overall supervision of the experiment; and (3) what relationships should exist between the operating, research, funding, and other organizations involved.

We have not arrived at any definitive answer to the whole question of the organization most suitable to operate an income maintenance experiment, but we do have a few observations which we feel may be helpful. With respect to the relationship between the organizations and the various levels of government, it now seems clear that, unless the number of actors is kept to a minimum, substantial, and perhaps insurmountable, operational problems will arise. Experimentation with income maintenance is exceedingly complex and delicate. Dealing with a panel study of relatively long duration, making variable payments to families in the sample, operating in a volatile political environment, and making constant adjustments in the experimental parameters as a result of things that are learned in the experiment or outside occurrences (e.g., FAP), means that the operating organization (as well as others involved) must be flexible in the extreme. Decisions must be made quickly and scientifically and new policies implemented rapidly. It is our strong recommendation, therefore, that income maintenance experiments be funded from one level of government directly to an operating agency or organization which has full power to make decisions and act on them.

We would add to that a second important consideration; that the organization operating the experiment have virtually no connection to any local agency or organization at the experimental site. On numerous occasions in New Jersey, the fact that the experiment was funded by OEO in *Washington* (as distinct from the local CAP agency, for example) got us out of very difficult situations. There is tremendous pressure by many local groups to help select the sample. First, this is the way things are done in most cities—those in power give out the jobs and decide on how the pie is to be divided. If any local agency is responsible in the least for the experiment, it will be impossible to distinguish sample selection from other (nonrandom) selections made routinely by the city government, and the experiment itself will become a political plum.[3] Second, it is important to establish at the outset that this is a *scientific* undertaking, not only to allay possible charges of rigging the selection process, but to deal with families who were not selected, to insure local officials that the experiment is not a political threat (again, because anybody giving out money is automatically regarded as having a good political base), and, as we will discuss later, to provide the firmest possible grounds for keeping the press away from the families. The fact that it is an experiment run by scientists has the additional advantage of diminishing ideological opposition to it among the lower-middle class and others in the area who might make it difficult to operate. ("We are certainly not committed to the idea of a guaranteed income, but we think it is important to find out about it once and for all," etc.) It was extremely helpful to us in New Jersey in this regard to use the two names, Institute for Research on Poverty at Wisconsin and Research and Plans Division of OEO.

The third important consideration is the organization which actually deals with the families and the local community. The staff in such an organization should have two main qualities: They should be academically oriented, to the extent that they understand the purpose of experimentation and are constantly attuned to analyzing, researching, and discovering, as opposed to merely operating, and they should be oriented toward the attitudes, views, and activities of the community, both because they must operate a program in that environment and because research is more effective if the researcher understands the experimental environment. The major difficulty here is that these two sets of qualities are rarely found in the same person. A community person who is excellent at dealing with the sorts of problems which arise in an urban area may never really grasp the nuances of experimentation. Over the course of the last year we have tried a number of different techniques, including operating a field office with strictly community people with light supervision from the central (research) office, operating with strictly research people, and a combination of these. Our feeling now is the organization should continue to hire locally, although this can be a function of how important this

---

[3] It appears that this may already be the case in Gary, where charges of favoritism in sample selection are already being leveled at the Model Cities agency six months before the experiment is to get under way.

factor is considered by each local community. (In our experience, for example, it appears very important in Paterson while it is of no importance in Scranton.) Along with local staff members, a field coordinator should be used—a person who is primarily research oriented but understands the problems of the local community. This person can provide continuous research direction to the field staff, bring his own research capabilities to bear in the local area, and maintain a standard set of practices by the office staff in the field. A very delicate balance must be maintained between an office which is in, and of, the local community and a scientific experiment which maintains some distance from involvement in local community problems and entanglements.

To sum up: A limited number of agencies or organizations should be involved, distant from any local relationships, research oriented but with the clear capability of operating with the blessing of the local community.

D. Special Problem of Interviewing

There is not a great deal that can be said about interviewing without going into considerable detail. Urban interviewing requires that all of the common interview problems be faced (e.g., reduction of sample bias through suitable call-back and other procedures; quality control, validation, etc.) in addition to the following unique urban requirements: (1) hire both interviewers and supervisors locally to insure rapport with the community; (2) devise a tighter organizational structure to assure that interviews and interviewers can be accounted for completely; (3) institute an effective training and retraining system which addresses itself directly to the problems of urban interviewing and local interviewers.

Interviewing in urban areas is sensitive, complex, and taxing work and requires an organization that understands the problems and attitudes which exist in cities. Our primary finding in this respect is that it is possible to interview on a very large scale (we did as many as 10,000 interviews in some cities), hold bias to a minimum, and achieve a rapid pace (1,000 interviews per week), provided that those doing the interviewing understand the difference between urban and suburban operations.

E. Sample Selection Methods

We will treat this section with considerable detail, since we have had substantial experience with it in New Jersey and because it is very likely that other experiments will include a selection process which is virtually identical to the one developed during a year of selection in New Jersey and Pennsylvania.

Besides selecting the sample which will remain in the study for a number of years, this selection process also includes (1) establishing the groundwork for the operating part of the experiment; (2) setting the tone of community relations; and (3) gathering the initial data upon which the experimental results will rest.

There are a number of sampling methods which could be used to select the sample; telephone interviews using reverse telephone directories to select families from certain areas, welfare case lists, insurance lists, mailings at random within certain areas, volunteers, selection through an existing community agency or through such organizations as churches and service groups, sign-ups at designated points throughout the city, or house-to-house canvasses. With the exception of the house-to-house survey method, all of the above introduce severe bias into the sample selection process. Volunteers and members of various organizations are self-selecting, not random; telephoning misses a large number of the poor who either have no phone or have unlisted phones (over half of the New Jersey sample have no phones); welfare lists are not inclusive of all eligibles, although they may be used later to check incomes and select a subset of the sample on welfare; community and neighborhood organizations immediately open the process to political accusations, favoritism, and other "nonscientific" practices; and so forth.

We would therefore recommend selection through house-to-house canvass-type interviewing. It is also probable that the following will hold as well:

1. In any given experiment a large number of interviews will have to be conducted, perhaps 10,000 or more
2. Accurate and up-to-date lists of dwelling units in the area will not exist and a separate "listing" operation will have to be undertaken
3. Current data on the city are either nonexistent or unreliable and sampling ratios will have to be determined through initial sample interviews, use of census and other relevant data, a coefficient of change added from previous experiments, and results as the interviews progress

Before the actual selection process begins the following steps should be taken.

1. Development of the Screening Instrument. The fact that interviewing will be conducted under the watchful eye of the community requires that a highly sophisticated and well-tested instrument be used during the screening process. Such an instrument requires careful pretesting in the community before its use. Specially developed techniques for eliciting meaningful income information from poor families should be employed to insure that eligible families are located quickly, comprehensively, and efficiently.

2. Definition and Characterization of the Experiment Site. Once the general area for the experiment is decided upon, it is easy to neglect further critical decisions on the precise location of the experimental target areas within the city. The determination of the exact boundaries of the house-to-house canvass is critical to both speed and the minimization of bias in the sample. As an example, the following procedure would be used to define a target area.

Examination of all relevant census and survey information on the area. City planning, Model Cities, census, and other maps and plans should be used to define a general area for the experiment. Particular attention should be paid to ethnic, age, income, and other relevant characteristics of the sample population as well as other considerations governing choice of area (e.g., an emphasis on the Model Neighborhoods).

Preliminary on-site examination. Relatively extensive and intensive discussions should take place with city officials, official and unofficial neighborhood leaders, and others with a knowledge of the community. Rough estimates of physical facilities requirements, interviewer travel problems, interviewer safety problems, and other operating considerations should be made at this time.

Tentative selection of target areas. Based on an analysis of the existing data on the area, discussions with residents, and the preliminary on-site examination, a tentative set of Census Tracts would be chosen for interviewing.

First-hand analysis of the site. Following the tentative selection of the site, a detailed examination of the target areas should be undertaken. This technique yields outstanding results in inner cities since they are continuously in a state of change. Every city block in the tentatively selected areas should be covered to determine whether it is residential, commercial, or vacant; its ethnic characteristics; any danger to interviewers; and so forth. In addition, areas not initially included in the target area should be investigated to determine if they should be included. All areas bordering on the target neighborhoods should be examined. As a result of this analysis, a new, final, target area should be drawn. In addition to providing a higher interviewing yield and insuring a lack of bias by including areas which might not have been noted as poor in the last survey of the area, this step eliminates the possibility of sending a lister or interviewer to a vacant interviewing segment or a woman alone to a dangerous segment, and gives the researchers an up-to-date picture of the total number of dwelling units which exist in the target area.

Sample interviews. As a final check on the selection of the site, a small number (50–100) of sample interviews should be administered in various parts of the target area. Particularly in the more doubtful fringe areas, these sample interviews provide a current picture of family characteristics, project more accurately the eligibility rate, and greatly help to determine an accurate sampling ratio. In addition, this step provides a final pretest of the screening instrument.

3. Determination of the Sampling Ratio. Based on the most recent census data and other data available on the city, an initial sampling ratio can be determined. This ratio would be modified as operations continue by (1) adding in a factor from other experiments on changes in family incomes and other characteristics since the last census, (2) use of the detailed on-site analysis to eliminate areas demolished for highways and other projects, and (3) use of the data from the sample interviews. The final sampling ratio which emerges would then give an accurate indication of the number of interviews which would be required and would enable the staff to draw up a realistic schedule for the screening and selection process.

If the above steps have been carried out completely, the selection process should proceed quickly and smoothly. Selection itself consists of the following:

Selection of segments for listing. A segment is most conveniently defined as a city block with a number assigned by the Bureau of the Census. Although these are often workable units for interviewing, problems may arise in using them because of the time between censuses, errors in the census, or the geographical particularities of the area being surveyed. Consequently, it is often desirable to combine some segments into working units of more manageable size or definition. This may require grouping up to ten segments together. After consolidating segments and determining the sampling ratio, the proper number of segments can be randomly chosen for listing. Since it is often necessary to interview more families than originally anticipated to arrive at a large enough sample, it is prudent to list more segments than one initially plans to interview. The extent to which the interviewing organization is flexible in changing the sampling ratio will be a critical ingredient in determining whether the schedule is met. The organization must develop a system for "over-listing" an adequate number of segments to allow for immediate expansion of the number of interviews if necessary.

Listing. Listing requires the notation of the address of every dwelling unit within each selected segment. Specially trained listers should survey each assigned segment within the target area using standardized techniques to insure full and accurate coverage of each segment. A set of ten to fifteen well-trained listers can usually list an area of 5,000 to 10,000 dwelling units in less than a week.

Preparation for screening. All dwelling units listed should be placed on individual dwelling unit cards. Each dwelling unit should have its own card to insure strict control and accuracy during interviewing. These cards form the basis for interviewer assignments and record keeping during the interviewing process.

Screening. All households within the selected segments should be interviewed. Randomly selecting whole segments rather than households insures much more accurate and complete coverage. (It is much easier to instruct interviewers to interview every household in a given block than a randomly selected number of households—he knows the area for which he is responsible and it is not necessary to burden interviewers with random selection techniques in the field.)

Quality control. Both during and after the interviewing, extensive quality control techniques should be used. These include telephone and on-site validation of up to 25 percent of each interviewer's work, a complete reading of each interview in the field, a rereading in the office, and a final computer error check.

Determination of eligibility and stratification. Based on the screening interview, families are declared eligible or not and stratified according to income, ethnic group, or other variables. Depending on the desired characteristics of the sample, a determination should be made as to which families would be interviewed in the second round (pre-enrollment interview).

Pre-enrollment interview. A longer interview is then administered to check on income information reported in the screening interview and to gather base-line information on the families before enrollment. In almost all income maintenance experiments it will be advisable to collect such "perishable" data prior to making the first transfer payment.

Redetermination of eligibility and final selection. Pre-enrollment interviews should be checked against the screening interviews for consistency and the more detailed income information on the pre-enrollment can then be used for a final eligibility determination. Coding can begin immediately.

Plan assignment. Eligible families are randomly assigned to the control or experimental groups and, within the experimental group, to each of the various treatments.

This selection process is a relatively time-consuming activity; it can become even more time consuming if the proper preparations are not made and if the organization is not flexible enough to make rapid changes as work progresses.

F. Enrollment Techniques

The enrollment period is the time the families have their first contact with the experimental agency as opposed to the interviewing organization. Experience in New Jersey indicates that misunderstandings, misconceptions, and attitudes created during enrollment are exceedingly difficult to change as the experiment progresses.

Enrollment should include the following: (1) a general introduction to the experiment, who sponsors it, why, how long it will last; (2) what the general benefits to recipients will be and under what circumstances they will continue to be members of the experiment (they may move, the family may split up, they may spend the money in any way they see fit, etc.); (3) the obligations of recipients including accurate reporting, change of address information, etc.; (4) further relevant information from the family—accurate weekly income, are they receiving welfare, other sources of income, do they plan to move; (5) making out the first income report form to begin the process of filing; (6) general encouragement to take advantage of the local office for assistance with filing or any other problems related to the experiment; and (7) careful explanation of their rights, including a brief explanation of the rules and information regarding right of appeal in cases of disagreement with a policy of the experimental agency.

The most general lessons learned in New Jersey about the enrollment process relate to the kind of personnel who do the best job and the nature of the training which should be provided. With respect to personnel, the first approach in New Jersey was that enrollers had to have a thorough theoretical background which would enable them to explain the negative income tax concept in detail to recipients. Accordingly, graduate students in the social sciences were used extensively for enrollment in Trenton, and largely in Paterson and Passaic. As in interviewing, however, it became clear that contact with the families should be made by staff members who understand the concept well enough, but who, in addition, thoroughly understand the attitudes and problems of recipients. Hiring was therefore changed from college students to community interviewing personnel.

The training procedures also evolved over the course of the experiment until it included the following stages:[4]

---

[4] Tangible evidence of improvements in both personnel and technique can be demonstrated from the fact that the refusal rate in Trenton (early training with graduate students) was 10 percent, in Paterson and Passaic (some community personnel with slightly refined training) was 8 percent, in Jersey City (all community people with new training scheme) was just under 2 percent and in Scranton (community people with final training technique) there was one refusal out of an enrollment of 165 families.

1. Introduction to the concept of income maintenance. Most enrollers have been interviewers and are very interested in the part they are playing in a larger national effort. It is important, therefore, to discuss in some detail the notion of income maintenance, what it is supposed to do and not do, who supports it, how it works, etc. This ordinarily takes about two hours.

2. Review of enrollment procedures. A thorough review of techniques, policies, and approaches for enrollment including a detailed discussion of each of the items in the enrollment packet. In New Jersey these include: brochure explaining the basic aims of the experiment; Rules of Operation in brief for the families; a Basic Payments Tables for the family's plan; an enrollment agreement for the husband and wife to sign; a calendar for the next six months with filing dates noted on it; an explanation of the method for filling out an income report form; an identification card for the family to enable them to cash their checks more easily; their first income report form which is filled out by them and given to the enroller to take back to the office; an information sheet on the family for reference by the enroller; a list of local contacts who would be known to the family that the family can call if there is doubt as to the legitimacy of the program; an enroller observation form on which any questions or problems or observations are noted by the enroller for inclusion in the family's file; and the family's first check. This procedure also takes about two hours.

3. A demonstration of enrollment by members of the staff. A brief run-through showing the approach, method, and a few typical problems is enacted by members of the staff for the benefit of enrollers.

4. A dry run by enrollers. Before sending enrollers into the field, a detailed set of practice sessions are administered to enrollers. The best procedure for this includes an assembly line arrangement where enrollers begin by introducing themselves and explaining the program to a member of the staff who makes it appropriately difficult, then proceeds to another staff member highly experienced with the use of the income report to tell him how to fill out the report (again, typical problems are posed to the enroller), and finally a session with other staff members who ask questions which are most likely to be asked. Each enroller is then given a list of questions which have been asked most often in the various New Jersey cities. The enroller studies the questions and asks about any of them which he finds puzzling. This activity takes each enroller about one hour.

5. A final pep talk. To avoid overwhelming the enrollers with the amount of information, a brief session is held either as a group or individually to assure enrollers that the process is very easy, that difficult problems arise only rarely, and that they are well prepared. This helps them to relax.

6. Retraining. After the first few enrollments have taken place, it is advisable to get together with the enrollers again and discuss

any unusual problems. At this point, the enrollers will want to do most of the talking. This session serves to review any difficulties as well as to build enthusiasm for the enrollment process in general.

Given an intelligent set of community people and a thorough training program (usually over a two-day period), enrollment should proceed rapidly. It is usually possible for an enroller to do between five and ten enrollments per day.

G. Counter-Attrition Methods

Income maintenance experiments combine the attrition problems normally associated with panel studies with added problems resulting from the fact that different families are receiving different payments, expectations may not be met, and various economic circumstances change during the course of the experiment. There are three distinct attrition stages: (1) refusals at the initial (screening or preenrollment) interviews; (2) refusals to be interviewed or dropouts during the experiment; and (3) changes in address and family splitting without word to the agency. The first two of these require preventive action, the latter remedial.

Initial refusals create bias problems for any study and are particularly troublesome at the beginning of a panel study of long duration. There are a number of steps which can be taken to minimize the refusal rate. The most effective is to use interviewers who can relate easily to respondents, since a relatively large number of refusals occur after a few minutes in a respondent's home. Assuming that interviewers are well trained and sensitive to respondent attitudes, it may still be necessary to "race-match" in some areas. Care should be taken during initial interviewing efforts to determine whether there is any evidence that refusals are a function of racial differences between respondent and interviewer. A third technique is to pay respondents for the time they take to answer questions. With respect to amount, we discovered that five dollars for each hour of respondent time got good results: five dollars was enough above the average hourly wage rate of respondents to seem attractive, but not so much higher that it made respondents suspicious (ten dollars created suspicions). While we have no hard evidence that five dollars is significantly better than nothing, we feel strongly that a payment of some kind helps to gain entrance to respondents' homes.

A fourth technique is to use a write-up about the program which is left at doors of respondents who do not open, are not home, or who do not want to answer. A few days later another interviewer can return and try again. This technique was very successful in Jersey City where a large initial refusal rate created some initial fears of substantial bias.

Fifth, the interviewing organization should be careful to make the proper community contacts to insure that various leaders know about the study and can respond positively if asked about it by potential respondents.

Finally, a well-written and thoroughly tested instrument insures that refusals are kept down by eliminating confusing, sensitive, or otherwise unsatisfactory questions.

Having taken whatever steps are necessary to minimize bias, it is still vital to determine what kinds of bias refusals are presenting. In order to do this in New Jersey, a sample of Jersey City respondents is being studied, including some who refused to be interviewed at the initial four tries, to determine the extent to which refusals are a function of income level, home ownership, race, age, ethnic group, or other characteristics traditionally associated with interview refusals.

Following sample selection, counter-attrition measures should be immediately instituted to minimize attrition during the panel study. A few lessons have been learned in New Jersey, although a great deal of work remains to be done on counter-attrition methods in panel studies.

The most important step is to develop an interest in participating or a sense of responsibility to the study without undue involvement which would tend to create a "Hawthorne effect." The best way of accomplishing this is to maintain brief, regular remunerative contact with sample families, bother them with long, taxing, sensitive interviews as little as possible, and make special provisions for notification of change of address. It is, of course, just as important for sample members to remember to notify the agency as it is for them to continue to open their doors when interviewers arrive. The New Jersey study makes a regular monthly payment to control group families in exchange for a card giving their current address. If there is no change, they still check a small box on the card and mail it in. Another payment is given in return for the quarterly interview. It is too early to determine the effectiveness of this method. However, a yearly bonus system, increasing for each year of participation, was found to be unsatisfactory, primarily because remuneration was deferred. Deferring a payment of $50 for a year makes it virtually useless as a counter-attrition procedure. Other techniques that were considered include: (1) a lottery for the sample families where a few members become eligible for a very large payment (e.g., a car or house)—rejected because of some legal difficulties and the problem of injecting a "gimmicky" quality into the study; (2) much larger interview payments—rejected because of the doubtfulness of responses elicited with a payment so large that sample members get suspicious or uneasy; and (3) a regular communication or "newsletter" to maintain interest—rejected because it was nonremunerative and might create "Hawthorne" type bias.

By far the most successful techniques have been small, regular payments in cash and an attempt to keep the interviews brief.

Having taken whatever steps are possible to elicit cooperation from the families in maintaining contact, the most difficult counter-attrition program still remains: locating those families who move and have not informed the agency. A number of successful techniques have been developed in the New Jersey study which we will list briefly here:

1. Inquire of neighbors—often successful although many neighbors tend to be suspicious of inquiries
2. Inquire of neighbor's children—get the names of the children from the interviews and ask other children where their friends have gone (this eliminates the suspicion problem among the adults and has been our single most successful technique)
3. Talk to others of the same name—many moves are within the same area and several families have been located by calling all of the names in the phone book corresponding to the lost family's name (relatives are often located in this way and are willing to give the new address of the family)
4. Use the school records at the children's school—particularly for local moves, but also often helpful for longer ones since schools are usually careful to list changes of address;
5. Post office—change of address forms are available at the post office or through the use of a postcard requesting change of address information on an individual
6. Inquiries of the landlord
7. Inquiries at stores and bars in the neighborhood—this has proved to be very effective
8. Inquiries through the public housing authority
9. Dial the same phone number—numbers are often left unchanged
10. Inquiries through the Department of Public Assistance or other assistance agencies in the community
11. Inquiries through the police
12. Inquiries through the Division of Employment Security
13. Inquiries through the local churches
14. Inquiries through state agencies for migrant workers
15. Inquiries through employers
16. Inquiries through a savvy community contact—there are a number of individuals in every city who know virtually everything that is going on—we have had great success in locating families, both within the city and those who have moved farther, through such people

Field office personnel should be extremely careful to use these techniques with sensitivity. They should be aware that families do not want some people to know where they are, and staff members should never discuss the experiment with any of these people of whom they are inquiring.

H. Confidentiality

The problem of maintaining the integrity of the sample population by protecting it from outside influences is central to this kind of experimentation. Aside from the problem of families telling one another that they are recipients (which does not seem to create serious difficulties for the experiment outside of some Hawthorne effect consideration), the sample is threatened primarily from the mass media and from existing governmental agencies whose aims may conflict with those of the experiment.

The major problem with the media is the assessment its representatives make about their audience: They are uninterested in why there is an experiment, what it is designed to find out, what a guaranteed income is, and what it means for the problems of poverty. The orientation is often toward "human interest" and, more importantly, toward public reinforcement of widely held (negative) stereotypes. In this regard, a newsman would prefer to interview a family himself rather than talk about the experiment with someone who understands what it is designed to do. Indeed, a great many newsmen have decided not to do a story at all after being refused access to families themselves. Barring a personal interview in which he can use the name of the family (very important for human interest), a newsman would like the following, in decreasing order of preference: an interview using no name, a telephone call to a family, a talk with someone on the staff who has just seen a family, a set of quotes from families, a set of family profiles, a description of the experiment. As one gets to the bottom of this list, the accuracy of the story increases, since the newsman discusses the experiment with people who view it with some perspective. Given the built-in conflict between accuracy and human interest, it is not surprising that there have been virtually no accurate articles or news programs about the experiment.

The real problem here is not the lack of accuracy, which we seem to have been able to absorb, but the critical difficulty in keeping representatives of the press, radio, and television away from the families. As we began the experiment, we held rather vague fears regarding the impact of the media on families made available for interviews. Our primary concern centered around the fact that they might no longer react in the same way to the receipt of our payments and would therefore cease to be valid experimental observations. Our experience to date is too limited to speak definitively about such reactions, although we have increasing reason to believe that our original assumptions about it were correct. In addition, one of the families interviewed has been subjected to a tragic set of events as a direct consequence of a television interview.

The key lesson of New Jersey is to be publicly firm about interviews with families from the beginning. We had a long series of arguments regarding whether we should make a limited number of families available to the media for interviews. Most of us felt that, since this was an important national experiment, we were using public funds, and we wanted to educate the public about the concept of income maintenance, it would be wise to provide some means for satisfying requests by the media ("satisfying" being defined as access to families). We therefore identified a few "typical" families and cooperated with one of the networks in producing an interview. As some of us had feared, this indicated to all other newsmen that the only way to do a story is to talk to families. The others are not satisfied without talking to families and would, of course, like to speak with individuals who have not as yet been interviewed so that their responses will be "spontaneous." Our policy for the last six months has been that no access is given to any families; the names of families already interviewed are "in the public domain" but we do not give them out either. It is very difficult for us to hold this line after initially giving way. Future experiments should decide on a policy in the beginning and follow it. We feel strongly that an income maintenance experiment is so delicate that the researchers have to insulate it as much as possible. In addition, the extent of the responsibility to the families selected cannot be overemphasized. Too often we have a tendency to consider them "lucky winners" in a contest, forgetting both the contribution they make as individuals to the experiment and the extent to which the experiment has an impact on their lives. The money from the experiment is not "extra" payment for having been selected to participate in an interesting undertaking; for many it represents their sole source of income. Under these circumstances tampering from the outside can have, from their point of view, an impact of major proportions. The experimenters have an ethical, as well as legal, obligation to tread very carefully with the rights of privacy of the families in the sample.

A second major area where confidentiality is important is in the relationship of the experiment to existing public agencies, in particular welfare and public housing. We made some assumptions in New Jersey which appear to have been relatively serious mistakes. In the first instance, we assumed that, if we told families to be sure to report our income to public housing and welfare people, they would automatically do so. However, since for some families our payments constituted a major source of family support, they were reluctant to report our payments and face a corresponding reduction in other forms of support. We have reminded families on several occasions that they should continue to inform the appropriate government agency of the extent of their participation in the experiment. It now appears that some more formal reporting arrangements should be used.

Second, we based some of our policies on the assumption that families would react in economically rational ways to the interaction of our payments with those of other agencies. The best example is the public housing case. Since we impute rent to families with subsidized housing, their payments increase when public housing raises their rents (although by not as much). Accordingly, we obtained a waiver from the various public housing authorities regarding the *eligibility* of our families for the three-year experimental period (i.e., they would be able to remain in the project despite an increase in income), but we agreed with public housing that there was no reason for the rents to remain at the same level. We explained this to the families. It now appears, however, that many poor families exhibit a basic fear of investigation by any government agency for any reason. Despite the fact that the family is much better off with a higher rent and our payments, the decision on the part of public housing to raise the rent constitutes a perceived threat of broader proportions. Similarly, the possibility of a welfare investigation represents a threat large enough for some families that they would prefer not to receive our payments at all. We have had a number of families drop out (and lose benefits) over the public housing and welfare problems; in addition, some families refused to enroll initially for the same reason. The best approach to this problem now appears to us to be a more rigid and formal agreement with public housing people either not to raise the rents at all or, if that is not feasible, to have the experimental agency make up the difference in rent without involving the family. The relationship between public housing and a national income maintenance system will, of course, be carefully worked out. Our experience has implications for further experimentation, however, since an experiment represents an additional, unofficial, and sometimes puzzling outside agency. The idea of our coming in for a three-year period and inducing agencies of government to begin investigation is troubling to the families.

The final erroneous assumption which we made in New Jersey (and potentially the most damaging) was that various welfare agencies would be well intentioned, cooperative, and attuned to the national importance of our efforts. Although we have developed a workable relationship with a number of agencies throughout the state, the possibility that a family may not report accurately and thereby have fraud charges brought against it remains a very serious problem. The experiment does not want to be in the position of continually forcing the families to report. (Indeed, one legitimate experimental finding is the accuracy of reporting.) In addition, it now appears that some families may not report payments accurately to the requisite agency at some point in the experiment, usually due to over-sight, but sometimes intentionally. If the welfare agencies appreciated the problems of this kind of experimentation and held a real interest in scientific inquiry, these situations could be worked out jointly. In many agencies, investigation is a goal in itself, however, and zealous case-workers and investigators are a continuing threat to the experiment. The result may be to create legal difficulties for some of the families on the basis of their participation in the experiment. To avoid this, some formal arrangement of a legal nature should be reached at a high level, tempo-rarily waiving the rights of the local agencies to investigate (usually read "harrass") families who are participating. The agreement should not be intended to exonerate, in advance, illegal behavior, but to give the ex-perimental agency latitude in order to operate.

The major recommendation of this section is that experiments of this nature can preclude serious difficulties, both for the families personally and for the experiment, by making a set of high level, formal agreements initially, commensurate with the importance of the undertaking. Both with respect to the media and in the case of the relationship with govern-mental agencies, strict confidentiality and a corresponding control over the experimental environment is the only way in which the sample can survive the experiment intact.

I. Effect of the Experiment Itself on Responses

One of the most common criticisms of the New Jersey experiment is that it does not last long enough to allow families to react to the receipt of the transfers in a "natural way," that is, in the same way they would were the payments part of a permanent national income maintenance program.

Within the larger area of uncertainty surrounding an experiment of relatively short duration are a number of related, specific criticisms: (1) the families will feel like guinea pigs and will react simply because they are part of an experiment ("Hawthorne effect"); (2) they will react to the aims of the experiment and use the money in atypical ways ("funny money"); (3) they will develop a conditioned pattern of responses to the quarterly interviews during the experiment and thus their answers will be a function of the fact that they have been interviewed previously; and (4) the relatively short duration of the experiment will make responses unnatural and atypical (they will be either getting used to it or looking toward the termination date).

At this point we cannot say a great deal that is definitive about any of these criticisms. With regard to the first point, we have developed an interview which will determine their awareness to being part of an experiment, how they feel about it, how it affects their behavior, and so forth. In the absence of tabulated results from this interview—currently being administered in Trenton—we have evidence collected from the contacts of our field office staff with the families. Our current impression from this source is that the families view us essentially as another agency; indeed, many of them are financially dependent upon the regular receipt of the biweekly checks. The efforts we have made to separate the interviewing (Urban Opinion Surveys) from the payments (Council for Grants to Families) appear to have been largely successful; the families themselves seldom confuse the two (e.g., ask an interviewer a question about their payments) and appear to be largely oblivious to our continued scrutiny of their activities. While none of these impressions is systematic enough to depend on, it is clear that all experiments should develop a means to measure the extent of the Hawthorne effect.

Second, we had been very wary that families would use our payments to do special things (i.e., socially valued activities like clothes for the children, home furnishings, saving) because of its source and because of the nature of the experiment.[5] However, it now appears that this is not going to be a problem. For families close to the poverty level, the luxury of regarding any payment as "funny money" simply does not exist. From a large number of office staff contacts with families, it is reasonably clear that our payments are added to any others the family receives and used with them for things the family typically buys. From these preliminary indications our payments do not appear to be segregated from other income, although the interview currently being administered is designed to obtain more systematic information on this point.

The nature of the responses on the quarterly interviews is a little more disturbing. As several members of the research staff had feared,[6] we are beginning to see some of the problems often encountered in a relatively lengthy panel study. In an early pre-test of the interview

---

[5] Some families agreed to enroll after being told that their participation was important: they had been selected to participate in the first try at a national income maintenance program. Under those circumstances, some families may have felt an obligation to spend the money in certain ways to support the overall goal.

[6] In particular, Myron Lefcowitz and David Elesh of the University of Wisconsin.

currently being administered in Trenton, one of the respondents indicated that he had never really thought about some of the things covered in the questionnaires and was now reading the newspaper and watching television more so that he would be better prepared for the questions. This is obviously a serious problem and must be countered in any panel study. The standard response is to use two control groups, one interviewed as often as the experimental group and the other only rarely, sometimes only at the beginning and the end of the study. We currently intend to use such a second control group to gauge the extent of bias in the response pattern of the regularly interviewed families.

The final specific criticism, that these families have a longer time horizon than three years and therefore none of their responses are particularly meaningful, is much more difficult to deal with. My current view is that three years is a lengthy enough period of time for these families that their responses settle down to those analogous to a national program after the initial suspicion and uneasiness about who is running the study vanishes (i.e., after the first six months to a year).

Nevertheless, the question of whether responses are valid in a three-year experiment and, if so, when are they most so, continues to worry us. The special interview which I discussed above addresses itself to the issue of time horizon, although it is not clear whether one can deal with that sort of question in an interview. We may decide that depth interviews with a relatively small group of families are the answer, or that we need to administer a special battery of psychological tests to determine whether or not we can depend on the responses.

The rather indecisive point of this section is that there appears to be some cause for alarm on Hawthorne effect grounds but that we will be able to test the extent of bias imposed by the experiment itself if we develop suitable techniques.[7] In any case, future experiments should investigate such techniques with care.

J. Phasing Out

Related to the concern above regarding how we affect the lives of the families while they are participating in the experiment is the problem of what arrangements can be made for them at the end of the experiment. The fact that we have fully or partially supported a number of these

---

[7] A particularly troublesome point is the fact that these techniques may themselves result in Hawthorne-like effects. The administration of a special interview may have a great deal more impact on the respondents than the quarterly interviews. We are therefore proceeding with our new questionnaire with great care, using only a small subsample of the Trenton experimental group.

families for three years and derived a great deal of useful information from them clearly vests us with some responsibility for their welfare after the experiment itself is completed.

There are two major possibilities: we will not have to do anything because some other program will take over for us, or we will have sole responsibility for letting the families down.

In the first instance, there are a number of things which could happen. First, FAP will become law and all families will have a guaranteed minimum income. The problem with depending on this, aside from the uncertainty of passage in Congress, is the different regulations under FAP and the New Jersey NIT: the training and work requirement under FAP, the fact that our families without children would not be covered, the different support levels and so forth. Second, we may want to use all of the New Jersey families as some sort of national control group for FAP, keeping them at the current levels and operating under the same regulations in order to test future rules which could be part of FAP. These families would be particularly valuable as such a control. Third, we might be able to make the case that these particular families, by virtue of their participation in the negative income tax program, would make excellent observations for some other experiment: a manpower NIT study like Seattle, a consumption study, a long-run set of experiments on fertility, retirement, family formation, migration, mobility, and so forth. There seems to be some indication that others might be anxious to take them on as experimental observations. Finally, we ourselves might decide that time horizon considerations were such that we wanted to observe them longer, and the decision as to how to phase out could be put off.

In the event that none of the above are feasible, however, the problem of phasing out becomes serious and delicate. It seems to me that we have three techniques which could be used, perhaps in concert. The first is a special training program for the families involved, with intensive reeducation, counseling, and placement efforts. If begun in time to give families six months of such training, we might have an impact on those in the sample who would be able to work. Second, a special effort could be made to involve other agencies in training, placement, and, particularly in the case of families without an earner, in additional financial assistance. The experiment would begin to act as an ombudsman for the families, insuring at the very least that all services normally available to the needy in each community are available to them. Finally, barring the funds to engage in the above, some thought should be given to a phase-down of the payments. It has become clear to us that many of the families in the experiment react only to concrete stimuli and not to written or oral information or instruction. We are no longer confident that our initial statements regarding the three-year duration or a warning near the end would suitably prepare the families for the cessation of payments. Consequently, if funds could be found, it would be desirable to carry families for a somewhat longer time at a lower level or, if no such funds were available, to start a lower payment six months before the end of the experiment and carry such a lower payment six months longer than the original termination date. In the event that most other remedies are closed off, this would seem a minimal way of making the approach of the end of the experiment more tangible.

It is not necessary that an experiment propose a definitive termination solution before beginning, because a great deal changes over the duration of the study. A number of promising solutions have occurred to us since beginning which still require investigation. Such solutions only arise as the experiment itself operates in a given location and as organizations and individuals in a position to help at the end become aware of it. Nevertheless, it is in keeping with the experiment's overriding responsibility for the livelihood of the families it selects to take effective steps to smooth the transition at the end.

MARGINAL TAX RATES ON EARNINGS IN EXISTING TRANSFER PROGRAMS FOR THE POOR*

Leonard J. Hausman

I. INTRODUCTION

What are the implicit marginal tax rates on earned income in transfer programs which are primarily directed at the poor? This question needs to be answered for a variety of reasons: (1) in conducting research on the work incentive effects of the tax rates in AFDC or in a negative income tax experiment, one wants to avoid errors in measuring the tax rate variable; (2) if a new income maintenance program is adopted, the designers of that program will want to consider how it will mesh with existing programs—or how existing programs should be changed to mesh with it; and (3) even if a new income maintenance scheme is not adopted, persons involved in altering existing programs will want to consider the relationship of their programs to others. What follows is largely a description of the tax rates that are currently in effect in the various transfer programs. Some attention is devoted to the relationships of tax rates in a few programs, and consideration is given at the end to how these programs might be modified if a universal plan of income support is adopted.

With an awareness of the fact that nominal and effective tax rates

* Robert J. Lampman originally suggested that a paper be written on this topic. The author is grateful to him and to Glen C. Cain, who made some very helpful comments.

are often quite disparate, I will describe the tax rates built into: (1) AFDC, AFDC-UP, and general assistance (GA); (2) benefits related to public assistance; (3) Medicaid and other health programs for the poor; (4) the food stamp, surplus commodities, and free school lunch programs; and (5) public housing, leased housing, and rent supplementation in private housing. There will also be a brief discussion of the tax rates on earnings in three other income support programs: unemployment compensation, survivors' insurance, and veterans' programs for nonaged, able-bodied persons.

II. PUBLIC ASSISTANCE

Until some new scheme like the Family Assistance Plan supersedes them, the 1967 Public Assistance Amendments have established three rate structures in AFDC and two in AFDC-UP; one other prevails in the decreasingly important GA program.

In AFDC, the tax structures will vary according to whether a state pays: (a) 100 percent of "needs"; (b) some variable amount of needs or; (c) some constant proportion of "need," i.e., some proportion of needs less other income. Illustrations of each of the three situations might be useful. In the group (a) states, the first $30 of the pooled monthly earnings of unit members who are not enrolled in school will be taxed at a zero rate; earnings above $30 will be taxed at a 66⅔ percent rate, i.e., benefits will be reduced by $2 for every $3 the family earns. In the group (b) states, the matter is more complicated. Initially, monthly earnings will be treated as they are in the first group of states; then a different rate will apply. Take a family in Delaware whose needs are valued at $200. In the absence of any nonwelfare income, assume that its AFDC payment would be $160. If the female head begins to earn $130 per month, her earnings will be taxed in a two step process. First, like the women in the group (a) states, she will have $30 of it taxed at a zero rate and $100 taxed at a 66⅔ percent rate. Thus she nets $63; and $67 remains as taxable earnings in the second step of the process by which her payment is determined. In this step, she is allowed to retain that part of remaining taxable earnings that is less than or equal to needs ($200) minus the potential maximum payment ($160)—thus up to $40—without any reduction of benefits. This mother, in effect, faces a zero rate on the first $90, and then a marginal rate of 66⅔ percent. The amount of earnings taxed at a zero rate will obviously vary among families and among the group (b) states, according to the relationship between needs and potential maximum payment. In the group (c) states, after the "30-and-⅓ rule" is applied to earnings, a family with needs and earnings like those of the family in the previous example will be treated as follows: needs ($200) minus remaining taxable earnings ($67) equals need ($133); payments equal 50 percent of need, or $66.50. This family's payment would have been $100 [=.50(200 − 0)] in the absence of any earnings. Thus, the mother faces a zero rate on the first $30 and a marginal rate [= reduced payments ($33.50)/taxable earnings ($100)] of 33.5 percent beyond $30.

A number of qualifiers are in order. First, no one is really sure that these are the procedures that the state will follow. They are the best (and very plausible) guesses of a person on the staff of the President's Commission on Income Maintenance Programs. Second, I have ignored three items that are deducted from gross earnings *before* the $30 and ⅓ rule applies: employee payroll deductions, such as income and OASDHI taxes and union dues; the standard employment expense allowance, for the incremental food, clothing, and laundry costs associated with employment; and other costs of employment, such as day care and transportation expenses. These three items will frequently exhaust all earnings. Third, children in the AFDC unit who are enrolled in school can earn any amount at a zero rate. Fourth, AFDC unit members who are enrolled in training programs or special works projects under the Work Incentive Program (WIN) face different (actually zero) tax rates on their training allowances or project wages. Fifth, unearned nonwelfare income is taxed differently. In some states, $7.50 of unearned family income is taxed at zero rate. Above that amount, it is taxed at a 100 percent rate in group (a) states; a zero and 100 percent combination in group (b) states; and a non-zero, non-100 percent rate in group (c) states.

The AFDC-UP program exists only in group (a) and group (b) states. Earnings of AFDC-UP unit members should be treated like the earnings of AFDC unit members who are in the same state, except that the SRS has established a special rule for fully employed AFDC-UP fathers: their benefits drop from wherever they are at 29 hours of employment to zero at 30 hours of work (or at whatever is a full-time work week in a particular industry). At some point, an AFDC-UP father faces a tax rate in excess of 100 percent. This is one way of creating a "notch problem," a situation where a working nonrecipient receives a lower total money income than a recipient who is working less. SRS developed this ruling, they claim, because a fully employed father is legally not entitled to receive AFDC-UP benefits, even if the 30 and ⅓ rule does not result in reducing his payments to zero at 30 hours of work. The SRS resolution of the conflict between these two aspects of AFDC-UP law appears to be a typical "cost-saving" welfare maneuver. Lastly, in GA, my best guess is that the constant 100 percent rate is now in effect universally.

III. BENEFITS RELATED TO PUBLIC ASSISTANCE

There are three types of benefits which an AFDC mother can or will lose as her payments are reduced to zero: day care and other welfare services, complete protection from liability for consumer debts, and a substantial degree of income security.

Welfare departments may subsidize in full the cost of day care for the children of employed welfare mothers. Where a child is placed in a day-care center for the entire working day, the costs of such care average about $1,500 per child per year. How the costs of day care to the mother vary as her earnings increase is a matter about which generalizations cannot easily be made. There will be great variation among local welfare jurisdictions on this matter as more mothers are placed in jobs under the WIN Program, because the SRS has distributed only guidelines, i.e., suggestions, and not requirements to the states. While on welfare, the costs of day care will be fully borne by the agency. SRS has told the states that they "are expected to continue services as long as necessary to sustain training or employment of a mother . . . after termination of assistance, to prevent recurrence of financial need, and until other satisfactory child care arrangements can be made";[1] and to consider charging the assistance terminee part of the costs of day care. Given the acute shortage of day-care facilities, one must be skeptical about the willingness of the states to keep the children of welfare terminees in day-care centers. The marginal tax rate on earnings that results from the phasing out of day-care services could thus be negligible or astronomical.

On the matter of the protection recipients receive from the liability for consumer debts, James Graham has written:

> The former client also subjects himself, *instanter,* to liability for past debts. In New York, creditors are prohibited by statute from attaching a client's earnings or utilizing other legal devices to compel repayment. But these protections expire with the last receipt of welfare assistance. Consequently, the study found, some clients never contemplate leaving the rolls because they feel they could not face the economic consequences. It is not uncommon, for example, for an employed recipient to deliberately keep his income below the budget level, receive token assistance, and retain his welfare immunity.[2]

---

[1] Social and Rehabilitation Service, "Guides on Federal Regulations Governing Service Programs for Families and Children: Title IV, Parts A and B, Social Security Act" (U.S. Dept. of Health, Education, and Welfare, April 1969), p. 25.

[2] James J. Graham, "Civil Liberties Problems in Welfare Administration," *New York University Law Review,* Vol. 43 (November 1968), pp. 885–86.

Graham provides no estimates of the extent of this behavior among recipients in New York, and I have no idea how common this debt-immunity is across the nation. Where the immunity provision exists, the implicit tax rate on earnings at the welfare margin can, again, far exceed 100 percent.

As of July 1, 1969, reestablishing eligibility for welfare was supposed to become a simpler matter than in the past for recipients who involuntarily lost their jobs within four months after leaving welfare. If this does happen, then the possibility of losing a substantial amount of payments while waiting to get back on the rolls is likely to be less of a deterrent to leaving welfare than it has been in the past. If eligibility is not going to be easily reestablished upon termination of employment, another situation will exist in which the implicit tax rate on earnings at the welfare margin can exceed 100 percent: a man whose monthly earnings of $400 made his family ineligible for any payments may find, after he loses his job, that he has to forgo three months and $600 worth of welfare payments before he is allowed to return to the rolls.

IV. MEDICAL PROGRAMS

The largest program of medical aid for the nonaged poor is Medicaid. Under this program, beneficiaries often receive, at no out-of-pocket cost to themselves, a vast array of diagnostic, physician, hospital, nursing home, and pharmaceutical services, at the facility and doctor of their choice.

This program too, however, has developed an income zone in which the implicit marginal tax rate on income can be greater than 100 percent. Before this is demonstrated, one must first know how eligibility for this program is established. Forty-eight of the fifty states had a Medicaid program as of March 1970. Of the 48 states that had Medicaid, 28 states admitted both the "categorically" and the "medically" needy to the program, whereas 20 states admitted only the categorically needy. The categorically needy are those who receive some cash assistance payments. Medically needy persons are those in nonwelfare families whose annual family incomes, net of taxes, are less than or equal to $1\frac{1}{3}$ of the welfare cost standard (or needs) for a similar family within a given state. Thus in New York, for example, if a particular nonwelfare family of four could get $3,000 on AFDC, its net income could rise as high as $4,000 before it would become ineligible for Medicaid.

Now the new AFDC tax rates on earnings and the Medicaid eligibility rules must be considered simultaneously to understand the tax rate problem in the group of 28 states. The break-even level (B) that results from the 30-and-$\frac{1}{3}$ rule is typically, though not universally: $B = 3/2A + $

360, where A is the income guarantee (or welfare cost standard) for a particular family.[3] B will always exceed the Medicaid cutoff line (C), because $C = 4/3A$ and $3/2A + 360 > 4/3A$. Since $B > C$, when an AFDC family earns the marginal dollar that reduces its welfare payment to zero, it simultaneously loses the most comprehensive medical insurance imaginable. Once again we find the familiar notch problem.

Return to the New York family of four to see why the *average* implicit tax rate on earnings that are equal to $D - B$, where D is any income level greater than or equal to B, may rise above 100 percent. Assume $D = \$5,000$; we know $B = \$4,860$ and $C = \$4,000$, if $A = \$3,000$. According to SRS rules, this family becomes eligible for Medicaid again when its income drops to C or below, of course, or when its medical expenses become equal to or greater than $D - C$. For earning the \$140 $(= D - B)$, this family thus forfeits all medical benefits of up to \$1,000 $(= D - C)$. If the family anticipates spending around \$140 or more on dental, medical, hospital, and pharmaceutical services during the year, it would be quite sensible to keep its income below \$4,860.

In the 20 states which allow only welfare families to receive Medicaid, recipients may also face an implicit tax rate of more than 100 percent when their earnings approach B. Not only are welfare families in these states with sizable medical needs induced to stay on welfare; but, because these states do not provide Medicaid to the medically needy, there is also a powerful incentive for near-welfare families to reduce their incomes to below A (not B).[4] The incentive problems created by this weird mess of welfare and Medicaid rules is somewhat dulled by the availability of alternative sources of low-cost or free medical care: OEO Neighborhood Health Centers, outpatient clinics in hospitals, federally financed maternal and child health care programs for the poor, and veterans' hospitals for those poor males who were in the military.

V. FOOD PROGRAMS

The surplus commodities and the food stamp programs are the two main public programs under which food is transferred to the poor. Within a county that has the surplus commodities program, all families that have

---

[3] B is generally higher than $3/2A + 360$, because annual Social Security taxes and the employment expense allowance should be added to the \$360.

[4] The problem of having welfare families whose incomes lie between A and B receiving both welfare and Medicaid while similar nonwelfare families with equivalent money incomes receive neither arises from the welfare rule which requires a family's income to fall below A before it can start to receive any welfare benefits.

incomes and assets below state-determined cutoff lines and all welfare families, regardless of their income levels, are eligible for such aid. The state-determined income cutoff levels for nonwelfare families vary substantially, but they generally fall below the Orshansky poverty lines. For example, the monthly income cutoff levels for families of four are $260 in Wisconsin, $195 in North Carolina, and $270 in Missouri. Cutoff levels for welfare families would vary among families and among states, according to their payment levels and tax rates. The current estimated retail value of the typical bundle of goods distributed monthly under this program is $15 per person. Thus, in a four-person family, even if the family values its food at only half the USDA estimated retail value, there is a loss of $30 in monthly income associated with the dollar of earnings that reduces payments to zero; or, for the nonwelfare family, the dollar of earnings that brings income over the income cutoff lines.

The food stamp program distributes benefits in a more reasonable manner, from the work incentive point of view. The benefit varies by region, welfare status, family size, and income. An illustration of how the program works should be useful. A family of four with a net monthly income of $175 is required to put up $56 in cash to receive $78 worth of food stamps; its transfer payment is thus $22 of food stamps. If its income rises by $20, it *must* put up $60 in cash to receive $80 in stamps, or a transfer of $20 of stamps. Thus, as its earned income increased by $20, it lost $2 of stamps and $4 of the increase were restricted to food stamp purchases if the family wanted any food stamps. Depending upon what part of the $4 it really wanted to use for food, the marginal tax rate on the $20 was somewhere between 10 and 30 percent. The tax rates are not constant among families of different sizes or across income classes for a given-sized family. They are typically higher for the lower-income classes and in the range of the illustration for the higher-income classes; at the highest income level, however, they will approach 100 percent.

The USDA also distributes food to poor people through the free school lunch programs. Some school districts use income cutoffs to determine pupil eligibility for these programs. I do not know what these cutoffs are. Most likely, though, eligibility is an all-or-nothing phenomenon at the Orshansky poverty lines.

VI. HOUSING PROGRAMS

There are three housing programs under which low-income families receive aid: public housing, rent supplements, and leased housing.

Public housing is the oldest and largest of the three programs, and rents are determined by local housing authorities. Rents vary with the operating costs of the project and with rents in the local private market, as well as with family size, family income, and the employment-related expenses of the employed head. There are three types of rules by which rents are set, given operating costs and local private rents: (1) all families pay the same rent for a particular type of unit; (2) public assistance recipients, who constitute roughly one-fifth of the perhaps 80,000 public housing project families, are charged the maximum rent that a local welfare department will pay for them; (3) tenants pay 21.7 percent of their family income net of taxes, employment-related expenses and, in some instances, part of the earnings of children and spouses. A project will use either rule 1 or 3; sometimes rule 2 will be used in combination with rule 3. Families operating under rule 1 face a zero tax on added earnings; families under rule 3 face a marginal rate of 21.7 percent.

In most projects, there is one other way in which the marginal rate can rise above zero in public housing. Rents in projects are generally supposed to be at least 20 percent below rents in the private market for similar apartments. Consequently, when a family's income passes the project's income ceiling, which again varies among localities and by family size, it is likely to face a sudden annual rent increase of about 25 percent when its income increases by a few dollars. For example, a family of four with a net income of $5,000 will pay rent of $1,085 per year. For comparable private housing, it should have to pay around $1,350 per year. When its income rises by a few dollars it will be evicted from the project and thus pay a "tax"—either by paying nearly $300 more in rent or by accepting lower quality housing.

Under the rent supplement and leased housing programs, beneficiaries live in privately owned housing and receive rent subsidies from the federal government. Beneficiaries generally pay a constant 25 percent of their net, adjusted family income in rent, and the 25 percent rate becomes the implicit tax rate on earnings. (Gross family income is netted and adjusted for employment expenses and family size.) In this program, unlike public housing, a tenant can remain in the dwelling unit forever; that is, no income ceilings exist. But, as in public housing, the federal government does exclude very low-income families by limiting the subsidy per family that it will provide.

VII. OTHER PROGRAMS THAT AID THE ABLE-BODIED NONAGED POOR

The survivors' insurance part of OASDHI, unemployment compensation, and death pensions to dependents of deceased veterans are all income-conditioned income maintenance programs which were not designed exclusively to aid the poor, but rather to support any insured families whose incomes were interrupted by the death or unemployment of a possibly nonpoor breadwinner. The implicit tax rates on income built into them as well as into the College Scholarship Service evaluation of parental ability to contribute to the expenses of an enrolled child are discussed in this section.

Benefits from the survivors' insurance component of OASDHI flow largely to female-headed families in which there are one or more orphaned children. Maternal orphans and paternal orphans whose mothers have remarried also receive aid under this program.[5] Benefits received by paternal orphan families are a function of the deceased father's earnings which determine the family's "primary insurance amount" (PIA), family size, and the earnings of the surviving mother. Generally, surviving mothers face either a constant zero tax rate on earnings or a tax schedule which combines zero, 50 percent, and 100 percent rates. Mothers in families in which the maximum family benefit can be reached when the mother is excluded from the beneficiary group—generally, all families which have three or more eligible children and two-children families with very low PIA's—face a zero rate on earnings. Mothers in other eligible families face a zero rate on the first $1,680 of annual earnings, a 50 percent rate on earnings between $1,681 and $2,880, and a 100 percent on earnings above $2,880, until only the mother's part of the family's benefit is reduced to zero.

In the unemployment compensation (UI) program, the states divide into four groups, with respect to the implicit tax rates on the earned income of UI recipients.[6] In by far the largest group of states, a small amount of earnings is taxed implicitly at a zero rate; then earnings are taxed at a 100 percent rate, until earnings equal what the UI payment would be at zero earnings; whereupon a rate of more than 100 percent applies, as the remaining UI payment is reduced to zero. In the second group, non-zero and non-100 percent rates apply over a substantial range of earnings; after which a variety of rates take effect. In the third group, a straight zero-100 percent combination is used. In the fourth group, weird zero, greater-than-100 percent, zero, greater-than-100 per-

---

[5] In maternal orphan families, the surviving father cannot receive any aid for himself. His children do receive benefits, if their deceased mother was covered under OASDHI. Thus there can be no price effect on the work effort of the adult head, but there can be an income effect.

[6] For a more detailed discussion of this matter, see Raymond Munts, "Partial Benefit Schedules in Unemployment Insurance: Their Effects on Work Incentive," University of Wisconsin, Institute for Research on Poverty, Discussion Paper No. 43 (April 1969).

cent schedules prevail. Munts' study indicates that the latter type of tax schedule strongly affects the work effort of UI beneficiaries in Wisconsin.

Two types of transfer programs exist for veterans: under compensation programs, transfer payments are made as a consequence of service-connected death or disability and are not income-conditioned; under pension programs, benefits are made as a consequence of nonservice-connected death or disability and are income conditioned. Able-bodied, poor adults can receive aid only under one of the pension programs and would always be females. Widows receiving nonservice-connected death pensions have their benefits determined by family size, assets, and other money income. The tax schedule for those widows who have children is as follows: a zero rate applies to the first $500 of annual income; the implicit rate is 12 percent on the next $500 and 24 percent on earnings between $1000 and $3100. A one-child family then loses $492 in benefits for the next $100 in earnings so that benefits are reduced to zero at the $3200 income level.

The College Scholarship Service (CSS) has developed detailed (implicit) tax tables which serve as the basis for their recommendations to cooperating schools for loans and grants for students.[7] Tables are available, for example, for families which itemize and for those which use the standard deductions on their federal income tax return. For "standard" families, the implicit tax rates on income that result from the CSS demand for parental financial support for the expenses of an enrolled child are zero on income up to the families' (Orshansky) poverty thresholds and then are typically 24 percent over a substantial range of income; for smaller families, the tax schedules become more progressive (the rates rise to about 28 percent), whereas for the larger families, they decline to 12 percent above roughly $12,000. The tax rates for families that itemize deductions on their federal tax returns are slightly more progressive. Allowances are also made for anticipated year-to-year variations in income.

There are other "status-conditioned" programs under which poor persons receive transfers in cash or in kind. Programs for Indians and the vocational rehabilitation program are two examples. For some of the poor, the existence of these programs probably mitigates the negative effect on work effort of the high marginal tax rates on earned income that are built into the programs discussed in previous sections.

---

[7] College Entrance Examination Board, College Scholarship Service, "Sample Case Studies, Charts, and Tables: 1968 Revision, Manual for Financial Aid Officers," Charts I and II, and "Part Five: Need Analysis, 1968 Revision," pp. 5–4 and 5–5.

VIII. SIMULTANEOUS PARTICIPATION IN TRANSFER PROGRAMS

It may be useful to briefly consider the question of what the marginal tax rate on earned income is when a person receives aid under a few programs in which there are non-zero and non-100 percent rates. The marginal rate is *not* necessarily the sum of the tax rates in each of the programs. Consider, for example, the marginal rate for a mother who receives AFDC, food stamps, and public housing. Assume that the AFDC tax rate, t_1, is 50 percent; that the food stamps rate, t_2, is 20 percent; and that the public housing rate, t_3, is 10 percent. If this mother's earnings increase by $100, her AFDC payment is reduced by 50 percent, or $50. If the food stamp administrators tax only the net increase in her money income ($50) at a 20 percent rate, her food stamp bonus declines by $10. The public housing authorities then note that her net income has increased by $40, to which they implicitly apply a 10 percent tax rate, and so her rent increases by $4. The total "tax" on the $100 of earnings is thus $64; and this 64 percent total marginal tax rate, R, is less than $50\% + 20\% + 10\% = 80\%$. The total marginal tax rates *after* each program adjusts its benefits to the *net* increase in income are:

$$\text{Stage 1}: r_1 = t_1$$
$$\text{Stage 2}: r_2 = t_1 + t_2 (1 - t_1)$$
$$\text{Stage 3}: r_3 = t_1 + t_2 (1 - t_1) + t_3 [1 - (t_1 + t_2 \{1 - t_1\})]$$

It is doubtful that any combination of current transfer programs works in such neat fashion. But if accounting periods, definitions of income, and administrative practices are somewhat coordinated, this formulation provides a notion of what R $(= r_3)$ looks like. Where only the initial, not the net, change in earnings is taxed after stage 1, R approaches $t_1 + t_2 + t_3$.

Under the Nixon Family Assistance Plan (FAP), the tax rate on earnings that arises from FAP alone will be either 50 or 66⅔ percent.[8] Where states guarantee more than the federal government guarantees, the implicit marginal tax rate on earnings will be zero and then 66⅔ percent, not 50 percent. This will be the case because the federal government will reduce payments at a 50 percent rate as earnings increase—above $60

---

[8] The tax rate problems that arise under FAP are discussed in depth in D. Lee Bawden, Glen C. Cain, and Leonard J. Hausman, "The Family Assistance Plan: An Analysis and Evaluation," available from the National Manpower Policy Task Force Associates, Washington, D.C.

of monthly earnings—and the states will add 16⅔ percentage points to the 50 percent; in other words, the "income tax base" for both the federal government and the states will be the initial change in earnings. After the federal guarantee is taxed away, state payments will continue to be taxed at a 66⅔ percent rate, until they are reduced to zero.

IX. CONCLUSION

When FAP is considered by Congress, attention ought to be devoted to the tax rates in other transfer programs, like the food stamp program. The present situation not only creates important work incentive problems because of high and erratic tax rates—the anywhere-near-rational poor person would be wise today to get on and hold on to AFDC and its associated benefits—but it also presents serious horizontal and vertical equity questions. How are these incentive and equity problems to be eliminated? A number of policy alternatives exist. One is to continue improving the tax structures within particular program areas; for example, on incentive and equity grounds, the food stamp program is better than surplus commodities, the rent supplement program is superior to public housing, and FAP will probably be better than AFDC and AFDC-UP. Improvements in each of these areas, as well as others, like the medical one, is thus one option.

Three specific improvements that could be made are: (1) Medicaid could be made compulsory in all fifty states and all FAP recipients made eligible for Medicaid benefits. Since Medicaid, like AFDC and probably like FAP, is a Social Security Act creature, improvements in the former that are consistent with the basic purposes of FAP could be made when FAP is enacted. As noted above, Medicaid presently exists in 48 of the 50 states; and, in 20 of the 48 states, only the "categorically needy" are eligible for benefits. The interstate and intrastate differences in eligibility conditions add to the migration and work incentive problems created by AFDC. When FAP is enacted, families previously ineligible for AFDC but now eligible for FAP could be covered under Medicaid—and this could be made compulsory in all 50 states. (2) Moreover, the implicit tax structure in Medicaid could be altered. Two very moderate, simple suggestions apply in situations where a family reaches its FAP-AFDC breakeven point (B). Recall that presently, in the 23 states in which the "medically needy" are eligible for Medicaid, a low-income family must pay for all medical costs equal to the difference between its net family income (D) and its Medicaid threshold income (C)—which is lower than B—after its income passes B. Thus, when its income passes

B, it loses an absolutely comprehensive medical insurance until its medical expenses rise to equal $D - C$. The suggestions are that the special Medicaid thresholds be eliminated and that families above the new FAP-AFDC breakeven points (B') pay medical expenses equal to ½ $(D - B')$ before they reestablish complete eligibility for Medicaid (and FAP).[9] This will keep the potential marginal tax rate on earnings above the break-even points down to 50 percent. (3) Other in-kind transfer programs could implicitly tax only net changes in money income. The total marginal tax rate on an increase in earnings will be the sum of the tax rates in the FAP and public housing programs, if both the FAP and public housing administrators use the increased earnings as their tax base. The total marginal tax rate on earnings will be lower than the simple sum of the FAP and housing tax rates, if the housing administrators use only the *net* increase in money income as their tax base. This change in other transfer programs should reduce the work disincentive effects that arise from a family's simultaneous participation in two or more transfer programs.

A second option is to substitute income-conditioned cash grants on a universal basis to all individuals and families who fall below some set of break-even lines; or, to slightly modify this, substitute cash for in-kind transfers in all areas except health, where an income-conditioned, universal health insurance system could be established. One danger of such an approach, of course, is that some families would be hurt, given the public's attitude on what incomes ought to be guaranteed to the poor. For example, take a family of four which lives in public housing and which receives AFDC, Medicaid, food stamps, and has one child in a day-care center in Chicago. Its AFDC guarantee is $280 per month or $3,360 per year. If the AFDC mother is employed and earns $200 per month, her monthly payment under the new AFDC tax rates might fall to $187 per month and her earnings, net of employment-related expenses, will be about $150 per month; her total, net money income is thus $4,044 per year. At that income level, she can remain in the housing project and implicitly receive a rent subsidy of roughly $60 per month, to use Smolensky's estimates.[10] The mother can also get $18 per month in food stamps at a monthly money income level of ($187 + $150 =) $337. If her child is in a day-care center, it costs roughly $125 per month. The

---

[9] Some limits would have to be placed on D. One possibility would be to allow D to be no greater than $3/2B$.

[10] Eugene Smolensky, "Public Housing or Income Supplements—The Economics of Housing for the Poor," *American Institute of Planners Journal* (March 1968), p. 96.

Illinois (and other states') Medicaid program is so comprehensive that, if its benefits were purchased in insurance form in the private market by such a family, it would cost no less than $450 per year.[11] On the annual basis, therefore, this family receives in-kind transfers valued at $2,886. Its total money and in-kind income is thus ($2,886 + $4,044 =) $6,930 per year. This family's welfare break-even point is at $5,760 of nonwelfare money income. Its in-kind transfers at that point might be worth roughly $2,200. Above $5,760, it would start to lose the other in-kind transfers at a very rapid rate. Such families are, of course, not too common; but I believe that not terribly rare, aggressive welfare families in major cities can accumulate such an income. To turn the major criticism of this second option: converting all transfer programs into one cash program would undoubtedly, given the present state of public opinion, result in lower guarantee and break-even levels for this type of family.

---

[11] This figure is somewhat below an estimate I received from a Mutual of Omaha agent on a major medical-hospital-dental insurance for a young family of four. Private, group insurance would be cheaper and would probably have far fewer deductibles.

NEGATIVE INCOME TAXES AND EDUCATION

Thomas I. Ribich

The interaction between a negative income tax and education is relatively unexplored territory. Those who have discussed the "technical" problems of a negative income tax, or have drawn up model legislation, recognize that special issues arise because of this interaction, but the discussions have been very brief and ungeneral. This paper attempts to provide some of the generality that has so far been missing, though it is little more than a rough outline of issues and possible answers.

Two types of negative income tax will be considered: (1) the "noncategorical" variety where low income is essentially all that is needed to qualify for negative income tax payments; and (2) the Family Assistance Plan where both an effort to seek work and children in the family are preconditions for payments. Several formulations of the noncategorical type have been put forward, but most have a good deal in common when it comes to education problems. The Family Assistance Plan will be dealt with in the form introduced to the U.S. Senate on October 2, 1969 (Bill S. 2986). Relatively less time will be spent on the Family Assistance Plan since its interactions with education are not as extensive as in the case of a full negative income tax.

The discussion is structured according to the educational decisions faced by four different types of individuals who, in loose terms, can be described as (a) the poor adult, (b) the affluent adult, (c) the poor youth, and (d) the affluent youth. The main aim will be to indicate possible sources of inequitable fiscal treatment and of resource misallocation that may result when a negative income tax and educational investment decisions interact. No attempt will be made to assess the quantitative importance of these problems. It is probably safe to say, however, that a number of the hazards discussed below will not involve large dollar amounts, but even such financially minor problems can endanger the political tenability of a negative income tax if they have the potential of giving rise to "shocking" stories of misused funds. Education, as it turns out, would seem to present numerous possibilities of this sort. The goal of this paper, then, will be to try to make clear the range of problems that might be involved and to provide a few suggestions that may help to avoid both the serious misallocation of funds and the appearance of scandalous tales.

I. POOR ADULTS

Most discussions of negative income tax legislation have worried mainly about the education problems involved with college-age individuals. These problems are unquestionably trickier than those encountered with adults, but the neglect of adults has led to the neglect of some problems that are worth direct consideration. It will help to deal with the adult questions first. The problems with adults are not only interesting in their own right but also provide an opportunity to explore beforehand some of the same issues that are involved in the more complex case of youths.

One general point should be made clear at the outset: under the proposals that are being most actively considered, a major (but usually unemphasized) implication of a negative income tax is that it serves as an automatic (or semi-automatic) subsidy for private educational investments. An individual who is currently spending a good part of his time earning income will find that if he chooses to spend some of that time in pursuit of education, the forgone earnings portion of his educational investment will be at least partially covered out of public funds. For some individuals the subsidy will of course not apply, since their incomes during an education program will not drop below the levels required for payment eligibility, but for many others the negative income tax will figure in decisions about undertaking full-time education or training. It would appear that nearly all versions of model negative income tax legislation contain this human investment stimulus, implicitly or explicitly, and the legislation outlined by President Nixon goes a step further than most by providing an automatic supplement (of $30 per month) to family assistance payments for individuals who undertake job-training programs.

Under a straight uncategorical negative income tax (NIT for short), the attractiveness of private investments in human capital will almost surely increase for adult individuals earning relatively low incomes and having insignificant sources of other income.[1] For such "poor" adults it is probably true that the human investments will be of a "practical" variety, aimed at increasing earning power. Thus, unlike the incentive under the NIT to choose more leisure, this deflection of choice would seem to be clearly in the spirit of an overall antipoverty campaign. But problems can arise.

First of all the widespread and automatic subsidization of education and training for poor adults is not clearly a good thing unless there is widespread underinvestment now in their education and training. The presence of underinvestment cannot be established with great certainty, though there is a fairly strong presumption in that direction: capital market imperfections are probably most relevant when it comes to educational investments in poor adults, and various studies suggest that training programs for unskilled adults have high payoff rates. Whether underinvestment is substantial enough and widespread enough to justify education subsidies as general as those implied by an uncategorical NIT is another question. Large numbers of individuals taking advantage of the subsidy could result in rates of return much lower than those observed "at the margin." And while there is little doubt that subsidies of this sort will end up raising the productivity and earnings of many who would otherwise find it impossible to finance personally their educational investments, it is quite possible that the total earnings gains (appropriately time-discounted) generated in this way will fall short of the total costs of education, including the social costs of foregone production.

A second problem is that an NIT which grants subsidies to individuals without questions asked—and that seems to be the way most plans are designed to work—could tempt individuals into foolish investments. Bad educational investments by the poor can be considered likely because of the existence of weak market knowledge. Poor individ-

---

[1] Although the private costs of educational investments will be lowered by a negative income tax, expected private returns will also be lowered because of the high effective marginal tax rate on income earned in the negative income tax range. That will tend to counteract the stimulative effect on private educational investments brought about by the lower private costs. If both the current income lost because of educational investment and the later income gained are changes that take place exclusively in the negative income tax range (i.e., below the break-even point), it could be argued that no alteration occurs in the net attractiveness of educational investments. It is likely, however, that a large part of the expected return (in most cases) will involve gains in income above the break-even point, where marginal tax rates are lower and approximately the same as they are presently. A negative income tax should therefore end up as a net inducement for making educational investments.

uals may very well choose bad investments, just as they often (apparently) make unwise consumer choices. Moreover, profit-seeking companies, aware of the new opportunities, may strive to "exploit" the poor as they have in such areas as retail sales and credit terms. A fair amount of "educational exploitation" already seems to take place in the form of matchbook-advertised correspondence courses and the like, which promise rapid entry into attractive occupations. A redoubling and reorientation of such get-affluent-quick schemes may very well accompany the introduction of a negative income tax.

At least from an economic point of view general overinvestment and widespread instances of bad investment in education are no more desirable, and perhaps less so, than the phenomenon of reduced work incentives. Like the straight work disincentive effect of a negative income plan, it reduces current work effort, and, on top of that, absorbs other scarce resources. Highly trained manpower devoted to education programs that have little or no payoff can be considered just as detrimental to overall economic welfare as the generation of outright idleness.

Some of the same considerations are relevant for the Family Assistance Plan (FAP). Educational investments undertaken by adults and financed by FAP payments are apparently limited to job training programs. But that does not mean there is no danger of overinvestment in human capital. While it is true that FAP offers no payments at all for single individuals and childless couples, the stimulus for human investment is clearly stronger than it is under most NIT plans for that large group of adults who are in families with children at home. FAP not only offers a special bonus of $30 a month for those engaged in training programs, it will also (a) introduce relatively more poor adults to the possibility of job training (or employment), (b) require some individuals to undertake job training in order to continue to receive FAP payments, and (c) establish an expanded network of job training programs to handle the expected increase in candidates. As under an uncategorical NIT, there will surely be many instances of new and worthwhile careers started as a result of the new human investments that are stimulated. But a greatly expanded program of job training still must face the likelihood that average returns will not be as great as those observed at the margin for programs in the past and that the total gain experienced by the trainees could fall short, perhaps substantially, of the total cost of training.

The problem of seriously misguided educational investments by individuals would not seem to be a serious problem under FAP. Local state employment offices are given a heavy responsibility for directing the nature and type of training received, and this will keep down the instances of misinformed choice. Individuals will still, presumably, have a measure of choice in the type of training they undergo, and it is intended that privately run training programs will handle some of the new candidates for training. But numerous provisions in the legislation make it clear that considerable effort is to be directed toward minimizing the number of wrong-headed decisions by individuals.

If and when a full uncategorical NIT is enacted, it would seem wise that public authorities continue to take an interest in the types of educational investments being indirectly financed by negative income tax payments. Under an uncategorical NIT, with a wide variety of educational investments financeable through NIT payments, it probably is not practical to run everything through the local state employment agencies, but it would seem advisable to expand the machinery for accreditation of educational establishments and provide a broadened public program of education counseling.

The problem of possible overstimulation of education and training investments is a more difficult issue to approach. For both a standard NIT program and FAP the possibility is present; but, also for both, we have little idea of how much human investment will be stimulated. From the NIT experiments that are now in progress, we may get a rough estimate of how much an uncategorical negative income tax will stimulate new educational investments of various kinds. For FAP, there seems to be no ready alternative but to wait and see how the interacting clauses of the legislation, in combination with the operation of the individual local employment offices, generates new enrollees for job training. Once we know the approximate amount of new human investment stimulated by a given program, it is still necessary to estimate what the influx of the newly trained workers will do to relative wages and hence to estimates of economic benefits. What is then required is research that goes beyond the usual "marginal change" assumption that characterizes nearly all previous studies of human investments, in order to get a reasonable estimate of returns for this more-than-marginal change.

There are special questions in FAP: under what conditions will an individual have a choice between job training and a job, if both are available? Will an individual be permitted to undertake training for a job he prefers, rather than accept an available job opening that is not to his liking, and still be permitted to collect FAP payments? Will it be possible for an individual to quit a job he dislikes or he feels is too low paid and undertake job training and collect from FAP in this instance also? As the legislation now reads, this decision appears to be left to the discretion of the U.S. Department of Labor (presumably in cooperation with the local state employment board) and will depend on the specific circumstances of each individual case (see section 431a). The apparent opportunity in FAP to alter the specific conditions under which an individual is permitted to take job training could be useful as a way to deliberately change the human investment stimulus of the legislation, in response to accumulating knowledge of payoff rates and also in response to changing conditions. It also brings with it some problems, which are treated in the following section.

II. AFFLUENT ADULTS

Individuals who are capable of or are presently earning incomes which are well outside the poverty range may nonetheless derive advantages from an NIT if they choose to engage full time in an education program. Unless there is mandatory income averaging over several years (which most would agree creates considerable difficulties), the NIT could be used to help the affluent adult who decides to make himself more affluent by obtaining further education. Such income gains could be considered a healthy overall development if it is thought that serious underinvestment in education characterizes affluent adults, but that would seem to be a more doubtful proposition than in the case of poor adults. Even if underinvestment in affluent adults can be demonstrated, use of NIT payments to encourage such income-increasing investments could be interpreted nonetheless as outside the spirit of the negative income tax law.

A second problem arising with affluent adults, and perhaps to some degree with poor adults, is that some individuals will choose to undergo education programs essentially for the "consumption" aspects of the experience. Some college-educated individuals, for instance, may simply decide to take a sabbatical from their regular jobs in order to round out their cultural background, financed partially by the negative income tax and perhaps some dissaving. This would very likely be considered even less socially laudable than education that leads to higher incomes and greater productivity among the already affluent.

FAP has some safeguards against such abuses, though it is not entirely clear how they will work out in practice. One safeguard is that only "job training" seems to count as an acceptable substitute for working. Though the precise limits of job training are not spelled out, it is apparent at least that undertaking recreational or avocational sorts of education are not considered justifiable grounds for taking off work and collecting FAP payments. A second line of defense is that all families with over $1,500 in "resources" other than "home, household goods, personal effects and other property . . . essential to the family's means of support" are ineligible for payments (see sections 442a (1) and 444a). A tough administration of these clauses could weed out a good many affluent individuals attempting to take temporary advantage of FAP for any purpose, including the acquisition of more education. There is apparently a third safeguard, in the form of income averaging, which is involved in section 442d of the legislation. All the clauses in that section bear on this issue, and the last one contains the open-ended statement that "the Secretary may, in accordance with regulations, prescribe the cases in which and the extent to which income received in one period . . . shall, for purposes of determining eligibility for and amount of family assistance benefits, be considered as received . . . in another period or periods." It would seem that these clauses could be used to deny payments to an individual who recently experienced substantial earnings and who quit his job to acquire training for purposes of getting an even better job.

While the existing form of the legislation can apparently be employed to correct abuses by the nonpoor who try to use FAP to finance additional education, it would still seem advisable to provide some guidelines that bear directly on the issue of when it is appropriate for an individual to quit a job in order to undertake retraining. This is required both to prevent abuses by those who already have adequate earnings and to assure individuals in substandard employment that there is a way out which can be financed from public funds. It is probably wise to permit at least some flexibility to adjust to regional differences and changing circumstances, but some general rules would seem needed to distinguish these two cases and to assure some reasonable uniformity of application.

This still leaves the problem of what is to be done if we move to an uncategorical NIT. One alternative is to keep approximately the same sort of restrictions as are in the present version of FAP, to control strictly the type of education that still permits eligibility for payments, and to inquire closely into past income and employment circumstances before eligibility is granted. But that would encumber the administrative simplicity of the NIT which is one of its major virtues. Moreover, it is not clear that we need go this far in inhibiting individual choice.

An alternative is to practice a limited and asymmetrical form of income averaging: payments could be allowed to occur relatively quickly if an individual's income drops to a low level for whatever reason, but a requirement might be made for automatic payback through the regular income tax system if it turns out that the individual earns ample income later on. This raises the problem that once an individual slips into the poverty range for whatever reason, the desirability of earning higher income is to some degree diminished by the higher tax rate paid. Such penalty rates could be made progressive, however, so that those who become truly well off later on repay somewhat more than what they collected, but those who never climb very far up the income ladder repay little or nothing. Such a provision is reminiscent of Milton Friedman's plan for financing college loans, though the purposes here are much broader, and the goal is not to make the program self-financing from the repayments (as it is in Friedman's plan) but rather to discourage one possible misuse of NIT payments and provide for at least some recompense from individuals who do misuse the system or whose poverty turns out to be a very temporary phenomenon. With a rule of this sort, truly affluent individuals would not be as tempted to use the negative income tax for undertaking educational investments and would also be discouraged from indulging in temporary leisure at public expense.

III. POOR YOUTHS

Under a straight NIT program, a youth who is really on his own and is also poor would seem to be no less deserving of payments than an older person. And if the indirect subsidization of education for adults is considered appropriate under NIT, there is little reason why it should not also be made available to independent young people who are genuinely poor. For young people who are clearly separated from their original families, the only problems that would seem to arise are the ones that apply to adults as well. These problems might be more severe quantitatively in the case of youths since young people are more inclined to attend school or acquire training and may also have generally weaker market knowledge than do adults. But they are of the same general nature as those treated above.

But all youths affected by the negative income tax cannot be thought of as having made a clean break with their original family: many young people who are making educational decisions are still at home, and many are capable of exercising the option to leave home or stay. A negative income tax can affect such decisions and special care in the drafting of legislation must be exercised to make sure perverse results do not occur. First of all, any variety of negative income tax should probably disallow separate filing for any individual below some minimum age, regardless of the circumstances. An orphan or a runaway, below 16 (or perhaps 18) years of age should simply be handled in some alternative way that recognizes the need for close guidance by an adult. The fact that he is going to school, or thinking about doing so, should not change matters.

Beyond this, the distinctions and judgments become difficult. The age at which a youth is considered responsible enough to care for himself does not necessarily correspond to the age at which his parents are thought to have no responsibility to help if the means are available. Eighteen-year-olds can join the army without parental consent, can vote in some states, and are perfectly free to leave home to seek their own livelihood. Yet colleges and universities look carefully into the financial circumstances of parents before deciding upon scholarship aid. That raises the question of who exactly qualifies as a "poor youth."

A young person above legal minor status who is from a poor family and has little earning capacity of his own should, it would seem, be included as eligible for negative income tax payments even if he is no longer financially integrated with his original family. And if he is involved in an educational pursuit, there is little reason why that should not be considered the same way it is for a poor adult. Separate filing would logically be allowed if separated from the family, regardless of whether or not the individual is in school.

But what about the youth from a poor family who is presently capable of earning a satisfactory living on his own, and the youth from an affluent family who is capable of earning only very little? Should the former be allowed negative income tax payments if he chooses to go to school away from home rather than work, but the latter be excluded in such a situation on the grounds that his parents are obligated to shoulder the burden of educational financing? Or should the judgment be the other way around, on the grounds that the capable youth from the poor background is not really a short-term or long-term poverty worry, but the inept son estranged from his affluent family is a worry on both counts? Perhaps both types of individuals could justifiably collect NIT payments—or maybe both should be excluded.

Even for young individuals who are clearly poor in all relevant respects, a number of issues must be handled with some delicacy. One question is what to do about scholarship income. (The same question can arise in the case of poor adults undertaking education, though it is likely to be a more major problem here.) One possibility is to consider all scholarship income, including that portion that simply covers tuition, as gross income for the purposes of calculating appropriate negative income tax payments. But that would seem to make an arbitrary distinction between individuals who happen to live where there are free schools (e.g., community colleges) and those who must pay tuition but are reimbursed for it.

In contrast, that portion of scholarship grants which goes beyond tuition and covers at least part of living expenses should justifiably be treated as income when calculating appropriate negative income tax payments. Care must still be exercised in making sure that the provisions of the legislation relating to such income does not unduly encourage or discourage family separations or lead to heavy bias in choice of schooling. Account must be taken of the fact that living away from home, if that is involved in an educational opportunity, entails extra expenses. Hence, if a youth remains financially integrated with his family and files his claim with his original family, then a fellowship that covers such extra expenses while in school should not be added into the income of the family that is left behind, thereby making that family ineligible for NIT payments. If living at home, fellowships (or paid living expenses associated with an education program) could justifiably be treated as income for the family.

The same sort of considerations would apply if no paid living expenses are involved: going to school away from home should be reasonable grounds for permitting separate filing by the individual or permitting the individual a full adult allowance if he files with his family. It would seem appropriate, however, to deny separate filing privileges if living at home, regardless of whether or not school attendance is involved.[2] Rules along those lines should come close to preserving the current relative desirability of leaving or staying at home, and should provide roughly the same degree of indirect subsidy for education and training as it does for poor adults.

Turning now to the youth from a poor family who is capable of earning a respectable (nonpoverty) income, a case could be made that his receipt of negative income tax payments while furthering his education is no less objectionable than it is for an adult who is capable of earning a comfortable living but chooses to improve his earning capacity, and collects NIT payments in the process. It would seem extremely difficult, however, to distinguish between such youths and those who are not capable of earning their own way. Youths in the relevant age category frequently have no full-time earnings records whatsoever, and it is doubtful that there is a reliable and objective alternative for determining what true earnings potential really is. One possibility is to exclude from NIT eligibility those youths who enroll in college, as compared to training courses, on the grounds that the individual able enough to tackle college work cannot be considered a real poverty problem. But the distinction between "college" and "work training" is inherently blurry: many junior colleges, for instance, offer curriculums that are quite similar to courses offered in "training" programs. The problem is further complicated by the fact that ability to tackle college is not tantamount to an ability to earn an adequate wage without college and also by the existence of pro-

[2] Though at age 21 or so, or if the individual is married, separate filing privileges would be appropriate.

grams which recruit into college ghetto youths who may fall shy of normal standards of ability.

In short, there is little choice but to treat all youths from poor families in an equivalent way, regardless of the particular type of education involved. Some instances may arise of unjustified collection of payments, but these should not be great in number, given the fact that most youths from poor families are fairly likely candidates for poverty during their own adult lives if special steps are not taken. Any alleged abuses would in any event have to rely mainly on conjecture since little or no full time earnings history will be available.

The rules under FAP are similar to some of the ones suggested above for NIT. In particular, scholarships for tuition and fees are excluded as income, and (by implication) grants which go beyond that are included. In some respects, however, FAP is less generous than the rules proposed above. An individual who is away at school will receive no extra payment to compensate for the extra expense, and no separate filing is permitted under any circumstances for an individual who is financially separate from his family. Not only does this mean a smaller educational stimulus for some poor youths, it also biases choice towards going to school nearby and/or toward staying financially integrated with the original family. Encouraging poor youths in school to stay with their families can be viewed as bolstering the traditional virtue of family cohesiveness, but it is not clear that rewarding a poor youth for staying in a depressed area or urban ghetto, in a family situation that may be less than wholesome, is all that wise a policy if our aim is to reduce the incidence of future poverty. Moreover, once a poor youth has left home it is not clear why that individual should not be as great a poverty concern as the youth still living with his family, and therefore just as worthy a subject for public payments. He will, in all likelihood, be a parent soon himself, and it would seem reasonable to encourage educational investments before an individual is tied down with family responsibilities.

FAP is more generous toward the educational investments of poor youths in some of its other provisions. Providing that the individual going to school (or in training) is living at home, any money he earns on the side is not counted as family income. More important than that, going to school can make the difference between whether or not the whole family is eligible for FAP payments. A family who has no children is automatically ineligible for payments; but children are defined as those under 18 *or* students under 21. A poor family with a youth between the ages of 18 and 21 and with no children under 18 therefore has a strong interest in seeing that this youth is enrolled in some sort of educational program. It would make the whole family eligible for payments when they otherwise would not be. This provision in the legislation runs some risk of prompting educational enrollments by poor youths who have little interest in picking up useful knowledge, but are simply playing the loophole. Moreover, given that an important purpose of the legislation is to provide more wholesome environments for young people so that their odds for future adult poverty is reduced, it is a questionable practice to exclude 18–21-year-old youths (and their families) just because the young person is not in school. The youth who is less willing or less able to enroll in an educational program is probably a greater risk for adult poverty than is the person who is enrolled.

It would seem, then, that the clauses in FAP pertaining to poor youths in school contain some instances of inequitable and inconsistent treatment. The number of individuals affected may not be very great, and the inefficiencies may not be extremely costly in total, but they cannot be dismissed as insignificant. Some adjustments would seem to be a good idea. But such adjustments turn out to be difficult. In particular, moving in the direction of the less restricted system runs into problems in the case of affluent youths, to which we now turn.

IV. AFFLUENT YOUTHS

This is surely the most difficult case of all to deal with. It is also the situation that has attracted the most attention from others who have pondered the interaction between a negative income tax and education. The reason is clear enough: the large and highly visible numbers of resident college students from affluent families create the potential for large-scale tapping of NIT funds which would lie clearly outside the spirit of such legislation, at least as viewed by the vast majority of the public.

The most common response to this threat has been to propose that all full-time students under 21, or at least college students under 21, be prevented from filing separately for NIT payments.[3] While that stipulation would effectively eliminate the possibility of youths from affluent families receiving payments while at school, it would also mean that a poor student separated from a poor family would also be excluded from filing separately. We therefore should have at least some reservation about this easy way out.

---

[3] See Christopher Green, *Negative Taxes and the Poverty Problem* (Brookings Institution, 1966), pp. 101–02; James Tobin, Joseph Pechman, and Peter Mieszkowski, "Is a Negative Income Tax Practical." *Yale Law Journal,* Vol. 77 (1967), pp. 1–10. Editors, "A Model Negative Income Tax Statute," *Yale Law Journal,* Vol. 78 (1969).

Tobin, Pechman, and Mieszkowski make an allowance for the poor youth in suggesting that "the adult basic allowance might be allowed for a person engaged in full-time study for his first college degree, and added to the basic allowance to which the unit would be entitled if the college student were not a member."[4] Thus, a student, though not permitted to file separately, would be given the same basic allowance as that allowed the first two adult members of the family, thereby permitting him to go as far toward covering the extra expenses of going away to school as would be the case if he were permitted to file separately. This would amount to a not very serious amendment to the previous section on poor youths. It would not necessarily exclude youths who are estranged from their families: if they can establish that their parents are also poor, they could still be eligible for a full adult allowance.

This now gets to the nub of the very serious dilemma faced in the case of youths from affluent families. While most of these youths who are away at college (or other types of school) are not estranged from their families and should justifiably be expected to receive support from home, some indeed are financially separated in all relevant ways. The latter would seem to be appropriate candidates for NIT payments. But to allow payments in that case would encourage estrangement of youths from their affluent families. The nature of the estrangement and its motivation could be of numerous varieties, and many would generally be considered undesirable. Affluent youths away at school, who are restive of whatever parental control is still being exercised, would now find it tenable to break off relations with their parents. Affluent youths who have the option might choose to go away to school against parental wishes. The initiative might also come from parents who might now be more inclined to let their offspring struggle through school on his own, with the help of a negative income tax. There might also be mock separations of youth from parents to take advantage of the provisions, perhaps with surreptitious gifts involved while the student is drawing from NIT funds.

The problem would seem to have no completely satisfactory resolution. Either we risk having some youths from affluent families really suffer hard times at school because they are truly out of touch with their families, or we encourage family separations of a generally disapproved sort and tempt the misuse of NIT funds. It would be reasonable to argue that the former of the two risks is the less weighty. A young student from an affluent family is not likely to be a poverty case for more than a short period and, more often than not, will best be described as a case of "voluntary" poverty. If he happens to really be a long-term problem, that will

---

[4] Op. cit., pp. 9–10.

be taken care of under the NIT when he reaches full adulthood; and in the (probably rare) instances where a young person from an affluent family is in a very serious state of poverty, that is perhaps better handled not by simply providing money but by individual attention of some kind, to help him with the other sorts of difficulties that are associated with the combined circumstances of youth, family separation, and student status as well as poverty.

By excluding students from affluent families from NIT payments, some varieties of undesirable choice distortion would be prevented, but others can appear. Perhaps the most worrisome difficulties are those generated if separate filing is permitted for youths who are *not* in school. Most NIT proposals would allow this, thereby making this portion of the NIT provisions parallel with the existing U.S. Revenue Code. Separate filing in the case of youths from poor families would seem to present no special problems, at least under the sorts of rules that were discussed above. If a student from a poor family is not at home, then he should be either permitted to file separately or be permitted to claim a full adult allowance if filing takes place with the family. If he leaves school or decides not to go, his basic allowance under NIT would remain essentially the same as if he were in school. But for a youth from an affluent family who is no longer living at home, the situation is quite different. If in school, he is to be denied NIT payments, but if not in school he can file separately and receive a full NIT allowance.

Several sorts of distortions can take place if this combination of provisions is instituted. Students estranged from affluent families who are having a rough time making ends meet while in school will find the risks reduced for leaving school or may simply drop out to take deliberate advantage of NIT. Moreover, the problem of youths encouraged to leave affluent families crops up again, only this time the departure would not be for the purpose of going away to school. Rather, affluent youths would be drawn into trying to make their own way in the world of work, knowing that there is always NIT to fall back on, and others would be drawn into leaving home without any intention of seeking a job, knowing that a period of youthful "exploration" is financeable from NIT payments. Among the lesser problems is that an NIT would end up supporting youths who are not able to earn very much on their own, but who could easily be supported by their parents. Among the more serious problems is that the NIT could become an important source of income for the widely publicized and socially disapproved communes of nonworking young people.

These problems would seem no less severe than the abuses that might occur if college students from affluent families were permitted to collect payments. Indeed, if nonstudents are permitted to file separately, it might be preferable to let students (even those from affluent families) file separately in order to not divert choices away from acquiring further education. But given the sorts of abuses that were discussed earlier, it is not clear that a net gain in equity would occur if this more liberal policy were followed.

The other major alternative is to disallow separate filing for any individual under 21. All individuals under that age floor could be required to show proof that their original family unit is incapable of financial support of their independence before NIT payments were made. All payments to underaged individuals would be determined not only according to the earnings of the given individual but also according to the income of the original family, whether or not estrangement has taken place. If the individual is unable or unwilling to provide such family-income information, then he would be excluded from NIT payments.

Such treatment for youths out of school would then be parallel to the treatment of in-school youths proposed above. They need not be excluded from other welfare services and payments in the community, but as in the case of the in-school youths, it is probably preferable for more individual attention to be given rather than just automatic payments. Moreover, the inquiry into family finances before granting NIT payments to nonstudent youths would be little different from the inquiries that are now made into family finances before awarding scholarships, or the proposed inquiry into family finances before awarding NIT payments to students. If this is justifiable in the case of college students, who are by and large more independent and responsible than their nonstudent counterparts, then it should be justifiable for this latter group as well.

Such requirements would complicate the administrative machinery to some degree, and that would have to be a consideration in deciding between requiring all youths to demonstrate that their parents are incapable of support and other alternatives for handling this problem. But the more powerful issues have to do with very broad questions of the role of young people in society. While young people are demanding and acquiring independence and political power, the complicated technology of our economy is demanding that a young person prepare a longer time for his life's work. Striking out on one's own at an early age makes good economic sense in fewer and fewer cases, yet independence from family is a powerful and increasingly common urge. The urge toward independence might be viewed as a rebellion against the lengthy preparation for work which has become increasingly onerous. For this reason, or perhaps for more subtle ones, social forces are out of step for young people; and the choice on this seemingly technical problem of a clause in a negative income tax law must make a decision on which of these two forces takes precedence, or must find some compromise that does not generate still more problems of equity and administration.

My own judgment leans towards the more severe test of requiring individuals under 21 to demonstrate that their parents are incapable of support. This is not based on a parochial view that economic considerations are overriding, but rather on the view that independent use of the negative income tax by young people (1) involves irresolvable equity problems, (2) would likely be politically untenable, given the preponderant adult attitude concerning young people, and (3) could result in a serious drain on NIT funds, which in turn could lead to lower payment levels for those people unquestionably deserving of payments. As far as the "youth revolution" is concerned, enforced unit filing would simply leave things unchanged with respect to the economic advantages of independence. That in itself can be considered a political compromise, given the apparent urge on the part of the adult population to work against the tendency toward complete and early independence.

Under FAP, the problem of affluent youth disappears altogether. Though not privy to the elements that went into the decision of the current administration to present a relatively watered down version of a negative income tax, I would not be surprised if one of the reasons was the unwillingness to confront the difficult problem of what to do about young people estranged from affluent families. It is hoped that the above discussion furthers the attempts to resolve that issue, thereby lowering one of the barriers to adopting a negative income tax law that is more far-reaching than the one that is currently under legislative consideration.

V. CONCLUSIONS

The above survey of interactions between negative income taxes and education is only a first attempt to spell out problems and possible solutions. Further study and actual experience with a negative income tax may very well uncover another layer of problems that are equally important and equally difficult to solve. Even the ones dealt with here have stopped short of comprehensive detail. Moreover, the solutions that are proposed are not wholly satisfactory and still leave some problems dangling. Additional rounds of thinking should be able to tailor solutions that fit the problems more closely. This paper does suggest, however, that at least the following should be given serious attention in the design of a full-scale NIT:

1. An attempt to determine the degree of underinvestment in education and training and how much stimulus will be given to such activities through various kinds of negative income tax regulations. Some idea is required on both of these issues before a reasonable decision can be made on the generosity of a negative income tax code when it comes to granting payments for those investing their time in educational activities.

2. An expansion of educational counseling and accreditation to keep pace with the induced expansion of educational investments (especially by unaffluent adults), which would thereby minimize the incidence of unworthy educational investments as this expansion takes place.

3. A provision in the legislation which requires at least some payback of negative tax payments received for those individuals who later end up earning substantial incomes, as a deterrent to affluent individuals who would use the negative income tax for educational investments or for financing leisure activities.

4. Basing negative income tax payments for all individuals under 21 on the income of their parents or guardians as well as their own income, as a relatively straightforward way of easing the multiple forms of undesirable preference distortion that can arise with young people under a negative income tax.

5. Allowing youths from poor families who are away at school to collect full adult allowances, paid either through the original family unit or filed for separately, provided it can be demonstrated that the original family unit is incapable of support. This, plus the exclusion of tuition scholarships and the inclusion of grants for living expenses in the income base for calculating payments, should allow a negative income tax to yield approximately the same degree of stimulus to education for poor youths as it would for poor adults, and should not create serious distortions in family unit decisions.

The Family Assistance Plan would seem to have fewer and less serious problems in its interactions with education, largely because of its more limited objectives and coverage. But here too it would be helpful to inquire into the amount of new human investments stimulated and what can be expected in terms of payoff rates. Some further elaboration of when it is appropriate to quit or leave a job to acquire training for a better job is also necessary. Finally, further thought is required on the issue of college-age youths. Inequities do seem to occur here, and some modification in the direction of favoring the family less and the youth more would seem to be feasible and advisable.

INSTITUTE FOR RESEARCH ON POVERTY DISCUSSION PAPER SERIES

INSTITUTE FOR RESEARCH ON POVERTY REPRINT SERIES

INDEX